Economics Lab

MW00573186

The new field of experimental economics has come of age, as signaled by the 2002 Nobel Prize in Economics. Laboratory experiments with human subjects now provide crucial data in most fields of economics.

This textbook introduces the world of experimental economics. Contributors including Reinhard Selten and Axel Leijonhufvud add to a book that sketches the history of experimental economics before moving on to describe how to set up an economics experiment and to survey selected applications and the latest methods. This user-friendly book demonstrates how students can use the lessons to conduct original research.

With their freeflowing, discursive yet precise style Friedman and Cassar have created a book that will be essential to students of experimental economics across the world. On account of its authoritative content, *Economics Lab* will also find its way onto the bookshelves of leading researchers in all fields of economics.

Daniel Friedman is Professor of Economics at the University of California, Santa Cruz, USA.

Alessandra Cassar is Assistant Professor of Economics at the University of San Francisco, USA.

Economics Lab

An intensive course in experimental
economics

Daniel Friedman and Alessandra Cassar

With contributions from Reinhard Selten and others

Routledge
Taylor & Francis Group

LONDON AND NEW YORK

First published 2004
by Routledge
11 New Fetter Lane, London EC4P 4EE

Simultaneously published in the USA and Canada
by Routledge
29 West 35th Street, New York, NY 10001

Routledge is an imprint of the Taylor & Francis Group

Typeset in Times New Roman by
Newgen Imaging Systems (P) Ltd, Chennai, India
Printed and bound in Great Britain by
T.J. International Ltd, Padstow, Cornwall

British Library Cataloguing in Publication Data
A catalogue record for this book is available from the British Library

Library of Congress Cataloging in Publication Data
A catalog record for this book has been requested

ISBN 0–415–32401–7 (hbk)
ISBN 0–415–32402–5 (pbk)

Contents

Illustrations

Plates

Figures

Tables

Contributors

Steffen Huck's research is split between theory and experiments. His work on endogenous preferences and learning combines both. Topics he is currently working on range from mergers in Cournot markets to the role of trust in contractual relationships. Recently he has also been working on limited memory and imperfect recall. He obtained his PhD from Humboldt University in 1996. Before joining University College London in 2002 he spent two years at Royal Holloway and two years traveling, visiting Queen Mary, UCL, Texas A&M, and Harvard. Since 2001 he has been deputy scientific director of ESRC Centre for Economic Learning and Social Evolution (ELSE).

Axel Stig Bengt Leijonhufvud was born in Sweden. He came to the United States in 1960 to do graduate work and obtained his PhD from Northwestern University. He taught at the University of California at Los Angeles from 1964 to 1994 and served repeatedly as Chairman of the Economics Department. In 1991, he started the Center for Computable Economics at UCLA and remained its Director until 1997. In 1995, he was appointed Professor of Monetary Theory and Policy at the University of Trento, Italy. His research has focused on the limits to an economy's ability to coordinate activities as revealed by great depressions, high inflations, and (recently) transitions from socialist toward market economies.

Rosemarie Nagel's 1994 dissertation was in the area of experimental economics on reasoning and learning in games, supervised by Reinhard Selten, University of Bonn. She was a postdoctoral student of Al Roth in Pittsburgh before she joined the faculty of economics of the Universdad Pompeu Fabra in Barcelona in 1995. Her work on the beauty contest game has received attention not only in academic circles but also in several newspapers where readers were asked to participate in the game. Currently, Rosemarie works on economic behavior in games and auctions.

Reinhard Selten graduated in Mathematics from the University of Frankfurt in 1957, obtained his PhD in Mathematics in 1961 and his Habilitation in Economics in 1968. From 1969 to 1996, he taught at the universities of Berlin, Bielefeld, and Bonn. Professor Selten's major research interests are in Game Theory, Oligopoly Theory, and Experimental Economics. In 1994, he was awarded the Nobel Memorial Prize in Economics for his pioneering work in non-cooperative game theory.

Seven groups of students contributed chapters in the last part of the book.

Acknowledgments

The authors of any book incur large debts and we are no exception. The book originated in the extraordinary summer school program organized through the Computable and Experimental Economics Laboratory (CEEL) of the University of Trento. Additional funding was generously provided by the Latsis Foundation and Fondazione Cassa di Risparmio di Trento e Rovereto. We are grateful for the support of these worthy organizations.

Our greatest personal debt is to Axel Leijonhufvud. He is the guiding spirit and the practical organizer of the Trento summer school program. We constantly looked to Axel for guidance in putting together the Intensive Course in Experimental Economics. He pushed us to write the book and put us in touch with the editorial staff at Routledge. At every stage we were sustained by his enthusiasm, good sense, and vast knowledge of local restaurants.

Our guest lecturers were all indispensable, each in his or her own way. Reinhard Selten lent us his prestige as a Nobel laureate, and helped us attract students as well as other guest lecturers and sponsors. More directly, he devoted his lectures to new material of interest to a wide audience. Massimo Egidi, Rector of the University of Trento, also lent his considerable prestige and support, and shared his ongoing research. Steffen Huck and Rosemarie Nagel shared their deep knowledge in their fields and spent uncounted hours with students, helping them to sharpen their research ideas.

Morena Carli handled all local arrangements with extraordinary aplomb and, under the guidance of Director Luigi Mittone and Technical Assistant Marco Tecilla, we and our students drew on the impressive resources of the Computable and Experimental Economics Laboratory.

Our thanks go especially to all the summer school students. Their eagerness to put into practice what they were learning spurred us to develop the material we presented. We are proud to include their work in the third part of this volume.

We would like also to thank Routledge Economics Editor Robert Langham, who made our book proposal a reality; Editorial Assistant Terry Clague, whose unfailing patience kept us on track; and Vincent Antony and all the staff at Routledge who guided us rapidly through the production process. We are grateful to two anonymous reviewers for suggestions that helped us improve on the first draft. Also contributing to the production of this book were senior colleagues who generously sent us vintage photographs: James Friedman, John Kagel, Martin Shubik, Charles Plott, and Vernon Smith. (Last minute technical glitches forced us to substitute a recent photo of Smith and to omit the Kagel-Battalio photo.)

Finally, our thanks go out especially to our families who gave us the space and support we needed to put the book together. Dan thanks Penny for everything, including her good nature and her good taste in prose. Alessandra thanks her mother for unlimited babysitting while we ran classes in Trento, and Rich for his support while we wrote the book back in Santa Cruz.

Part I
Introductions

An intensive course in experimental economics

Daniel Friedman

For two weeks, 18–29 June 2001, twenty economics graduate students from around the world gathered to learn how to run economics experiments. Despite the distraction of a stunning setting – a cliff-top hotel overlooking Trento and the Adige valley – the students made remarkable progress. Students sorted themselves into eight groups and on the last day, each group presented the results of an original pilot experiment. After returning home, many students continue to run laboratory experiments and to show others how to do it.

The structure of the summer school contributed to its success. Morning lectures began with an overview of the history and purposes of economics experiments, and then alternated between presentation of laboratory methods and surveys of applications. Methods lectures covered experimental control, emphasizing induced value theory; design, including the proper use of randomization and disposition of focus and nuisance variables; data analysis, including qualitative summaries as well as hypothesis tests; issues concerning human subjects and laboratory facilities; and project management. Applications topics included the mysterious efficiency of double auction markets; the successes and failures of institutional design, including spectrum auctions and California electricity markets; the successes and failures of game theory and learning theory in predicting bargaining behavior; and the promises and pitfalls of behavioral economics.

Afternoons usually featured guest lecturers. Distinguished guest lecturer and 1994 Nobel laureate Reinhard Selten lectured on his new theory of impulse balance equilibrium and laboratory applications, and also lectured on his recent theory of imitation equilibrium and applications to oligopoly. Guest lecturers Massimo Egidi, Steffen Huck, and Rosemarie Nagel surveyed laboratory discoveries in their fields: social learning, oligopoly, and coordination games. Program Director Axel Leijonhufvud lectured briefly on adaptive economic processes, and Peter Howitt gave a talk on themes for the next summer school that inspired one student project a year ahead of schedule!

Most important, the student groups met several times a day to hammer out a research question, design an experiment, and run a pilot session. The groups had scheduled afternoon meetings as well as impromptu meetings over meals, during coffee breaks, and late at night, in balconies, lobbies, and eventually in the CEEL facilities at the University of Trento. The groups worked with Teaching Assistant

Alessandra Cassar, and often consulted with the summer school director and guest lecturers. Our students' areas of applications went beyond what is covered in this book, to include two projects inspired by macroeconomic questions, and one in public good. Altogether, it was an intense learning experience for everyone!

This volume is intended to capture the essence of that summer school and to make it available to economists everywhere. We have written up most of the lectures, and edited the student project papers. We have tried not to homogenize everything as in a normal textbook, however. An intensive course works better when there is more than one voice, and we have tried to preserve the informal flavor of lobby discussions by sprinkling the text with comments in boxes.

Several monographs and textbooks on experimental economics appeared in the early and mid-1990s; we draw on and acknowledge these excellent books in subsequent chapters. The present volume makes four sorts of contributions:

- surveys of applications that have progressed rapidly in the last few years;
- streamlined and unified presentation of methods;
- original material by the distinguished guest lecturer and other contributors; and
- seven examples of early project development by our student groups.

This volume will serve as a helpful reference book for experimental economists, but it is primarily intended as a self-contained introduction to economists who want to develop a laboratory experiment but are not sure how. It can serve as a primary or secondary text in a formal course, or as the backbone of a do-it-yourself course.

1 The Trento Summer School

Adaptive economic dynamics

Axel Leijonhufvud

This Summer School in Experimental Economics is the second in a series. The first, on Computable Economics, was directed by "Vela" Velupillai. Next year, the third one, on Adaptive Economic Processes, will be run by Peter Howitt. And we hope to go on to Behavioral and Institutional Economics, for example. It may not be obvious what they have in common.

They are all part of our ongoing program in Adaptive Economic Dynamics – as we call it "for want of a better name." Although we – and some other colleagues – have made common cause in these efforts, the chances are that no two of us would explain what we are about in exactly the same way. What follows, therefore, is my own perspective on the matter.

The economic theory of recent decades has been built on the basis of the optimality of individual decisions and the equilibrium of markets. This "neoclassical" economics is often criticized, but it has many achievements to its credit. Indeed, it embodies most of what economists know and the tools of what they know how to do. If you are to become an economist you had better learn it!

Yet, neoclassical economics is the subject of constant criticisms from within and from without. But the notion that one might somehow abandon it, in favor of one or another alternative, founders on the enormity of the prospective cognitive loss. Those "schools" that have defined themselves largely in opposition to neoclassical economics have remained marginal.

We had better accept, therefore, that for now and for the foreseeable future, neoclassical economics is the core of our subject. Instead of looking for an alternative theory to replace it, we should try to imagine an economic theory that might transcend its limitations. Easier said than done! To get a start on it, it may help to compare how optimality and equilibrium are understood in modern theory with how they were understood in neoclassical economics many decades ago.

The architecture of modernity: choice, optimization, equilibrium

A brief summary of how a modern neoclassical model is built up may run as follows:

- *All* behavior is conceptualized as *choice*.
- Choice is formalized as constrained optimization.

- The solution to a choice-problem is a *plan*.
- If this plan is to explain *observed behavior*:

    - the agent must know his opportunity set in all relevant dimensions;
    - this information must be objectively true (as observed by the economist);
    - the agent must be able to calculate the optimum.

- When this behavior description is applied to *all* agents, it follows that the system as a whole must be *in equilibrium*.[1] If observed actions are to be interpreted as realizations of optimal plans, the state of the system must be such that all plans are consistent with one another.
- In modern general equilibrium theory, this conception is transposed into a temporal framework where opportunity sets have to be defined over all future periods. Uncertainty about the future can be represented only in the form of objectively knowable stochastic distributions. If at any given date, the probability distribution has to be defined over k possible states for the next period, the dimension of an agent's opportunity set will be: n goods $\times t$ periods $\times k^t$ contingencies, where n and k are arbitrarily large and t is usually taken to be infinite.
- In modern macroeconomics based on intertemporal general equilibrium (IGE) theory, the economy is represented as following an *intertemporal equilibrium time-path*. Such a trajectory is basically ballistic, not adaptive. There is no sequencing of decisions. The information required for each individual optimization problem to have a solution includes the equilibrium prices for all future (contingent) markets, which means, in effect, that *everyone's choices have to be reconciled before anyone's choice can be made.*
- In modern theory, the escape from this logical impasse is sought in the postulate of *rational expectations*. Past experience in a closed system of stationary stochastic processes enable agents to forecast the required future prices.
- An equilibrium time-path is a sequence of states where no one learns anything they did not know to begin with.[2] The construction, on the other hand, raises the question of how these rational expectations were learned once upon a time. This has also become a front-line question in recent years given greater urgency by the finding that IGE models very often have multiple equilibria.

Complaints, complaints,…

A list of the more common complaints directed against constructions of this kind would include the following:

- the conception of "rationality" attributed to the individual agent in standard choice theory;
- the treatment of firms and other organizations (including governments) as if they were individual decision-makers;

- "situational determinism," the practice of assuming that individuals or firms are always perfectly adapted to their external environment, so that inquiry into internal structure or functioning becomes otiose (cf. Latsis, 1972);
- the interpretation of the economy's motion as always in equilibrium;
- the treatment of time as simply the $(n + 1)$th dimension of the commodity space;
- the treatment of uncertainty as probabilistic and based on stable underlying frequency distributions;
- the lack of room for fundamental novelty – innovation, emergence, evolution;
- the explanation of institutions (money, firms) as market imperfections or market failures; and
- the theory's isolation from neighboring disciplines (sociology, cognitive psychology, etc.).

All the properties of the model that were stressed in the brief summary above, and the corresponding complaints, stem directly from the commitment to constrained optimization as the (exclusive) way to represent *how people make decisions*.

An older tradition

In the older neoclassical literature, the optimality conditions for an individual agent were commonly understood as a state that the agent would attain by some entirely unspecified or at best sketchily described process of trial and error. Similarly, equilibria were understood as rest states of processes of market interaction. Thus, both individual optima and collective equilibria were understood as point attractors of dynamical systems. *Static* theory dealt with what economists thought they knew about the properties of these attractors. Applied economic theory was largely couched in terms of *comparative statics*, all of which rested on the presumption of underlying adaptive dynamics that would carry the system from a historically given state to a new point attractor.

Statics comprised almost all of formalized economic theory. Economists knew little in substance about the dynamics of either individual adaptation or market interaction and the mathematics of such processes were on the whole beyond what they (or not so long ago, anyone) could do. *Adaptive dynamics was the unfinished business of neoclassical theory*. And so it largely remains. Intertemporal equilibrium is a generalization of the earlier statics that does not tackle the dynamic issues.

Two traditions

Elsewhere (Leijonhufvud, 1998), I have summarized the contrasts between these two ways of apprehending the core of economic theory in the form of a table, which is convenient to reproduce here. I have labeled the two traditions "classical" as opposed to "modern" in order to emphasize that the focus on *process* as opposed to the properties of optima and equilibria has its roots in the "magnificent dynamics" of the British Classical school.

	Classical	*Modern*
Objective of theory	Laws of motion of the system	Principles of efficient allocation
Individual motivation	Maximize utility or profit (intent)	Maximize utility or profit (performance)
Individual behavior	Adaptive "Procedural rationality" (often gradient climbing)	Optimizing choice "Substantive rationality"
Behavior and time	Backward-looking, causal	Forward-looking, teleological
Cognitive competence	Capable of learning Well-adapted "locally"	"Unbounded"
Role of institutions	Essential in guiding behavior, making behavior of others predictable	Problematic: why use money? why do firms exist?
Equilibrium concept	Constancy (point attractor)	Mutual consistency of plans

In the "classic" camp, I would put not only Ricardo and Marx, but also Marshall and Keynes. Examples of "moderns" would be Arrow and Debreu and later Lucas, Sargent, and Prescott. The great teachers of my own generation, Hicks and Samuelson, would move back and forth between the two as the problems they dealt with would dictate.

Marshall's laws of motion

Let us take Marshall as an example of the road not taken. The core of Marshall, I want to argue, is what we today would call an *agent-based model*:

- Marshall started from individual demand-price and supply-price schedules, $p^d(q)$ and $p^s(q)$ – not from demand and supply functions, $q^d(p)$ and $q^s(p)$, as Walras did. That is why he drew his diagrams (correctly) with quantity on the horizontal, price on the vertical axis, as we still do (incorrectly) today.
- These demand- or supply-price functions are not based on underlying optimization experiments. The demand-price is obviously not the "optimal" price that the consumer would pay for a given quantity. So, Marshall does not build from maximization.
- Instead, the demand- and supply-price schedules give rise to simple decision rules that become the "laws of motion" of the agents:
  - *For the consumer*: if demand-price exceeds market-price, increase consumption; in the opposite case, cut back.
  - *For the producer*: if supply-price exceeds the price realized,[3] reduce output; in the opposite case, expand.

And we should imagine a similar rule for the price setter.

- – *For the middleman*: if inventory turnover slows down, reduce prices to both customers and suppliers; in the opposite case, raise them.

- These are gradient climbing rules. The *substantively rational* agents of modern economics would presumably come up with something a good bit more clever, but Marshall's agent may still be granted a degree of *procedural rationality* in convex environments characterized by the continuity on which he so much insisted.
- Marshall presumed that the process of market interaction among agents obeying these laws of motion would settle down into the short-run equilibrium, characterized by the constancy (zero rate of change) of industry output.
- From this aggregate equilibrium, once obtained, optimality conditions get in by the backdoor. What is the "representative firm" doing, when industry output is at rest? It also is at rest, which requires that its supply-price equals the market price. Under competitive conditions, of course, its supply-price is simply its marginal cost.
- The various "Laws of Motion" of Marshall's theory do not all operate on the same timescale. Thus, his hierarchy of market day, short- and long-run equilibria, which have no counterpart in modern economics. In retrospect, this was a clever and surprisingly successful attempt to tame the dynamics of the theory and bring it within the ambit of static analysis, where a little calculus would go a long way.[4]

Tackling the unfinished business

The unfinished business of the "old" neoclassical economics is full of problems. But these problems are also opportunities. The apprentice economist will have a hard time adding value to intertemporal general equilibrium theory. But the unfinished business offers him or her a lot to do.

Marshall's theory has seen hardly any formal development for over half a century, so it is not surprising that we find it pretty primitive by present-day standards. It has one great virtue that the modern optimality/equilibrium economics has altogether lost, namely, a consistent focus on *process*. But gradient climbing is too simplistic a decision procedure in most environments and will not work in many of them. The presumption that all the dynamic processes assumed will go to point attractors is unfounded. The rank-ordering of adjustment speeds does not hold in general – prices certainly do not always move faster than output rates – and cannot be so simply ordered across a system of multiple markets. The older neoclassicals had the best possible reason for not modeling the dynamics explicitly, namely – it could not be done. But their statics, which has become the foundation of modern theory, was founded on the unproven faith that the unspecified dynamics would always converge in good order on the static equilibria.

In order to move towards a future economics *not* based on optimization and equilibrium, we should strive for a change in perspective at several levels at once:

- from equilibria, conceived of as states where all individual plans are consistent with one another – to temporal processes of interaction, which may or may not converge to equilibria, conceived as states of rest;
- from substantive rationality in the sense of Herbert Simon – to procedural rationality, analyzing how agents calculate what actions to take and on the basis of what information;
- from assumptions of complete knowledge of opportunity sets – to an emphasis on learning from and adapting to unfolding events;
- from risk as knowable probability distributions – to genuine uncertainty, including also undecideability;
- from economic institutions as the "market imperfections" of transactions cost theory – to institutions as defining the essential rules of the game that govern the interactions of agents.

Standard theory relies on optimization methods to *deduce* behavior. Going beyond optimization will mean less reliance on deduction. Economists will have to study how people actually behave, how decisions are reached, implemented, and monitored in organizations, and how various types of markets function. Such a *behavioral economics* must bridge our traditional disciplinary boundaries towards the cognitive sciences and organization theory. *Experimental economics* will then become steadily more important.

Institutional economics in the broad sense is about the rules that govern the interactions between economic agents. The rules constrain the strategies that people may use and consequently make their actions more predictable. The rules under which people interact also help determine what people will learn from experience and therefore to what equilibria interactive adaptive processes may converge.

A theory that sees the economy as a system of interrelated dynamic processes running in parallel is going to be far more difficult than Marshallian economics to handle. Analytical methods will not take us very far in investigations of complex adaptive systems. So we envisage increasing use of *agent-based models* and of computer simulation in general. Computable and experimental economics will complement one another for two reasons. First, agent-based modeling will be the only way for us to build macromodels from the bits and pieces of behavioral economics and experimental results. Second, past experience with complex dynamic models shows that the problem of imposing some discipline in the use of simulations is a serious one. Agent-based modeling needs to keep as close contact with analytical results as possible but, beyond that, one has to look to experimental economics and to calibration methods to discipline the enterprise.

If economics evolves in the directions that we hope to see it take, it will raise new questions and will require rather different skills from those that our graduate programs have concentrated on. Imagine, for example, a future adaptive macromodel written for some object-oriented platform such as Swarm. The algorithms comprising such a model would have behavioral interpretations[5] in terms of individual adaptation and market processes. The set of these algorithms compute the state of the economy period by period. The mathematics appropriate for working with this kind of representation would be recursion theoretic, discrete, constructive, and *computable*. And uncomputability in such systems would introduce a genuine uncertainty not reducible to probabilistic risk.

So that, very roughly, is how our series of Summer Schools hang together.

Notes

1 Although the term is otiose within the theory since it will not allow any non-equilibrium states.
2 Except the actual outcome of the lottery that determines the state of nature in each period.
3 Note the *ex post* formulation. I interpret the "Laws of Motion" as feedback-governed decision rules.
4 Quite a bit further, as a matter of fact, than Marshall would trust it!
5 In contrast to today's computational economics where the algorithms designed to find the numerical solution to large general equilibrium models bear no relation to the behavior of the agents populating the models.

References

Latsis, J. (1972) "Situational determinism in economics," *The British Journal for the Philosophy of Science*, August, 23: 207–245.
Leijonhufvud, A. (1998) "Mr Keynes and the Moderns," *European Journal of the History of Economic Thought*. Also in Pasinetti, L. and Schefold, B., eds, *The Impact of Keynes on Economics in the 20th Century*, Cheltenham: Edward Elgar.

2 Economists go to the laboratory

Who, what, when, and why

Daniel Friedman and Alessandra Cassar

> Experiment! Make it your motto day and night. Experiment, and it will lead you to the light....If this advice you only employ, the future will offer infinite joy, and merriment...Experiment...And you'll see!
>
> (Cole Porter, 1933)

Experiments are a special form of play. Puppies, cubs, humans, and assorted other creatures play just for the fun of it. Play is also adaptive and serves a vital purpose: it helps us learn. We playfully engage the world and thus come to understand it better.

An experiment actively engages some small piece of the world. We design and run an experiment and record the results in order to learn about that piece. This form of learning is the essence of science.

Science is a general-purpose learning engine with two components, as depicted in Figure 2.1.

Theory compactly organizes the existing body of knowledge. Using current theory and deductive logic, you can generate predictions about the world. These predictions tell you what to look for and tell you which observations are surprising. The surprising observations suggest (via induction) how theory might be improved. The improvements suggest new things to look for and lead, sooner or later, to new surprises. Over time, the empirics (the accumulated observations and techniques) become broader and deeper and theory becomes more sophisticated.

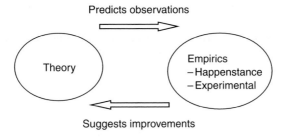

Figure 2.1 The engine of science.

Experiments turbo-charge the engine of science. Happenstance data – observations that already exist – sometimes include just what you need to test a crucial prediction, but you are rarely so lucky. Naturally occurring processes often do not allow you to observe a key variable, separate the effects of different variables, or infer causality. In an experiment, you actively engage the world and create a learning opportunity that would not otherwise exist. Experiments are play – with a scientific purpose.

History of experimentation

Science in the ancient world emphasized close observation of naturally occurring processes, not experiments (e.g. the Greek philosopher Aristotle 384–322 BC). One can find or infer scattered episodes in Greece, China, and elsewhere, but no consistent tradition. Prior to Bacon (1561–1626) philosophers regarded experiments as faintly disreputable (Lloyd, 1984).

Physics emerged first from natural philosophy as a separate scientific discipline and, at the same time (around 1600), developed the first experimental tradition. Galileo, for example, observed swinging chandeliers and balls rolling down the street and, on the basis of this happenstance data, formed some hypotheses not found in Aristotle. More importantly, he actively engaged the natural world by constructing pendulums of various weights and lengths, and ramps at various angles, to test and refine his hypotheses. Such experimental data later allowed Newton and others to develop more powerful theories.

Chemistry emerged as an experimental science two centuries later. Boyle, Lavosier, Priestly, and others developed laboratory techniques (involving balance scales, flasks, burners, etc.) that tested predictions of the new molecular theory. This work touched off cycles of new laboratory technique and new theory that accumulate to this day. Biology was long thought to be inherently nonexperimental since it dealt with life itself, but in the second half of the nineteenth century, pioneers such as Pasteur and Mendel developed laboratory techniques that spurred theory and new techniques at a pace that continues to accelerate.

Psychology long seemed even more remote from the laboratory, but by the beginning of the twentieth century pioneers such as Wundt and Fechner introduced influential laboratory techniques. Economics is just the latest discipline to go experimental.

Why did not experiments emerge earlier? The discussion to this point suggests that a discipline becomes experimental when two conditions are met: its theory matures sufficiently to generate laboratory-testable predictions and pioneers develop useful laboratory techniques. Innovations in one discipline can spur innovations in a neighboring discipline, but you cannot simply transplant theory or lab technique. To the extent that they look at different aspects of the world, the disciplines need to organize knowledge differently, and each must develop its own theory and its own lab techniques.

History of experimental economics

Economic theory before the 1960s had little room for laboratory experiments. Macroeconomics referred to prohibitively large-scale events, and had little connection to microeconomics. But microeconomics of that time referred mainly to competitive equilibrium. Economists were not interested in testing the underlying assumptions that all agents (firms and households) choose optimally and that equilibrium prices ensure consistency of choices. They were interested in the consequences of these assumptions in the field (Friedman, 1952).

Meaningful economic experiments became possible with the emergence of new theories in the 1960s. Game theory, industrial organization, general equilibrium, social choice, search theory, voting theory, etc. offered competing ways to understand microeconomic data, and in some cases multiple equilibria emerged from a single theory. By the early 1970s, many economists began to recognize the potential of experiments to distinguish among the many alternatives.

Fortunately, useful laboratory techniques had already appeared. Chamberlin (1948) reported 10 years of classroom demonstrations intended to convince his students that competitive equilibrium is not able to explain everything. Vernon Smith (1962) (see Plate 2.1) advanced Chamberlin's techniques considerably, as we will see in Chapter 3, by introducing salient payments, repeat trials, and a more realistic market institution. Shortly thereafter, he launched the first experimental economics lab, at Purdue University, and began to build interest among his colleagues, including Charles Plott (see Plate 2.2).

About 1950, a separate experimental tradition began among Princeton game theorists, including John Nash, John Milnor, Martin Shubik, and Lloyd Shapley (see Plate 2.3). They played out many games among themselves, usually for bragging rights but sometimes for real money. The 1952 RAND conference in Santa Monica brought these game theorists together with psychologists, cyberneticists, and other applied mathematicians. The conference volume (Thrall *et al.*, 1954) included five papers reporting experiments with games or individual choice tasks.

Early in his academic career in Germany, Reinhard Selten launched a long-term experimental research program on oligopoly theory, inspired, in part, by the RAND conference volume. Back in California, Siegel and Fouraker (1960) reported a landmark program on bargaining and oligopoly experiments launched about the same time. Other teams undertaking experimental economics research in the 1960s included James Friedman (see Plate 2.4) and Austin Hoggatt at Berkeley, and Raymond Battalio and John Kagel at Texas A&M.

Everything came together in the 1970s: ripening theory, innovations in laboratory technique, and a critical mass of individual researchers (including talented newcomers such as Al Roth, initially at the University of Illinois). As indicated in Figure 2.2, the decade began with a number of different research teams pursuing their own topics in their own way, and ended with a common identity and a unified methodology spanning topics from individual risky choice to market equilibrium. Permanent laboratories were established in Arizona, Caltech, Pittsburgh, Indiana, and elsewhere.

Plate 2.1 Vernon L. Smith received the Nobel Prize in 2002 for having established laboratory experiments as a tool in empirical economic analysis, especially in the study of alternative market mechanisms. Vernon L. Smith, Oslo, 2002. Photo: © The Nobel Foundation.

Plate 2.2 Charles Plott (center) with two Caltech graduate students in the late 1970s.

Plate 2.3 Martin Shubik "gaming" with a graduate student in the late 1960s.

Plate 2.4 Jim Friedman in the late 1960s.

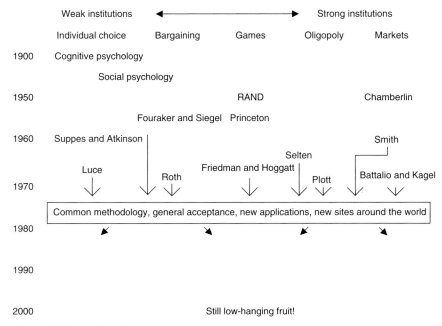

Figure 2.2 Evolution of experimental economics.

Experimental economics really took off in the 1980s. Financial markets, auctions, asymmetric information models, institutional engineering, voting, and dozens of other new applications opened to the new methodology. Young researchers flocked in, including one of the authors, and new labs sprang up. Mainstream economic journals began to print experimental articles on a regular basis.

The 1990s saw continued rapid growth, especially in Europe, and consolidation of gains. The Economic Science Association, formed in 1986, began to bring together North American and European experimentalists on a regular basis. The 1998 launch of *Experimental Economics* signaled that experimentalists were confident that they had a permanent place in the economic mainstream and that ghetto-ization was no longer a concern.

How will experimental economics fare in the 2000s? There is still low-hanging fruit to attract young researchers. Graduate students, and even undergraduate students, can still find significant new topics and produce publishable research. Eventually, it will become a boring mature field, where it takes years of work for talented researchers to produce meaningful results. The work of Trento Summer School 2001 students (collected at the end of this book) demonstrates that day has not yet come!

Divergence from experimental psychology

In 1960, Vernon Smith visited Stanford University and picked up some key lab techniques from psychologist Sidney Siegel (who unfortunately died in mid-career a year later). Since then, however, the techniques of experimental economics have diverged from those of cognitive and social psychology. New researchers can avoid unnecessary problems if they are aware of the differences.

Hertwig and Ortman (2001) identify four principal methodological differences:

- *Script versus open-ended.* Economists (drawing on Siegel's tradition) almost always include detailed formal written instructions for subjects defining their roles, interactions, and payoffs. Psychologists in recent decades seldom use written instructions and usually are quite casual about describing the task to the subjects.
- *Repeated trials versus one-shot.* Economists since Smith (1962) typically have subjects repeat the task or interactions several times, and focus on data from later repetitions when they are sure that the subjects are fully adjusted to the environment. Psychologists more commonly just give the subjects one shot at any particular task.
- *Salient pay.* Economists almost always pay subjects in cash based on performance. Psychologists seldom pay cash, and when they do, they usually pay a flat amount unrelated to performance.
- *Deception.* A large fraction of social psychology experiments attempt to mislead the subjects as to the true nature of the task. Deception of any kind is taboo among experimental economists.

It seems to us that these differences in lab methods spring from differences in the nature of the disciplines:

- *Role of theory.* Economics has a core theory that assumes self-interest, rationality, and equilibrium. Theory in psychology is more descriptive and eclectic. Hence, psychologists are less concerned with salient rewards, repeated trials, etc. that give economic theory a better shot.
- *Role of institutions.* Following a suggestion by Sunder in Friedman and Sunder (1994), Figure 2.2 presents a spectrum of economic situations based on the institutional constraints. Personal preferences are the dominant influence in individual choice tasks but play a minor role for firms in strong institutions such as markets. Cognitive psychologists prefer to work at the weak institution end of the spectrum, while social psychologists study quite different social constraints. By contrast, economic analysis emphasizes the institutional constraints, as we will see in Chapter 3.

Laboratory versus field data

The connection to traditional econometrics is in some ways as important as the connection to experimental psychology. A pair of related distinctions will help clarify the connection. First, traditional econometrics works with happenstance data, which occur naturally, as opposed to laboratory data, which are created in an artificial environment to inform the investigator. Second, traditional econometrics works with uncontrolled processes, as opposed to the controlled processes that are the hallmark of experimental science.

Laboratory data and experimental controls usually go together, but all combinations are logically possible. Penicillin reportedly was the byproduct of a laboratory experiment where the controls failed. Field experiments have become increasingly important in recent years. The idea here is to impose some controls on naturally occurring processes. For example, Lucking-Reiley (1999) used a website with different auction formats to sell collectible cards. By matching the cards and timing of auctions, he achieved considerable control and sharp comparisons of the auction formats.

Despite these increasingly important distinctions, we will save space in the rest of the book by assuming (unless otherwise stated) that lab data are experimental (i.e. properly controlled) and that field data are happenstance.

What are the comparative advantages of lab and field? Field data that have already been collected and compiled are the least costly, but it is typically very expensive (and often prohibitively expensive) for most investigators to collect new field data. Lab data are generally in between, depending on the subject pool; later, we will note that computerization tends to increase fixed cost but decrease marginal cost.

Validity is at least as important as cost, and again different considerations cut both ways. Good laboratory technique ensures that lab data are internally valid, that is, replicable by any other competent investigator. Nonscientists generally collect field data for their own purposes; it is up to the user to assess whether the data would be substantially the same if the user herself collected and compiled it properly.

Good laboratory technique cannot ensure external validity, however. Will regularities observed in a laboratory experiment generalize well to the larger, ongoing economy outside the lab? As discussed at greater length in Chapter 3, the experimentalist must rely on theory and judgment as well as laboratory robustness tests. Field data, to the extent that the relevant variables are observable, have automatic external validity in their native habitat. Whether or not you can generalize from regularities observed in one field setting to another, for example, from eBay auctions to large wholesale markets, involves pretty much the same issues as generalizing from lab data.

Two empirical studies shed light on external validity. Cox and Oaxaca (1991) generated market data in the lab and used standard econometric tools to try to recover the true supply and demand functions. On the whole, the results were rather discouraging. Resnick and Zeckhauser (2002) used experimental controls to demonstrate that buyer ratings have a modest but significantly positive impact on price in eBay auctions. Earlier studies on quite large happenstance data samples more often found a negative or insignificant effect.

Simulations

An increasingly popular practice is to write a computer program that approximates (or sometimes embodies precisely) a theoretical model. Running the program and compiling the output often provides new insights into the theoretical model. By our definition, such simulations are part of theory, not empirics, because they do not involve actual people and events in the world.

Simulations are increasingly useful in their own right. For information on agent-based computational economics, see the web-site maintained by Leigh Tesfatsion http://www.econ.iastate.edu/tesfatsi/ace.htm. Computational models are also increasingly helpful in conjunction with laboratory experiments. Examples go back to Hoggatt *et al.* (1978), and in Chapter 8 you can find a discussion of Cason and Friedman (1997) in which robot buyers are used as experimental controls.

Purposes of experiments

The discussion so far has emphasized experiments that are intended to advance economic science. The most direct way to do so is to design a laboratory environment that can discriminate among alternative theories. For example, Fiorina and Plott (1978) investigate committee decisions in a two-dimensional choice space, represented abstractly on a classroom blackboard. They consider more than a dozen rival theories, of which only three can account reasonably well for their data. Friedman and Ostroy (1995) test two different theories of market price determination, find that one does poorly in a first experiment, but the other also does poorly in a second experiment. The data suggest a modified theory, which performs well in a crucial third experiment.

Other studies test the predictive power and robustness of single relevant theory. Notable examples include Smith (1962) for competitive equilibrium, and Plott and Sunder (1982) for rational expectations equilibrium. One of the original purposes of the experiments is to calibrate or tune a theoretical parameter, for example, the typical degree of risk aversion in Binswanger (1981). A final scientific purpose is to find empirical regularities to help extend theory into a new area. For example, Plott and Smith (1978) compared two major market institutions, posted offer and continuous double auction; it was several years before a coherent theory emerged that could distinguish among market institutions (see Friedman and Rust, 1993).

Many experiments are conducted for very practical, nonscientific purposes. Some are intended to guide policy choices in industry or government. A related purpose is to create or "tune" a new institution required by a client. Such institutional engineering, as well as policy analysis, are discussed in Chapter 15.

There are also experiments for the practical goal of influencing consumer purchase decisions, or voter turnout and choice. These are major activities studied by academic researchers, especially in business schools and public policy schools. However, so far most of the work comes from the experimental psychology tradition. Perhaps in the future economists will contribute as much to the experimental work as they do to the underlying theory, but in the meantime we do not have much to say on this topic.

Some experiments have mainly a pedagogical purpose. In later chapters, we will mention complementarities and divergences between pedagogical and scientific experiments. Here, we will just point to a large and rapidly growing body of materials to help teachers run experiments in the classroom. Since 1992, Greg Delemeester at Marietta College and his collaborators have collected noncomputerized classroom experiments and presented the results in *Classroom Expernomics*. Arlington Williams of Indiana University has maintained a website for computerized classroom experiments for many years. Charles Holt at Virginia now has an outstanding collection of user-friendly computer programs for this purpose. Bergstrom and Miller (1999) is a supplementary textbook for Principles of Economics classes aimed at instructors who want to use experiments in the classroom. These materials allow instructors to give their students direct experience in key economic environments, and breathe life into the abstractions of competitive equilibrium, oligopoly, principal/agent problems, etc.

Further resources

- Home page of the Computable and Experimental Economics Lab at University of Trento, Italy; http://www-ceel.gelso.unitn.it/
- Al Roth's game theory and experimental economics page; http://www.economics.harvard.edu/~aroth/alroth.html
- Charles A. Holt's *Y2K Bibliography of Experimental Economics and Social Science*; http://www.people.virginia.edu/~cah2k/y2k.htm
- ESA – Economic Science Association Website and links to the journal *Experimental Economics*; http://www.economicscience.org/

References

Bergstrom, T.C. and Miller, J.H. (1999) *Experiments with Economic Principles: Microeconomics*, 2nd edn, Irwin: McGraw-Hill.

Binswanger, H. (1981) "Attitudes toward risk: theoretical implications of an experiment in rural India," *Economic Journal*, 91: 869–890.

Cason, T. and Friedman, D. (1997) "Price formation in single call markets," *Econometrica*, 65(2): 311–345.

Chamberlin, E. (1948) "An experimental imperfect market," *Journal of Political Economy*, 56: 95–108.

Cox, J.C. and Oaxaca, R.L. (1991) "Tests for a reservation wage effect," in J. Geweke, ed., *Decision Making under Risk and Uncertainty: New Models and Empirical Findings*, Boston, MA: Kluwer Academic Publishers.

Fiorina, M.P. and Plott, C.R. (1978) "Committee decisions under majority rule: an experiment study," *American Political Science Review*, 72: 575–598.

Friedman, D. and Ostroy, J. (1995) "Competitivity in auction markets: an experimental and theoretical investigation," *Economic Journal*, 105(428): 22–53.

Friedman, D. and Rust, J. (1993) *The Double Auction Market*, Reading, MA: Addison-Wesley.

Friedman, D. and Sunder, S. (1994) *Experimental Methods: A Primer for Economists*, Cambridge: Cambridge University Press.

Friedman, M. (1952) "The methodology of positive economics," in M. Friedman, ed., *Essays in Positive Economics*, Chicago, IL: University of Chicago Press.

Hertwig, R. and Ortman, A. (2001) "Experimental practices in economics: a challenge for psychologist?" *Behavioral and Brain Sciences*, 24: 383–403.

Hoggatt, A.C., Brandstarter, H., and Blatman, P. (1978) "Robots as instrumental functions in the study of bargaining behavior," in H. Sauermann, ed., *Bargaining Behavior: Contributions to Experimental Economics*, Tubingen: J. C. B. Mohr, pp. 179–210.

Lloyd, G.E.R. (1984) "Hellenistic science," in F.W. Wabeck *et al.*, eds., *The Cambridge Ancient History. Vol. VII, Part 1: The Hellenistic World*, 2nd edn, Cambridge: Cambridge University Press.

Lucking-Reiley, D. (1999) "Using field experiments to test equivalence between auction formats: magic on the Internet," *American Economic Review*, 89(5): 1063–1080.

Plott, C.R. and Smith, V.L. (1978) "An experimental examination of two exchange institutions," *Review of Economic Study*, 45(1): 133–153.

Plott, C.R. and Sunder, S. (1982) "Efficiency of experimental security markets with insider information: an application of rational-expectations models," *Journal of Political Economy*, 90: 663–698.

Porter, C. (1933) "Experiment," *Nymph Errant* (revised in 1943 for the un-produced film "Mississippi Belle").

Resnick, P. and Zeckhauser, R. (2002) "Trust among strangers in Internet transactions: empirical analysis of eBay's reputation system," in M.R. Baye, ed., *The Economics of the Internet and E-Commerce. Advances in Applied Microeconomics*, vol. 11, Amsterdam: Elsevier Science.

Siegel, S. and Fouraker, L.E. (1960) *Bargaining and Group Decision Making – Experiments in Bilateral Monopoly*, New York: McGraw-Hill.

Smith, V.L. (1962) "An experimental study of competitive market behavior," *Journal of Political Economy*, 70(2): 111–137.

Thrall, R.M., Coombs, C.H., and Davis, R.L. (1954) *Decision Processes*, New York: John Wiley and Sons.

Part II
Laboratory methods

3 First principles

Induced value theory

Daniel Friedman and Alessandra Cassar

Your first visit to an economics laboratory may not impress you very much. You will not see a lot of expensive and arcane scientific equipment. You will probably just see a group of young people playing some strange game. The game may resemble some real-world scenario or some theoretical model, but it is unlikely to be a close replica of either. The players may be even less impressive...maybe you recognize some from your photography class and you know they are not exactly hot-shot traders!

This chapter introduces the underlying scientific principles for a controlled economics experiment. After reading it you will know what really matters – it is not the surgical mask and white gown!

The key principles took a definite form in the 1970s and were first written out in Smith (1976, 1982) and Plott (1982). While these longer articles are still worth reading, you can find a summary in Smith (1987). The notation in some of these articles comes from the mechanism design theory originating in Hurwicz (1972); it is a bit heavy for most readers. The streamlined account in this chapter draws on Friedman and Sunder (1994: chapter 2).

Creating an economy in the laboratory

A microeconomic system is a complete, self-contained economy. It consists of a set of agents and the institutions through which they interact, for example, buyers and sellers operating in a particular type of market, or voters deciding under the majority rule. This general description applies equally well to theoretical models, to naturally occurring economies large and small, and to artificial economies in the laboratory.

The agents are the individual participants in the economy. Each agent has his or her own characteristics. These include type (e.g. a buyer), endowments of resources (e.g. time, goods, cash), information (e.g. regarding others' endowments or preferences), technology (e.g. production functions), and preferences over outcomes.

The institution specifies which interactions are allowed among the agents. The institution consists of a message space (or choice set) for each agent type (e.g. a range of allowable bid prices in an auction, or {top, bottom} in a simple matrix game), and by an outcome function, given the agents' choices (e.g. the winner and price at auction, or a payoff matrix for a simple game).

This theoretical structure has several uses. First, it allows us to predict what the economy will do. Typically, we assume optimization and equilibrium, and often we get a unique prediction of what each agent will do and what the overall outcome will be (e.g. competitive equilibrium). The traditional way of advancing economic knowledge is to test these predictions against observations in the field, and to refine the model descriptions (of agent characteristics or the institution) and the observations when significant discrepancies are found.

A second use is crucial for our purposes. By using the theoretical structure to guide lab implementation, we can test direct predictions and also comparative statics. For example, we can examine the effects of changing agents' information or the market institution. With proper implementation we achieve *replicability*, the hallmark of controlled laboratory work in any science. Replicability means that any competent investigator can produce functionally similar data.

So how do you do it? You recruit human subjects to fill some or all of the agent roles. If appropriate, you construct computerized agents, sometimes called bots or robots, for the other agent roles. To control the institution, you simply give the agents the desired message spaces and enforce the outcome function.

Check the list of agent characteristics once more. Creating chosen types and numbers of agents seems straightforward in the laboratory, as does creating chosen endowments of resources, information, and technology – but what about preferences over outcomes? Human subjects may have their own homegrown preferences and it is hard to know what they are. There is an ingenious trick you can use, as we now will see.

Induced value theory

Induced value theory, arguably the key methodological innovation for experimental economics, is based on the idea that the proper use of a reward medium allows an experimenter to *induce* pre-specified characteristics in the subjects so that their innate characteristics become irrelevant. Three conditions are sufficient: monotonicity, salience, and dominance.

Monotonicity means that in a suitable reward medium, more is always better (or, alternatively, less is always better). For example, we can safely assume that (other things being equal) every human subject prefers more cash earnings to less, prefers more grade points to less, and prefers less tedious work to more. Later, we will mention some practical and moral advantages of cash payments over grade points and aversive reward mediums. The point for now is just that all three of these reward mediums seem to satisfy monotonicity.

Salience means that, for each agent, the reward corresponds to a clear outcome function, for example, profit or utility, and the subject understands this. Salience connects the outcomes in the microeconomic system to a reward medium that the subject cares about. The connection cannot work properly unless the subject is fully aware of it.

Dominance means that the reward increments are much more important than the other components of subjects' utility that are affected by the experiment. Privacy helps. Subjects might have rivalrous or altruistic motives toward other subjects or toward the experimenter, but these motives cannot upset dominance if the subjects do not know how their own actions affect others' payoffs or the experimenter's goals.

A little math may help make the point. Assume that the subject's unobservable preferences over the reward medium (M) and everything else (Z) can be represented by $V(M,Z)$. Monotonicity can then be expressed as

$$\frac{\partial V(M,Z)}{\partial M} > 0$$

(or <0 for an aversive reward medium), salience roughly as

$$\frac{\partial M}{\partial a} \neq 0$$

where a indicates the action chosen by the subject, and dominance as

$$\left| \frac{\partial M}{\partial a} \right| \gg \left| \frac{\partial Z}{\partial a} \right|$$

Suppose you want to induce smooth preferences, for example, Cobb–Douglas, represented by $U(x_1,x_2)$ where x_1 and x_2 are intrinsically worthless objects such as red and blue pieces of paper, and $\Delta M = U(x_1,x_2)$ is the relationship (which you choose and explain to the subjects) between the number of blue and red slips they hold and the amount of the reward medium. The induced preferences can then be represented as $W(x_1,x_2) = V(M_0 + U(x_1,x_2), Z_0 + \Delta Z)$, where M_0 and Z_0 are the subject's unobservable initial endowments and ΔZ is the subject's non-pecuniary proceeds from the experiment. By Hicks' (1939) Lemma, two utility functions are equivalent if they have the same marginal rate of substitution (MRS) everywhere. So to prove that the pre-specified preferences U are equivalent to the induced preferences W, we only need to show that the true MRS^W is equal to the chosen MRS^U. This can be done in one line, using subscripts to denote partial derivatives:

$$\text{MRS}^W = \frac{W_{x_1}}{W_{x_2}} = \frac{V_M U_{x_1} + V_Z \Delta Z_{x_1}}{V_M U_{x_2} + V_Z \Delta Z_{x_2}} = \frac{V_M U_{x_1}}{V_M U_{x_2}} = \frac{U_{x_1}}{U_{x_2}} = \text{MRS}^U$$

where the first equality is just the definition of MRS, the second is obtained by applying the chain rule and the salience condition, the third holds (as a close approximation) by dominance, the fourth holds by monotonicity, and the last is again the definition of MRS.

In a way, induced value is a familiar idea. Concert tickets, frequent flyer miles, or even dollar bills have almost no intrinsic value. Their values are induced via their own reward mediums: a seat in the concert or airplane, or general purchasing power. The classic work of Lancaster (1966) extends this point to most goods and services: their values are induced by their underlying features, for example, crunchiness and flavor for breakfast cereals. Using cash to induce value in the laboratory is just an extra link in a long chain.

Some bad (and good) examples

One of the best ways to practice new ideas is to use them to spot errors. None of the bad examples below are fictitious, but prudence demands that we disguise personal identities.

Most psychological experiments involve no cash payment or other salient reward. Some involve a flat cash payment, for example, US$10.00 for every participant. But despite the suggestions of some authors, flat payments are not salient either. Check the definition again if you are not sure why.

Experiments with no salient rewards are not experimental economics, properly speaking. Of course, they still have their uses, even within economics. (Indeed most macroeconomic data published by national governments rely largely on questionnaires.) The objection here is to the improper labeling. For example, a senior macroeconomist several years ago asked subjects to evaluate alternative life cycle consumption plans, and paid them all with cash and free food. Since the payments were unconnected to the choices, it was not experimental economics but rather a questionnaire.

In general, questionnaires are not economics experiments. They do not have salient payments, and what people say they would do in hypothetical situations does not always reflect what they actually do. But the choices need not be hypothetical. For example, one of our students tested the effect of TV advertisements by inviting guests to choose among different brands of beer in his refrigerator before and after some brands were advertised during the Superbowl. Even though he used an unusual reward medium, the payments were salient because the friends drank the beer they chose.

A subtler problem with salience is illustrated in an article published in a top economics journal by a famous psychologist in the mid-1990s. The article reported human subject behavior in a task where choice A tended to reduce the future productivity of choice B, but subjects were not told about this externality and it was difficult or impossible for them to detect it. Payments are not salient when subjects do not understand the connection between their actions and the range of possible future outcomes. Hence, we disagree with the author's conclusion that he had demonstrated irrational economic behavior.

Tournament rewards can cause insidious problems. Several inexperienced experimentalists we know have casually thrown in an extra prize for the subject with highest score. This can induce risk-seeking behavior (as we will see in later chapters) and also can induce attempts to lower other subjects' scores. Both effects undermine dominance for the preferences that the experimenter intended to induce.

External validity: the sun will rise tomorrow!

Nowadays experimental methods are widely accepted by economists, but occasionally (especially if you are working in a new field) someone may question whether your data are representative of the real world. The issue here is generally called external validity. (Internal validity refers to replicability: will other investigators get the same laboratory results?)

External validity is a fundamental issue for any laboratory science. It goes back at least to Galileo and Newton, whose critics did not believe that the behavior of balls on inclined planes had any relation to planetary motion.

Such criticisms cannot be rejected by deduction. Deduction does not even allow us to conclude that the sun will rise tomorrow, just because it rose every day so far. We have to rely on induction. The general principle of induction states that behavioral regularities will persist in new situations as long as the relevant underlying conditions remain substantially unchanged. External validity is a special case of this principle: regularities observed in laboratory (or field) experiments can be expected in similar situations in the naturally occurring world.

Induction relies on existing theory to suggest which conditions are relevant and what represents a substantial change. It also relies on empirical work to keep the theory up to date and to test the suggestions, directly or indirectly.

The point is that an honest skeptic of external validity bears the burden of guessing what makes the lab environment substantially different than the real world. For example, he may think that traders in the real world have much higher stakes, or that they are more experienced. Now you can devise a new experiment designed to see how much difference these things make: do you actually get different results when you use more experienced subjects or higher stakes? Use skepticism constructively to advance the research.

The contrast between laboratory and "real world" is often exaggerated. As Plott (1982) says, laboratory experiments feature real people operating under real rules for real stakes. Laboratory processes differ mainly in that they are simpler than naturally occurring processes. But simplicity is a virtue!

General theories apply to special cases, and these offer the sharpest tests. It is hard to imagine a general economic model that applies to some aspect of the naturally occurring economy but does not apply to any laboratory economy. Some sort of laboratory economy normally can be constructed as a special case. If the model fails to capture what is observed in the simplest special cases, then it needs some serious reconsideration.

Does this mean you need to construct your laboratory environment to mimic a formal model as closely as possible, or that you should try to fully replicate some part of the "real world?" Neither is wise. Formal models often omit crucial details regarding the institution, and sometimes include behavioral assumptions that you would like to test rather than induce. The real world is often too complex to approximate closely in the laboratory, and futile attempts to do so would decrease the scientific value of your experiment. Simpler is better.

The best laboratory environment depends on your research question. The goal is to create an environment that offers the best opportunity to learn something useful, especially about the questions that motivate your research. Later chapters will give you many helpful ideas. But you already know enough to appreciate a few simple tips.

Seven easy pieces of practical advice

1   Motivate the subjects by paying them in cash right after the experiment. This will help you achieve monotonicity and salience.
2   Find subjects with low opportunity costs and steep learning curves. This will give you dominance and salience at a low cost. Undergraduates are usually a good choice.
3   Create the simplest possible economic environment in which you can address your issues. Simplicity promotes salience and reduces ambiguities in interpreting results.
4   Avoid "loaded" words in your instructions in order to promote dominance. For example, if you label the choices in a prisoner's dilemma game as "Loyal" and "Betray," subjects may respond to these words in their own idiosyncratic and uncontrolled manner. Interpretation of subjects' behavior is easier if the labels are "Action A" and "Action B."
5   If dominance becomes questionable and budget permits, try a proportional increase in rewards.
6   Maintain the privacy of subjects' actions and payoffs, and your experimental goals. Subjects' innate preferences may have rank-sensitive components (malevolent or benevolent) that compromise dominance.
7   Never deceive or lie to your subjects in any way. Aside from morality, a scientific reason is that you lose salience and dominance once subjects suspect that the instructions are not on the level. This can also create problems for other experimental economists, and they will resent it. Papers that use deception generally get a bad reception at economics seminars and from economics journal referees.

You should feel free to ignore any of this advice once you fully understand its logic. We personally have violated the first four items on rare occasions, and know of a couple of good studies violating item 6. We have not yet seen an exception to item 7 that we would endorse.

Philosophically inclined readers may want to read a more systematic discussion of experimental methodology. Among the classic articles, we personally have learned most from Lakatos (1978).

Roth's webpage http://www.economics.harvard.edu/~aroth/alroth.html#short includes several recent methodological pieces and cites. Smith (2002) contains, among other things, a recent discussion of the Duhem–Quine problem: pure tests of a scientific theory are impossible; one can perform only joint tests with auxiliary hypotheses.

An historical note: Smith's accounts of induced value list five "precepts." Three of them correspond to our three sufficient conditions: monotonicity (which Smith calls non-satiation), salience, and dominance. Privacy, which we include in dominance, is listed as a separate precept. The final precept, parallelism, refers to external validity.

References

Friedman, D. and Sunder, S. (1994) *Experimental Methods: A Primer for Economists*, Cambridge: Cambridge University Press.

Hicks, J. (1939) *Value and Capital*, Oxford: Oxford University Press.

Hurwicz, L. (1972) "On informationally decentralized systems," in C.B. McGuire and R. Radner, eds, *Decision and Organization*, Amsterdam: North Holland, pp. 297–336.

Lakatos, L. (1978) *The Methodology of Scientific Research Programmes*, vols 1 and 2, Cambridge: Cambridge University Press.

Lancaster, K.J. (1966) "A new approach to consumer theory," *Journal of Political Economy*, 74: 132–157.

Plott, C.R. (1982) "Industrial organization theory and experimental economics," *Journal of Economic Literature*, 20: 1485–1527.

Smith, V.L. (1976) "Experimental economics: induced value theory," *American Economic Review*, 66(2): 274–279.

Smith, V.L. (1982) "Microeconomic systems as experimental science," *American Economic Review*, 72: 923–955.

Smith, V.L. (1987) "Experimental methods in Economics," in J. Eatwell, M. Milgate, and P. Newman, eds, *The New Palgrave: A Dictionary of Economics*, vol. 2, New York: Stockton Press.

Smith, V.L. (2002) "Method in experiment: rhetoric and reality," *Experimental Economics*, 5(2): 91–110.

4   The art of experimental design

Daniel Friedman and Alessandra Cassar

Your purpose determines the appropriate design for your experiment. It defines the *focus variables*, those whose effects you want to understand. But other things – the *nuisance variables* – may also have an effect and you need to account for them or you may reach incorrect conclusions.

For example, you might want to know what sorts of actions by others encourages a person to behave more altruistically, so your focus variable is others' actions. You should worry that altruistic behavior might also be affected by how you phrase instructions, so the wording of instructions is an important nuisance variable. On the other hand, if your purpose is to discover how phrasing can affect choices, then the wording of instructions is the focus and others' actions are an important nuisance. It all depends on your purpose.

The whole point of experimental design is to deal appropriately with both kinds of variables. You want the effects of your focus variables to come through sharply, and not be confounded with the effects of nuisances. There are two basic devices to separate out the effects, *control* and *randomization*. These complementary devices help to achieve *independence* (sometimes called design balance) among the variables affecting the outcomes.

This chapter is intended to help you understand these devices and the underlying ideas, so that you will know how to choose the most appropriate design for your purpose. The ideas turn out to be rather intuitive, but sometimes the terminology is a bit odd. Below you will see jargon like crossover and blocks, and in the wider literature you may encounter jargon like split-plot. These words hearken back to the roots of experimental design in agricultural experiments. The classic text is Fisher (1935), and we have found Box *et al.* (1978) very enlightening.

Control

You, the experimenter, can freely choose the values of many sorts of variables. For example, you can choose the institutions, say two different auction formats, and you can choose what sorts of cost to induce on the sellers. The deliberate choice, or control, of key variables is what distinguishes experimental data from happenstance data.

You basically have two options for controlling a variable. You can hold it *constant*, keeping it at the same level throughout the experiment. Or you can vary it between two or more levels, in which case it is called a *treatment* variable. For example, you can keep the same trading rules throughout your experiment, or you can have two different institutions like posted price and English auction. As you hold more variables constant, the experiment become simpler and cheaper, but you also learn less about the direct effects and the interactions among variables.

Sometimes it takes some serious thinking and careful work through the theory before you can decide on the right control variable. Chapter 17 includes a prime example. The project is one of the few to consider nonlinear dynamics in the laboratory. Model predictions were given in terms of behavioral variables that should be observed (or inferred), so the control variables had to be picked indirectly.

Here are the standard rules of thumb on deciding which option to use:

1 Control all the variables that you can. It may be costly, but do not settle for happenstance unless you really have to.
2 Control your focus variables as treatments. Only by changing their level you can discover their effects.
3 For most treatments, two levels are sufficient for you to detect their effects. Detecting nonlinear effects requires more than two levels, but nonlinearity usually is not the main issue.
4 Separate the levels widely so that the effects will be evident.
5 Most nuisances should be controlled as constants, to economize on the design.
6 Nuisances that you think might interact with a focus variable, however, should be considered as treatments. An example of a possible interaction is a person might behave more altruistically after someone does him a favor when the instructions encourage altruism than when the instructions do not encourage altruism. In this case, an experimenter using the first sort of instructions would reach a different conclusion than one using the second sort. Both instructions should be used so that the interaction can be detected and incorporated in the conclusion.
7 Vary treatment variables *independently*.

Most of these rules are obvious once you think about them, but the last deserves further comment.

Independence

Treatment variables are *independent* if knowing the value of one variable does not give any information about the level of the other variables. The reason why you want to vary the treatment variables independently is simple. If two variables are dependent then their effects are harder (or impossible) to separate. Leamer (1983) makes the point well in his satire of the Monetarist–Keynesian controversies of the 1970s. Leamer begins by supposing everyone accepts the fact that certain plants grow better under trees. One camp, the Aviophiles, argues that the cause is bird droppings, while another camp, the Luminists, argues for shade. Since shade and droppings are very highly correlated, the field data are inconclusive. A field experiment could settle the argument. Control the birds, say, by putting netting over some of the trees so that the two focus variables are independent. Then, you can check whether the plants grow as well under the dropping-free trees. Leamer's point is that experiments are more difficult to conduct for macroeconomic issues.

How do you make control variables independent? This is easy for variables you control as constants: they are trivially independent from all other variables. As for treatment variables, the first thing you might think of is to run *all conditions*, that is, all possible combinations of the treatment variables. For example, have equal acreage in each of the four conditions shade and droppings, no-shade and droppings, shade and no-droppings, and no-shade and no-droppings. We will see soon that there are more economical designs that also achieve independence.

Randomization

We are not yet out of the woods. The weather, or having an experiment late in the evening or during finals week, or something else might have an effect on your subjects' behavior. Some potential nuisance variables are not controllable, so independence seems problematic. For example, trees might grow more often on slopes facing north, and you do not have the time and money to change the landscape contours. The lack of control is especially serious when the nuisance variable is not even observable and may interact with a focus variable. For example, some subjects intrinsically are more altruistic than others in ways that are almost impossible to measure accurately. What if you happen to assign the more altruistic subjects to the first instruction conditions? Your conclusions might be completely wrong.

This insidious problem has an amazingly simple solution. About 80 years ago, the British statistician R.A. Fisher showed how randomization ensures independence. Assign the conditions in random order and your treatments will (eventually, as the number of trials increases) become independent of all uncontrolled variables, observable or not. For example, do not assign the first half of the subjects to arrive to the encouraging instructions; the first half may be intrinsically more (or less) altruistic. Instead, use a random device to choose which instructions to use for each subject. Randomization ensures independence as the number of subjects (or other random assignments) increases.

Efficient designs

Now that the principles are clear, let us go through some classical design schemes. For example, if your treatments are three institutions and two different subject pools, their combination gives you six conditions to cover. If you could run them simultaneously, there would not be any time issues. Usually, this is impossible due to software limitations, different oral instructions, etc. So, now you have to decide on the appropriate way to conduct the sessions. Here are some of the options:

1 *Completely randomized.* In each session you draw the condition randomly (with replacement) from the list of possible conditions. (That is, the chosen condition is an independent, identically distributed random variable with the uniform distribution on the set of possible conditions.) This design is effective, but it can become very expensive! In fact, by bad luck of the draw, your budget might be exhausted before you run one of the conditions.

2 *Factorial.* This design is similar to the completely randomized design, except that the conditions are drawn without replacement until you exhaust your finite number of copies (replications). For example, if you have six conditions to cover and you want to replicate them four times each, you need a "3×2 factorial design with four replications" that requires twenty-four sessions (run in *random* order, of course). This design allows you to neutralize the effects of nuisances that did not even occur to you as well as known but uncontrollable nuisances.

   Factorial design not only achieves complete independence among control variables in moderate numbers of trials, but also allows the examination of all the interactions. The design, however, has two disadvantages. First, the number of conditions, hence the required number of trials, grows explosively with increased number of treatment variables (or levels in each treatment). Second, it is not quite as robust to experimenter error as the fully randomized design. If you make a mistake in assigning the treatments in one session, the design is no longer factorial.

3 *Fractional factorial.* One way to decrease the required number of runs is to deliberately confound some treatments with high-order interactions that you believe are negligible. See Friedman and Sunder (1994) for a full explanation. This design allows you to reduce considerably the number of trials, but it is less robust than a full factorial designs. Of course, if you make an error in assigning treatments in this design, you can always revert to full factorial or randomized designs.

4 *Crossover.* You can run more than one condition in the same session. For example, suppose you have a two-level treatment (A and B) and you can subdivide each session into four blocks (or sequences) of trials. Then you can run your first session with treatment sequence ABBA, the second session with BAAB, and so on. This design can be economical. It is also conservative in the sense that if the treatment effects linger, then the contrast observed between the A and B runs will understate the true effect. See an example of a balanced design (variant on ABBA) in Chapter 18.

5 *Within-subjects* and *between-subjects.* Each subject sees all levels of a treatment variable in a within-subjects design. In the between-subjects design, each subject just sees one level, but different subjects (possibly in different sessions) see different levels. As with the crossover design, the

within-subjects design is conservative. But it controls for subjects' personal idiosyncrasies, which sometimes are an important nuisance.

6   *Matched pairs.* The idea of controlling for nuisances by varying only one treatment appears in its purest form in the matched pairs design. A classical example is the boys' shoes experiment testing the durability of a new shoe sole material. Instead of giving either the old or the new soles to different boys, each boy received one old and one new sole randomly assigned to the left or the right foot. In this way, nuisances such as the subject habits and level of activity are controlled.

As another example, consider the experiments that allowed Team New Zealand to win the 1995 America's Cup, ending the longest winning streak in sport history. (Team US had held the cup for 132 years!) Instead of building two different boats and testing the keels separately for each model, New Zealand built two virtually identical boats and tested different keel configurations by racing the two boats against each other, thus also controlling for weather and sea conditions. This design helped them improve at a rate of 20–30 s per month versus the traditional 7–15 s per month.

One clever way to get matched pairs in the laboratory is to have subjects make two decisions each trial for two environments that differ only in one treatment. For example, Kagel and Levin (1986) have subjects bid the same value draw in both a small group auction and a large group auction. More recently, Falk *et al.* (2003) use a similar dual trial design to isolate neighborhood effects.

Other, less classical designs sometimes are useful:

7   *Baseline neighborhood.* In this design, one picks a baseline condition (combination of treatment levels) and changes one treatment at a time. For example, one of the authors currently is investigating how ten different variables affect the strength of the sunk cost fallacy. Pilot experiments disclosed a baseline combination that seems strong. A factorial design is infeasible because even one replication with only two levels for each treatment would require $2^{10} = 1,024$ sessions. The plan is to just vary one treatment at a time (e.g. the instructions or the cost differential) from the baseline in crossover type run sequences for each subject. This design will not tell us much about how the variables interact, but it will give a first look at the main effects.

Important nuisances

In choosing your design it is worth thinking through what nuisance variables are likely to be important and how you will deal with them. Here is a checklist of standard nuisances.

1   *Learning.* Subjects' behavior usually changes over time as their understanding of game deepens during a session. If this is a nuisance, you can control it by keeping it constant: use only the last few periods or runs. You can control it as a treatment too, by using a balanced crossover design.

2 *Experience*. This problem is similar to learning, but occurs across sessions. To avoid it, it is good practice to keep the experience of the subjects under control. Keep a database to track which subjects already came and played in a particular experiment. The easiest solution is to use only inexperienced subjects, but often you want to confirm the results with experienced subjects. Unless it is part of your research question, do not mix experienced and inexperienced subjects in the same market or game session.

3 *Boredom and fatigue*. Try to keep your sessions no more than 2 h (unless required by your treatment), and shorter is even better. You may save some money and time by running fewer but longer sessions, but you may pay too high a price. Salience and dominance are compromised when your data come from tired or bored subjects.

4 *Extracurricular contact*. Pay attention and try to prevent any uncontrolled communication among your subjects during a session. During a restroom break, they may decide to collude! So, if you cannot monitor them, change the parameters after each break; this will thwart most collusion attempts.

5 *Self-selection*. Try to have a long list from which you can choose your subjects. When the subject pool is potentially important, you should actively choose balanced subject pools. For example, if you advertise a finance experiment in a finance class and in a biology class and let them show up at the door, you probably will end up mainly with finance students.

6 *Idiosyncrasies of individual subjects or pools*. A subject or a group with a particular background may lead to unrepresentative behavior. We had once a scheduler that was member of a sorority, and after a couple of sessions we realized our subjects were exclusively first year female members! Try to avoid these obvious occurrences, and replicate with different pools to take care of phenomena not so visible.

We conclude with a final piece of advice.

KISS: keep it simple! More elaborate experimental designs usually cause more problems for beginners than they solve.

References

Box, G.E.P., Hunter, W.G., and Hunter, J.S. (1978) *Statistics for Experimenters*, New York: John Wiley and Sons.

Falk, A., Fischbacher, U., and Gächter, S. (2003) "Living in two neighborhoods – social interactions in the lab," No iewwp150 in IEW – Working Papers from Institute for Empirical Research in Economics – IEW.

Fisher, R.A. (1935) *The Design of Experiments*, Edinburgh: Oliver and Boyd.

Friedman, D. and Sunder S. (1994) *Experimental Methods: A Primer for Economists*, Cambridge: Cambridge University Press.

Kagel, J.H. and Levin, D. (1986) "The winner's curse and public information in common value auctions," *American Economic Review*, 76: 894–920.

Leamer, E. (1983) "Lets take the con out of econometrics," *American Economic Review*, 73: 31–43.

5   Dialogues with the data

Daniel Friedman and Alessandra Cassar

One of the pleasures of laboratory methods is that good experimental design makes for simple and clean data analysis. Happenstance data often require advanced econometric techniques to scrub away things like multi-collinearity, heteroskedasticity, endogeneity of explanatory variables, etc. But analyzing data from a well-designed experiment normally needs only basic and simple techniques. This chapter will cover the basic techniques that we have found most useful. Some of them are very familiar to economists and some are less familiar, but all of them are straightforward.

Many people dislike data analysis, and think of it as complicated and not very enlightening. In this chapter, we will try to get you to think of it as a conversation, where you encourage the data to reveal its secrets. Do not think of yourself as an inquisitor prepared to "torture the data until they confess"; you will not learn anything new that way. Think of yourself rather as an analyst in the tradition of Rogers (1995), giving the data the opportunity to tell its own story and to offer its opinion on interesting questions, always insisting on honesty and clarity.

A note from the teaching assistant:

My own first experiment was a goofy venture that I barely made it through! But I learned much quicker than if everything went right and maybe you too can learn from my adventures... I started my first experiment at the beginning of the surfing season. Without much knowledge on subjects recruitment, I found myself knocking door to door in the dorms desperately looking for twelve subjects who were not either frantically busy with their finals or guiltlessly out enjoying the weather. And, still now, I cannot help but wonder: where did my beginner's luck go? In any case, I am still fond of those data, and I will use part of it in this chapter to show you step by step how to start analyzing your data.

Your dialogue with the data should begin right away, even before the data actually exist. As soon as you get an idea for an experiment, you should think at how you will analyze the data. Knowing ahead of time which statistical techniques to use will help you plan the design. Analyze your pilot data right away. Improvements in design will almost certainly occur to you!

> At the beginning of my project, I was so excited about the idea that I wanted to test that I did not put much thoughts on how I would analyze individual behavior. As I will explain later, a fixed-effect logit model is a simple statistical approach that takes care of homegrown preferences, and it is useful in situations in which you are interested in isolating how individuals reacts to different treatments. To use this technique to best advantage, I should have made each pool of subjects play all possible treatments. But I did not and I ended up with an unbalanced "panel."

There are two main phases to data analysis. The first, which we will call qualitative or descriptive, is intended to get yourself (and your readers) acquainted with the data. Unlike standard macro or finance data, your data probably come from a newly created environment unfamiliar to most readers, so the first phase is especially important. The second phase, which we will call quantitative or formal, distills the information the data reveal about your research questions.

Qualitative phase

Getting acquainted with a new dataset is important for several reasons. First, it will help you spot outliers and anomalies. These should always be investigated and their source identified. Is the string of zero responses from subject #3 because his computer connection failed, or because he left to go to the restroom, or is it his conscious choice? If a conscious choice, do you have to reconsider your theoretical approach and your statistical technique?

Likewise, a good qualitative analysis of the data will help you spot unexpected regularities. You may decide to test theories whose relevance had not occurred to you. The descriptive analysis will also help you see which techniques will be appropriate for the quantitative analysis to follow.

Graphs and summary statistics are usually the best devices for getting familiar with the data you obtained. Sometimes, you may want to report all your raw data in an appendix or on your webpage. For most purposes, however, this is too much, and a good graph or summary table will do the job.

Which graphs should you use? Look in the existing literature for good examples and adapt them to your purposes. A classic reference on effective presentation of quantitative information via graphs and charts is Tufte (1983).

Most people use computer packages like EXCEL in this first phase, but it is worth investing time using a serious statistical package, because you probably will need it in the quantitative phase. We will refer mainly to SAS, but there are good alternatives including STATA, SPSS, LIMDEP, and EVIEWS.

Table 5.1 reports the raw data from two runs (called *loc07fir* and *loc07thi*) of session 7 of that first experiment. In this session, twelve subjects played several iterations of the coordination game. They were located in a circle, with one neighbor on each side. The treatment variable was the amount of information available to each subject: NONE, if they saw only the past actions of their neighbors, FULL if, in addition, they could see neighbors' payoffs and the average action chosen by the entire group. The idea was to test whether agents, with appropriate information, actually do imitate successful behavior, and, if so in the context of local interactions, whether this possibility of imitation improves the overall outcome.

Staring at these raw data will not tell you much, and you would go numb if I showed you similar data for the rest of the session and all the other sessions. So I will show you how to use SAS to generate descriptive statistics and graphs. The best way to learn how to program in SAS is to steal somebody else's code and to adapt it for your own purpose. You can start stealing mine, and begin building your own library of programs.

The first step is to read the data in and create a permanent SAS dataset. A simple program for reading in the raw data (here from space-separated text file called loc07fir.prn) starts like this:

```
libname library '~/ExpBook/sas/sasdata';
options ls=78 ps=max obs=max;
data rowdata;
  infile '~/ExpBook/sas/sasdata/loc07fir.prn';
  input period player0 player1 player2 player3
    player4 player5 player6 player7 player8 player9
    player10 player11;
proc print;
run;
```

The output of this file looks similar to the input: a table with eighty rows and thirteen columns. Each line represents a period, and the entries are the actions of the twelve agents plus the period indicator.

For SAS to do all the tests of this chapter, though, you want your dataset to be structured differently. You need to have each line containing the information relevant to a single agent. Say the first eighty lines correspond to the first agent, the second eighty lines to the second agent, and so on, and as many columns as you need to make sure that each line-agent will have the necessary information to perform all the subsequent tests. Experienced SAS users would do this quickly using a MACRO, but the following lengthy procedure is a good way to start.

Table 5.1 Data from the first and third runs of session 7 of LOCAL[a]

Period	Treatment: Information FULL (loc07fir)												Treatment: Information NONE (loc07thi)											
	Action chosen by player #												Action chosen by player #											
	0	1	2	3	4	5	6	7	8	9	10	11	0	10	8	1	9	5	11	3	7	6	4	2
1	1	1	0	0	0	0	1	0	0	0	0	0	0	1	1	1	1	0	1	1	1	0	0	1
2	0	0	0	0	0	1	0	0	1	0	0	0	0	1	1	1	1	0	1	1	1	0	1	0
3	0	0	0	1	1	0	1	0	0	1	0	0	0	1	1	1	1	1	1	1	1	1	1	0
4	1	1	0	1	0	0	1	0	0	1	1	0	0	1	1	1	1	1	1	1	1	1	1	1
5	1	1	0	1	0	0	0	0	0	1	1	0	0	1	1	1	1	1	1	1	1	1	1	1
6	1	0	0	1	0	0	0	0	0	1	1	0	0	1	1	1	1	1	1	1	1	1	1	1
7	1	1	0	0	0	0	0	0	0	0	0	0	0	1	1	1	1	1	1	1	1	1	1	0
8	0	0	0	0	0	1	0	0	0	0	0	0	0	1	1	1	1	1	1	1	1	1	1	0
9	0	0	0	0	0	0	0	0	0	0	0	0	0	1	1	1	1	1	1	1	1	1	1	0
10	0	0	0	0	0	0	0	0	0	1	0	0	0	1	1	1	1	1	1	1	1	1	1	1
11	0	0	0	0	0	0	0	0	0	1	0	0	0	1	1	1	1	1	1	1	1	1	1	1
12	1	1	0	0	0	1	1	0	0	1	0	1	0	1	1	1	1	1	1	1	1	1	1	1
13	0	0	0	0	0	0	0	0	0	1	0	0	0	1	1	1	1	1	1	1	1	1	1	1
14	0	0	0	0	0	0	1	0	0	1	0	0	0	1	1	1	1	1	1	1	1	1	1	1
15	0	0	0	0	0	0	0	0	0	0	0	0	0	1	1	1	1	1	1	1	1	1	1	1
16	0	0	0	0	0	0	0	0	0	0	0	0	0	1	1	1	1	1	1	1	1	1	1	0
17	0	0	0	0	1	0	0	0	0	0	0	0	0	1	1	1	1	1	1	1	1	1	1	0
18	0	0	0	0	1	0	1	0	0	0	0	0	0	1	1	1	1	1	1	1	1	1	1	0
19	0	0	0	0	0	0	1	0	0	0	0	0	0	1	1	1	1	1	1	1	1	1	1	0
20	0	0	0	0	0	0	0	0	0	0	0	0	0	1	1	1	1	1	1	1	1	1	1	0
21	0	0	0	0	0	0	0	0	0	0	0	0	0	1	1	1	1	1	1	1	1	1	1	0
22	0	0	0	0	0	0	0	0	0	0	0	0	0	1	1	1	1	1	1	1	1	1	1	0
23	0	0	0	0	1	0	0	0	0	0	0	0	0	1	1	1	1	1	1	1	1	1	1	0
24	1	1	0	0	1	0	0	0	0	0	0	0	0	1	1	1	1	1	1	1	1	1	1	0
25	1	0	0	0	0	1	0	0	0	0	0	0	0	1	1	1	1	1	1	1	1	1	1	0

(continued)

Table 5.1 (Continued)

Period	Treatment: Information FULL (loc07fir)												Treatment: Information NONE (loc07thi)											
	Action chosen by player #												Action chosen by player #											
	0	1	2	3	4	5	6	7	8	9	10	11	0	10	8	1	9	5	11	3	7	6	4	2
26	0	0	0	0	0	0	1	0	0	0	0	0	0	1	1	1	1	1	1	1	1	1	1	0
27	0	0	0	0	0	0	0	0	0	0	0	0	0	1	1	1	1	1	1	1	1	1	0	1
28	0	0	0	0	0	0	0	0	0	0	0	0	0	1	1	1	1	1	1	1	1	1	1	0
29	0	0	0	0	0	0	0	1	0	0	0	0	0	1	1	1	1	1	1	1	1	1	0	0
30	0	0	0	0	0	0	0	1	1	0	0	0	0	1	1	1	1	1	1	1	1	1	0	1
31	0	0	0	0	0	1	0	1	1	1	0	0	0	1	1	1	1	1	1	1	1	1	1	1
32	0	0	0	0	0	1	1	1	1	1	0	0	0	1	1	1	1	1	1	1	1	1	1	1
33	1	0	0	0	0	1	1	1	1	1	1	1	0	1	1	1	1	1	1	1	1	1	1	1
34	1	1	0	0	0	1	1	1	1	1	0	0	1	1	1	1	1	1	1	1	1	1	1	1
35	1	1	0	0	0	1	1	1	1	1	1	1	1	1	1	1	1	1	1	1	1	1	1	1
36	1	1	0	0	0	0	1	1	1	1	0	0	1	1	1	1	1	1	1	1	1	1	1	1
37	1	1	0	0	0	0	1	1	1	1	1	0	1	1	1	1	1	1	1	1	1	1	1	1
38	1	1	0	0	0	0	1	1	1	1	0	0	1	1	1	1	1	1	1	1	1	1	1	1
39	1	1	0	0	0	0	1	1	1	1	1	0	1	1	1	1	1	1	1	1	1	1	1	1
40	1	1	0	0	0	0	0	1	1	0	0	0	1	1	1	1	1	1	1	1	1	1	1	1
41	1	1	0	0	0	0	0	1	1	1	0	0	1	1	1	1	1	1	1	1	1	1	1	1
42	1	0	0	0	0	0	0	1	1	0	0	0	1	1	1	1	1	1	1	1	1	1	1	1
43	1	1	0	0	0	1	1	1	1	1	0	0	1	1	1	1	1	1	1	1	1	1	1	1
44	1	1	0	0	0	0	0	1	1	0	0	0	1	1	1	1	1	1	1	1	1	1	1	1
45	0	0	0	0	0	0	1	1	1	0	0	0	1	1	1	1	1	1	1	1	1	1	1	1
46	1	1	0	0	0	0	1	1	0	0	0	1	1	1	1	1	1	1	1	1	1	1	1	1
47	0	1	0	0	0	0	0	1	0	0	0	1	1	1	1	1	1	1	1	1	1	1	1	1
48	1	0	0	0	0	0	1	1	0	0	0	1	1	1	1	1	1	1	1	1	1	1	1	1
49	1	1	0	0	0	0	0	1	0	0	0	0	1	1	1	1	1	1	1	1	1	1	1	1
50	1	0	0	0	0	0	0	1	0	0	0	0	1	1	1	1	1	1	1	1	1	1	1	1
51	1	0	0	0	0	0	0	1	0	0	0	0	1	1	1	1	1	1	1	1	1	1	1	1

(Data matrix, rows 52–80; entries of 0 and 1, with dashes "—" indicating missing/unrecorded observations)

52	1	0	0	0	0	0	0	1	0	0	0	1	—	—	—	—	—	—	—	—	—	—	—	—	—	—	—	—	—	—	—	—	—
53	0	0	0	0	0	1	0	0	1	0	0	0	—	—	—	—	—	—	—	—	—	—	—	—	—	—	—	—	—	—	—	—	—
54	0	0	0	0	0	0	1	0	1	0	1	0	—	—	—	—	—	—	—	—	—	—	—	—	—	—	—	—	—	—	—	—	—
55	0	0	0	0	0	1	1	0	1	1	0	1	—	—	—	—	—	—	—	—	—	—	—	—	—	—	—	—	—	—	—	—	—
56	0	0	0	0	1	1	1	0	1	0	1	0	—	—	—	—	—	—	—	—	—	—	—	—	—	—	—	—	—	—	—	—	—
57	1	0	0	1	0	1	1	0	1	0	0	0	—	—	—	—	—	—	—	—	—	—	—	—	—	—	—	—	—	—	—	—	—
58	0	0	0	0	0	0	1	0	0	0	0	0	—	—	—	—	—	—	—	—	—	—	—	—	—	—	—	—	—	—	—	—	—
59	0	0	0	0	0	0	1	0	0	0	0	0	—	—	—	—	—	—	—	—	—	—	—	—	—	—	—	—	—	—	—	—	—
60	0	0	0	0	0	0	1	0	0	0	0	0	—	—	—	—	—	—	—	—	—	—	—	—	—	—	—	—	—	—	—	—	—
61	0	0	0	0	0	1	1	0	1	0	0	0	—	—	—	—	—	—	—	—	—	—	—	—	—	—	—	—	—	—	—	—	—
62	0	0	0	0	1	1	1	1	1	0	0	0	—	—	—	—	—	—	—	—	—	—	—	—	—	—	—	—	—	—	—	—	—
63	0	0	0	0	0	1	1	1	0	0	0	0	—	—	—	—	—	—	—	—	—	—	—	—	—	—	—	—	—	—	—	—	—
64	0	0	0	0	0	0	1	0	0	0	0	0	—	—	—	—	—	—	—	—	—	—	—	—	—	—	—	—	—	—	—	—	—
65	0	0	0	0	0	0	1	0	0	0	0	0	—	—	—	—	—	—	—	—	—	—	—	—	—	—	—	—	—	—	—	—	—
66	0	0	0	0	0	0	1	0	0	0	0	0	—	—	—	—	—	—	—	—	—	—	—	—	—	—	—	—	—	—	—	—	—
67	0	0	0	0	0	0	1	0	0	0	0	0	—	—	—	—	—	—	—	—	—	—	—	—	—	—	—	—	—	—	—	—	—
68	0	0	0	0	0	1	1	0	0	0	0	0	—	—	—	—	—	—	—	—	—	—	—	—	—	—	—	—	—	—	—	—	—
69	0	0	0	0	0	1	1	0	0	0	0	0	—	—	—	—	—	—	—	—	—	—	—	—	—	—	—	—	—	—	—	—	—
70	0	0	0	0	0	1	1	0	0	0	0	0	—	—	—	—	—	—	—	—	—	—	—	—	—	—	—	—	—	—	—	—	—
71	1	0	0	0	1	1	1	1	0	0	0	0	—	—	—	—	—	—	—	—	—	—	—	—	—	—	—	—	—	—	—	—	—
72	1	0	0	1	1	1	1	1	0	0	0	0	—	—	—	—	—	—	—	—	—	—	—	—	—	—	—	—	—	—	—	—	—
73	1	0	0	1	1	1	1	1	0	0	0	0	—	—	—	—	—	—	—	—	—	—	—	—	—	—	—	—	—	—	—	—	—
74	1	0	0	1	1	1	1	1	0	0	0	0	—	—	—	—	—	—	—	—	—	—	—	—	—	—	—	—	—	—	—	—	—
75	1	0	0	1	1	1	1	1	0	0	0	0	—	—	—	—	—	—	—	—	—	—	—	—	—	—	—	—	—	—	—	—	—
76	1	0	0	1	0	1	1	1	0	0	0	0	—	—	—	—	—	—	—	—	—	—	—	—	—	—	—	—	—	—	—	—	—
77	1	0	0	1	0	0	1	0	0	0	1	0	—	—	—	—	—	—	—	—	—	—	—	—	—	—	—	—	—	—	—	—	—
78	1	0	0	1	0	0	1	0	0	0	0	0	—	—	—	—	—	—	—	—	—	—	—	—	—	—	—	—	—	—	—	—	—
79	1	0	0	1	0	0	1	0	0	0	0	0	—	—	—	—	—	—	—	—	—	—	—	—	—	—	—	—	—	—	—	—	—
80	1	1	0	1	0	0	1	0	0	0	0	0	—	—	—	—	—	—	—	—	—	—	—	—	—	—	—	—	—	—	—	—	—

Note
a Action 1 (0) corresponds to playing *Top* (*Bottom*) in the Coordination Game Payoff Matrix:

	Top	*Bottom*
Top	5	−1
Bottom	4	1

For each subject X of each run, execute the following:

```
data subjectX;
  set rowdata (keep= period playerX);
  playerid=X;
  rename playerX=play;
  addvar; /*add here all the variables you need*/
*proc print;
run;
```

Now combine the data by:

```
data library.coif7fir;
  set subject0 subject1 subject2 subject3 subject4
    subject5 subject6 subject7 subject8 subject9
    subject10 subject11;
  info='full';
  session='loc07fir';
proc print;
quit;
```

Using the same code and just substituting the name of the file of the second run (loc07fir.prn), you have now both runs in a format that SAS likes. When all your runs are ready, you can build your main dataset:

```
data library.all;
  set library.coif7fir library.coin7thi /*add all
    runs*/;
proc print;
quit;
```

Now you are ready for all sorts of data analysis. Let us begin by preparing a graph of the average choice each period under each treatment. To find these averages type:

```
data average;
  set library.all;
run;
proc sort data=average;
  by session period playerid;
run;
proc means data=average noprint;
  var play;
  by session period;
  output out=meandata mean=avplay;
run;
proc print data=meandata;
run;
```

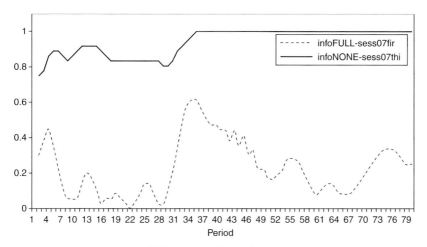

Figure 5.1 Frequency of payoff dominant choices (three-period average).

Import the variable `avplay` (from the SAS output) in EXCEL, and you will easily be able to obtain Figure 5.1.

Now, let us prepare some descriptive statistics. The following SAS program gives you the data to construct Table 5.2.

```
data average;
  set library.all;
  if period<=20 then time=1;
  if 20<period<=40 then time=2;
  if 40<period<=60 then time=3;
  if 60<period<=80 then time=4;
  if period>80 then time=5;
run;
proc means data=average;
  var play;
  by info time;
  output out=meandata mean=avplay;
run;
proc print data=meandata;
run;
```

Well-chosen descriptive statistics and graphs can give the reader (or the experimenter!) the impression that the main questions are answered. It is hard to tell from the raw data in Table 5.1, but looking either at Figure 5.1 or at Table 5.2, it seems clear that treatment NONE promotes convergence to the payoff dominant equilibrium while treatment FULL does not. If that were the research question, it seems we are done. Do we really need any formal statistical tests?

Table 5.2 Percentage of payoff-dominant choices (and standard errors)

Treatment	Periods				
	1–20	*20–40*	*40–60*	*60–80*	*1–80*
FULL	15.8%	30.0%	26.3%	20.4%	23.13%
	(0.37)	(0.46)	(0.44)	(0.40)	(0.42)
NONE	85.4%	90.0%	100.0%	100.0%	93.85%
	(0.35)	(0.30)	(0.00)	(0.00)	(0.24)

The tradition in most natural sciences is no, descriptive statistics are sufficient. A few economists (some of them quite eminent) agree, but most economists will not be convinced without formal tests. Why? We will explain in a moment, but even if you are not convinced, you might still want to cater to your readers' prejudices and use formal tests anyway.

Quantitative phase

Research questions in experimental economics often come down to "Does treatment X affect outcome Y?" For example, does having information about neighbors' payoffs increase coordination on the better outcome? The other common form of research question is "Is outcome Y better predicted by model $M1$ or $M2$?" For example, are subjects more inclined to imitate or to make a best reply?

To start answering the first question, you could compare the average choices across treatments. The SAS code is:

```
proc means data=average;
   var play;
   by info;
run;
```

obtaining $\overline{Y}_{none}=0.939$ and $\overline{Y}_{full}=0.231$. Since $\overline{Y}_{none} > \overline{Y}_{full}$, you may be tempted to conclude that indeed the treatment affected the outcome.

But the observed difference might be due to experimental error, and we need statistical techniques to evaluate that possibility. In natural sciences, the experimental error is often known to be very small relative to the observed differences, so formal tests are redundant. In experimental economics, sample sizes are usually not especially large and the scale of experimental error is hard to know in advance. So, the general topic is worth discussing before introducing specific statistical tests.

What is an independent trial?

Experimental error is easiest to control by running many "independent" trials, but what is a trial in experimental economics? Is it the action of a single player in each period, the average group action each period, or is it the run average (e.g. the mean over all subjects all time)? In the first case, the trials are not independent, because two players with the same neighbor share a common history that may cause their choices to be correlated. But in the second case, individual subjects and groups may have idiosyncrasies that persist from one period to the next and create positive correlation. It seems reasonable to assume independence across runs, but even there it is possible that there are lingering effects of history or experimenter idiosyncrasy.

There is no easy answer to this question and no real consensus among experimental economists. The most conservative position (more prevalent in labs with generous budgets!) is that when subjects interact, an entire laboratory session is a single trial. Our position (probably the more common view) is that each choice is a trial, possibly interdependent with other trials. How that interdependence is taken into account depends on the theoretical framework and the purpose of your experiment. For example, if you are testing whether agents imitate or apply best reply, you should use individual data (since the models predict individual choices), and adjust the sample size in light of the observed correlation. For checking the statistical significance of a treatment, it is best to be conservative and do the tests on run averages; your results will be stronger this way. If you chose a more aggressive definition of trial, consider including a caveat with the test results and remind the reader that the trials may not be independent. If possible, try to bound the effect that this might have on your results.

Sources and consequences of experimental error

The fundamental problem of experimental error is that imperfections in the set of observations might cause different results on replication.

The imperfections can take several forms. The first is measurement error. Recording mistakes can happen. To minimize this sort of error, try to automate your procedures where possible and always cross-check the data.

> Losing your data is the most extreme form of measurement error. I have lost data by forgetting to use a new name for a new data file, and overwriting data that had not been backed up. I hope you never do this! An easy way to avoid this is by selecting an acronym or short name for your experiment, for example, LOCAL. Each session can than be labeled chronologically, for example, LOCAL-1, LOCAL-2, LOCAL-3, and so on.

A second form is loss of control, sometimes subtle. Some sorts of social inter- action might be affected by the experimenter's attitude while instructing subjects, or the scheduler might say too much at the phone. The solution again is to be aware of the possibilities, to automate where possible, and to minimize "on the spot" discretion.

In one of my first experiments I realized too late that a group of close friends were showing up all the time. So at the end of my sessions did I have independent trials? Probably not! Also, I had a scare in the first session. Since that night was my very first pilot, I overestimated how long the session would last, and I finished the treatments I had planned almost an hour early. I had then the greedy thought of getting a second sample from the same subjects, so I continued, but I forgot to change the matching procedure in the control file. Luckily, the program crashed right away and I had to re-enroll the subjects, and ended up with a new random matching. So, I got useful data despite myself!

A third form of experimental error, one that can never be completely eliminated, is sampling error. Your actual data constitute a finite sample, and it might or might not be a good representative of the population of possible out- comes given your treatments. The goal here, given your finite resources, is to get a sample whose distribution is as close to the population distribution as possible.

Sampling is a serious problem when there are unrecognized relationships among relevant variables, so the data represent a small and atypical portion of the population. The good news is that experimental control allows you to avoid the worst sampling problems of field data. In particular, by using a classic experimental design you can eliminate:

- insufficient variation (so you do not have to worry about multicollinearity);
- omitted variables (so you will not have identification problems).

There are two main design tactics for reducing sampling error in the lab:

- Make the sample as close as possible to a classic random sample where each observation is independently selected from the population distribution.
- Take a balanced sample. Subdivide the population into segments and draw observations with frequency proportional to the weight of the segment in the population distribution. Voter surveys use this strategy.

The randomization scheme in your experimental design is the way you deal with unrecognized sources of sampling error. You might consider including randomization over different subject pools or even different labs if you think that your subjects or lab procedures may interact strongly with the key variables.

Formal tests

Formal statistical tests tell you whether differences in observed outcomes across treatments are due to chance alone (sampling error) rather than to the treatments (differences in the underlying population distributions), and whether one model is really explaining the data better than another, or just got lucky. The tests offer precise estimates of model fits and treatment effects. To do this, the test statistic must assume something about the nature of experimental error, and estimate its impact.

Traditionally, statisticians assumed that the error distribution belonged to a known family that can be computed easily. This approach is called "parametric statistics" and includes tests such as the "*t*-test," the "*F*-test," which we will go over briefly. An alternative approach has become more popular in recent decades as computer power developed. It makes fewer assumptions about the population distribution (other than independence!), but usually is less powerful when the parametric assumptions are true. This approach is known as "nonparametric statistics" and we will cover some essential tools it provides such as the "sign test," the "chi-squared test," the "Mann–Whitney test," etc. For a more complete description of nonparametric tests read Conover (1998). See Box *et al.* (1978) for an insightful overview of both parametric and nonparametric approaches, and see Chapter 7 of Friedman and Sunder (1994) for a brief summary of some of the key ideas (e.g. "reference distributions").

Normal distribution

If you feel comfortable assuming that the underlying population is normally distributed (the central limit theorem can be a good justification) then you can use several classic test statistics. Returning to our example, we might want to know whether in the first period the subjects were equally likely to choose each of the two available pure strategies (coded *Top* = 1, the payoff-dominant choice; and *Bottom* = 0, the risk dominant one). We can then impose the parametric structure that the mean choice $\bar{x}$ is distributed as a normal with unknown mean (μ) but known variance (σ^2): $\bar{x} \sim N(\mu, \sigma^2)$. The null and the alternative hypotheses of a two-side test can be specified as:

$$\left. \begin{array}{l} H_0:\ z=\mu=0.5 \\ H_1:\ z\neq\mu=0.5 \end{array} \right\} \quad \text{where } z=\frac{\sqrt{n}\,(\bar{x}-0.5)}{\sigma},\ z \sim N(0,1)$$

With the first line of data of Table 5.1 (e.g. under the treatment FULL) we can easily compute the mean: $\bar{x} = 0.25$. Assume the population variance is 0.2, then, since $n = 12$,

$$z = \frac{\sqrt{12}(0.25 - 0.5)}{\sqrt{0.2}} = -1.94$$

From the standard normal table, the probability of just by chance drawing an observation $z \leq -1.94$ is 0.026 (one-tailed test), and $|z| \geq 1.94$ (two-tailed test) is approximately 0.052. At the 5 percent level of significance (or 5.2 percent to be more precise), we can reject H_0 that the true mean is $z = \mu = 0.5$ and $\bar{x} = 0.25$ is due to sampling error.

The t-test

If you do not know the population variance, you can obtain the sample estimate:

$$s^2 = \frac{\sum_{i=1}^{n}(x_i - \bar{x})^2}{n-1}$$

A normal population with unknown mean and unknown variance has the Student t-distribution, published in tables and known to statistical computer packages.

Now you can compare the same normalized sample mean $t = \sqrt{n}\,(\bar{x} - 0.5)/s$ to tabulated values for the Student t with degrees of freedom $df = n - 1$. In the example, you obtain approximately $p = 0.04$ for the one-sided test and 0.08 for the two-sided test. These probabilities are higher than before, when your reference distribution was the normal with known variance, and now you cannot reject so confidently H_0. You conclude (at the 5 percent level) that $\bar{x} = 0.25$ might be due to sampling error after all.

Several of our student projects show how to use t-test and significance levels in different scenarios. In particular, go to Chapter 18 for an example in which the design and tests meet professional standards. With a few more sessions of data (and perhaps a *KS* test), this student paper is ready for journal publication.

Pooled t-statistic

Similar logic applies to testing hypotheses of the form: "treatment A promotes higher performance than treatment B." Assume that measured performance under A is distributed as $A \sim N(\mu_A, s^2)$ while performance under B is $B \sim N(\mu_B, s^2)$.

The pooled t-statistic is evaluated as:

$$t_P = \frac{(\bar{x}_A - \bar{x}_B)}{s\sqrt{(1/n_A) - (1/n_B)}} \quad \text{with degrees of freedom } df = n_A + n_B - 2$$

For sufficiently large absolute values of t_P you can confidently reject H_0 that the A and B populations have the same mean. If the two populations might have unequal variances, you can use a slightly more complicated version called the two-sample t-test.

In SAS you use PROC TTEST. It reports *p*-values both for the regular pooled *t*-test and the two-sample version, and tells you which version is appropriate. The CLASS statement identifies the variable on which the two populations differ, for example, the information condition. So to compare the average coordination under the two treatments, you run:

```
proc ttest data=meandata;
  class info;
  var avplay;
run;
```

The output looks like:

```
                        TTEST PROCEDURE
  Variable: AVPLAY

  INFO  N      Mean       Std Dev    Std Error     Minimum      Maximum

  full  80  0.23125000  0.16978879  0.01898296  0.00000E+00  0.66666667
  none  80  0.93854167  0.08253175  0.00922733  6.66667E-01  1.00000000

  Variances          T      DF    Prob>|T|

  Unequal    -33.5101  114.4     0.0001
  Equal      -33.5101  158.0     0.0000
  For H0: Variances are equal, F' = 4.23 DF = (79,79)   Prob>F' = 0.0000
```

The *F*-statistic for testing whether the variances from the two groups are equal is 4.23 with a *p*-value of 0.0000. Because the *p*-value is so small you would conclude that the two variances are Unequal, and use the third to last line reporting a two-sample *t*-test. This value of *t* is -33.5101, and the *p*-value is 0.0001. We can conclude that at 5 percent level of significance (or even the 0.01 percent level) the two means are different.

Paired (or matched) t-statistic

If the design is such that the A and B trials occur in *n* matched pairs then you can often sharpen the *t*-test. The basic idea is that some sorts of experimental error affect both parts of the matched pair in the same way, so taking differences across the pair eliminates those errors. For example, you eliminate the effects of individual differences in testing a $120 anti-stretch marks maternity cream by putting it only on half of the subjects' bellies (randomizing between left and right side). Opportunities are rare to design such perfectly matched experiments, but often you can apply this test in situations in which the same group of subjects participates in different treatments (e.g. ABBA design).

You can also use it to reduce errors due to sequencing or learning effects. To illustrate, recall Figure 5.1 comparing treatments FULL and NONE. To test whether the observed difference is significant, take the matched pair differences $x_D = x_A - x_B$, period by period and compute their mean $\bar{x}_D$ and standard deviation s_D. The matched t- statistic is:

$$t_m = \frac{\bar{x}_D}{s_D \sqrt{n}}$$

which, for sufficiently large values, would allow you to confidently reject H_0 that A and B populations have the same distribution.

To run this test, SAS uses PROC MEANS. The matched t-test looks at the differences between two measures that are dependent or correlated and tests whether or not the mean difference equals zero. In SAS, create a new variable that is the difference between the two measures, and test whether the difference is equal to zero:

```
proc means data=average noprint;
  var play;
  by info period;
  output out=meandata mean=avplay;
run;
data delta1;
  set meandata;
  if info="none" then avtop=avplay;
  if info="full" then delete;
run;
data delta2;
  set meandata;
  if info="full" then avbottom=avplay;
  if info="none" then delete;
run;
data delta;
  merge delta1 delta2;
  by period;
  diff=avtop-avbottom;
run;
proc means data=delta n mean std t prt;
  var diff;
run;
```

The output looks like:

Analysis Variable : DIFF				
N	Mean	Std Dev	T	Prob>|T|
80	0.7072917	0.1596595	39.6231216	0.0001

With a *t*-statistic of 39.62 and a *p*-value of 0.0001 you can again confidently reject the null hypothesis and conclude that the average coordination of the first and third run of your session is indeed different. (The absolute value of the *t*-stat here is a bit larger than in the corresponding pooled test, so we gained a little power. It did not make a difference this time because the pooled test already was quite decisive.)

Nonparametric tests

The tests discussed so far assume that the underlying populations are normally distributed. You may prefer nonparametric statistics when this assumption is not attractive. For example, observations of efficiency in most market experiments cluster near the upper bound of 100 percent, so the distribution is very skewed, not at all normal.

In general, the null hypothesis is of the form "treatments A and B yield populations of observations with the same distribution." If H_0 is true, then the actual assignment of the observed outcomes to A or B trials is equivalent to a random assignment. Some useful non-parametric test statistics give the probability that a difference between the A and B trials at least as extreme as observed could have come from a random assignment. If the probability is small, then we reject H_0 and conclude that the treatment effect is significant.

Binomial test

The binomial test is one of the simplest and most widely applicable tests. The sample consists of observation of n independent trials with two possible outcomes, say "class 1" or in "class 2." Each trial has the same specified probability p of producing a "class 1" outcome. Call O_1 the number of observations in "class 1" and $O_2 = n - O_1$ the number of observations in "class 2." The test statistic is then the number of times the outcome is "class 1": $T = O_1$.

In the coordination game example, let an individual player selection of the payoff dominant choice be class 1 and the risk dominant choice be class 2. Imagine we want to test whether, in the first period, agents choose the payoff-dominant action with a probability greater than 2/3.

To find the desired counts of how many subjects chose each action under the two treatments, you can use PROC FREQ:

```
proc freq data=frequenc;
  tables info*play / chisq exact;
  by period;
run;
```

The output gives you a contingency tables from which you can take the desired statistics: $T = 3$ and $n = 12$.

```
----------------------------------- PERIOD=1 -----------------------------------
                    TABLE  OF  INFO  BY  PLAY

        INFO                          PLAY

        Frequency  |
        Percent    |
        Row  Pct   |
        Col  Pct   |          0 |          1 |  Total
        ------------------------------+----------------+
        full       |          9 |          3 |     12
                   |      75.00 |      25.00 | 100.00
                   |      75.00 |      25.00 |
                   |     100.00 |     100.00 |
        ------------------------------+----------------+
        Total      |          9 |          3 |     12
                   |      75.00 |      25.00 |
                   |     100.00 |     100.00 |
        ------------------------------+----------------+
        Total                 9            3         12
                          75.00        25.00     100.00
```

The null distribution of T is the binomial distribution with parameters $p = 2/3$ and sample size n. For the null hypothesis $H_0: p \geq 2/3$ with one-sided alternative $H_1: p < 2/3$, the rejection region is the lower tail of the null distribution for T. To find it, you consult a table of the binomial distribution (of Y with parameters n, p) and look for a number t such that $P(Y \leq t) = \alpha$. Here, α is the p value you seek, also known as the size of the test. When $n > 20$ you can use the normal approximation; see Conover (1998) for details.

In our case, if the target α is 0.05, you can chose either the critical region consists of $T \leq 4 = t$ with an actual $\alpha = 0.0255$ or $T \leq 5 = t$ with an actual $\alpha = 0.0846$. Either way, we can confidently reject H_0 for both treatments since $T = 3$ is less than our critical value t. You can construct an upper-tailed test or a two-tailed test in a similar fashion.

Signs test

The signs test is just the binomial test with $p^* = 1/2$ applied to matched pairs. There should be some natural basis for pairing the observations; if not, the Mann–Whitney test (described below) is more powerful. For the matched pair data count the number r of paired differences that are positive and the number w that are negative. The test statistic is equal to the number of "plus" pairs: $T = r$. The null distribution of T is the binomial distribution with $p = 0.5$ and $n = r + w$.

Assume, for example, that the same subjects play under both treatments and compare their payoffs at the end of the two runs. Suppose $r = 11$ of the twelve subjects made more money under the treatment NONE and only $w = 1$ made more money under the treatment FULL. A two-tailed test has as null hypothesis that positive and negative differences are equally likely, that is, H_0: $r = w$ and H_1: $r \neq w$. From the same binomial table as before, you need to select the t value corresponding to $\alpha/2$. If you want α to be approximately 0.05, then $t_1 = 2$ and $t_2 = 10$ are the lower and upper bounds of the rejection region. Since our statistic $T = 11$ is sufficiently large ($T \geq n - t$) you can reject H_0 of no differential effect.

A problem with our example is that we used the sign test between treatments used at different times during the same session that were not balanced as in an ABBA design. We do not have precisely matched pairs because one observation in each pair is "before" and the other is "after," so differencing across pairs will not eliminate the time sequence as a source of experimental error. Other sorts of problems can be mitigated by variants of the signs test, for example, the McNemar variation; see Conover (1998).

Chi-squared test

When matched pairs are not possible or not meaningful (e.g. we cannot match up observations before and after a treatment), we can test the same hypothesis as before by drawing a random sample from the population before the treatment and comparing it with another random sample drawn after the treatment. The additional variability introduced by using two different random samples might obscure the treatment effect, but perhaps not completely. The chi-squared test is appropriate in this case, and it also can be used as a conservative test even when you do have good matched pairs.

To construct the test statistic, consider a random sample of n_1 observations drawn from one population (say before a treatment is applied) and classify each observation either in "class 1" or in "class 2," with the total numbers in the two classes being O_{11} and O_{12}, respectively, where $O_{11} + O_{12} = n_1$. A second random sample of n_2 observations is drawn from a second population (or the first population after the treatment is applied) and the number of observations in the two classes is O_{21} and O_{22}, respectively, where $O_{21} + O_{22} = n_2$. The test statistic is then:

$$T = \frac{\sqrt{N}(O_{11}O_{22} - O_{12}O_{21})}{\sqrt{n_1 n_2 (O_{11} + O_{21})(O_{12} + O_{22})}}$$

The exact distribution is difficult to tabulate because of all the possible combination of O_{ij}, so the large sample approximation is used, that is, the standard normal distribution.

To continue our example, we obtain the frequency table with the same procedure (PROC FREQ), this time including all periods:

```
                       TABLE OF INFO BY PLAY

        INFO                   PLAY

        Frequency |
        Percent   |
        Row Pct   |
        Col Pct   |          0 |          1 |   Total
        ---------------------------------------+
        full      |        738 |        222 |     960
                  |      38.44 |      11.56 |   50.00
                  |      76.88 |      23.13 |
                  |      92.60 |      19.77 |
        ----------+------------+------------+
        none      |         59 |        901 |     960
                  |       3.07 |      46.93 |   50.00
                  |       6.15 |      93.85 |
                  |       7.40 |      80.23 |
        ----------+------------+------------+
        Total              797         1123       1920
                         41.51        58.49     100.00
```

This output gives us all the necessary information to calculate the test statistic. Be aware that the chi-square reported in the output (see below) is actually a different, but related, test: the Pearson's chi-square. Our test is:

$$T = \frac{\sqrt{1920}((738)(901) - (222)(59))}{\sqrt{(960)(960)(797)(1123)}} = 31.45$$

For a two-tailed test at the 5 percent significance level, first recall (or look up in a table) that 0.975 quantile of a standard normal random variable is 1.9600. Hence, the null hypothesis is rejected when the statistic is greater than 1.96 or less than -1.96 (two-tailed test). Since the observed value is much greater than 1.96, we reject the null hypothesis that the probability of selecting the payoff dominant action is the same in both runs. This does not necessarily mean that the treatment with NONE achieve a better results than FULL: this might in fact be due to learning. But, once we analyze all the data from our experiment, by putting together all runs of all sessions, when NONE and FULL come first and second in similar proportion (e.g. ABBA design) and still finding the same results, then we may conclude that the treatments were significant.

Fisher's exact test

Again we summarize the N observations in a 2×2 contingency table, but now we consider the case that both of the row totals, r and $N - r$, and column totals c and $N - c$ are determined beforehand and are therefore fixed and not random. The test statistic T now is the number of observations in the first cell (row 1, column 1). The exact distribution of T when H_0 is true is given by the hypergeometric distribution:

$$P(T = x) = \frac{\binom{r}{x}\binom{N-r}{c-x}}{\binom{N}{c}} \qquad x = 0, 1, \ldots, \min(r, c)$$

$$= 0 \quad \text{for all other values of } x$$

For large samples, as in most of these tests, you can use as an approximation the standard normal distribution. If row totals or column totals or both are random, it is more accurate to use the chi-squared test statistic, but also when row totals, column totals or both are not fixed the Fisher's exact test is still valid. That is, this exact test finds the p-value for one subset of the sample space that has exactly that given row and column totals. However, the power of this test is usually less than the power of a more appropriate approximate test.

```
             STATISTICS FOR TABLE OF INFO BY PLAY

 Statistic                        DF          Value           Prob
 ----------------------------------------------------------------
 Chi-Square                        1         989.015          0.001
 Likelihood Ratio Chi-Square       1        1124.316          0.001
 Continuity Adj. Chi-Square        1         986.104          0.001
 Mantel-Haenszel Chi-Square        1         988.499          0.001
 Fisher's Exact Test  (Left)                                  1.000
                      (Right)                              6.50E-246
                      (2-Tail)                             1.30E-245
 Phi Coefficient                               0.718
 Contingency Coefficient                       0.583
 Cramer's V                                    0.718

 Sample Size = 1920
```

In our example, from the SAS output, we can reject the hypothesis that the two probabilities are the same in favor of the left-tail alternative that under NONE coordination on the payoff-dominant action is higher.

Mann–Whitney test and Kruskal–Wallis test

The tests based on the binomial distribution or contingency tables can also be used when outcomes are measured as real numbers. For example, you can simply split the range of possible observations into two bins labeled "class1" and "class2." That crude classification, however, disregards useful information contained in the data. With real-valued data (or even data measured ordinally), statistics based on rank are usually more powerful.

Consider two random samples, one of size n from population 1: $X_1, X_2, \ldots, X_n$, and the other of size m from population 2: $Y_1, Y_2, \ldots, Y_m$. Combine both samples and assign ranks 1 to $n + m = N$ without regard to which population each value came from. Denote $R(X_i)$ as the rank assigned to a member X_i of the first population. If several sample values are equal (tied), assign to each the average of their possible ranks. The test statistic is the sum of the ranks assigned to those values from the first population:

$$T = \sum_{i=1}^{n} R(X_i)$$

T is approximately a normal random variable, and the approximation is quite good if n and m are greater than 20 and there are few ties. When T is far below (or above) its mean, we have evidence that the values from the first population tend to be smaller (or larger) than the values from the other population, and we can reject the null hypothesis.

This procedure is known as the Mann–Whitney test, and is the nonparametric counterpart of the parametric two-sample t-test. The extension to more than two independent samples, called the Kruskal–Wallis test, uses a chi-square approximation instead of the normal, and that is what you find in SAS.

An example from SAS:

```
Kruskal-Wallis Test (Chi-Square Approximation)
CHISQ = 123.00  DF = 1  Prob > CHISQ = 0.0001
```

Wilcoxon signed ranks test

The signs test analyzed matched pairs of data by reducing each pair to a plus, a minus, or a tie, and applying the binomial test to the resulting single sample. The Wilcoxon signed ranks test also reduces the matched pair to a single observation by considering the difference $D_i = Y_i - X_i$, but keeps track of the magnitude of D_i as well as the sign.

To find the test statistic, drop the $D_i = 0$ observations and rank the remaining data by absolute value as in the Mann–Whitney test. The Wilcoxon signed rank test statistic is the sum of the ranks of observations that originally had a positive sign:

$$T^+ = \Sigma(R_i \text{ where } D_i \text{ is positive})$$

If the number of non-zero pair differences $n > 50$, the unit normal approximation works well:

$$T = \frac{\sum_{i=1}^{n} R_i}{\sqrt{\sum_{i=1}^{n} R_i^2}}$$

We can reject $H_0: E(D) = 0$ (i.e. the pairs have the same distribution) at level α if T is less than the normal $\alpha/2$ quantile or greater than its $1 - \alpha/2$ quantile.

```
                    NPAR1WAY  PROCEDURE

        Wilcoxon Scores (Rank Sums) for Variable AVPLAY
                  Classified by Variable INFO


               Sum of    Expected    Std Dev        Mean
   INFO    N   Scores    Under H0    Under H0       Score

   full   80  3240.50000   6440.0  288.485527   40.506250
   none   80  9639.50000   6440.0  288.485527  120.493750
                Average Scores Were Used for Ties


      Wilcoxon 2-Sample Test (Normal Approximation)
      (with Continuity Correction of .5)


      S = 3240.50    Z = -11.0889 Prob > |Z| = 0.0001


      T-Test Approx. Significance = 0.0001


      Kruskal-Wallis Test (Chi-Square Approximation)
      CHISQ = 123.00  DF = 1        Prob > CHISQ = 0.0001
```

In our example, $T^+ = 3240.50$ and its unit normal approximation $T = -11.0889$. The *p*-value of 0.0001 allows us to confidently reject the null hypothesis that mean choice is the same under FULL as under NONE.

Bootstrap

The Wilcoxon and the Binomial tests are very simple to compute but, by looking only at the order of observations, they still ignore useful information. Since computing power is now cheap, one way to overcome this problem is by using nonparametric procedures that are computationally demanding but use all sample information.

To illustrate, suppose we are interested in finding an approximate 95 percent confidence interval for the population standard deviation of the number of subjects choosing *Top* in the final period under the treatment information NONE. This is a rather complicated statistic, but the bootstrap method can find it in a straightforward manner. The available data consists of the following observations for ten independent runs:

Original observations:

Run	1	2	3	4	5	6	7	8	9	10	
# *Top*	12	10	9	12	12	9	10	12	11	12	10 obs.; $\bar{X} = 10.9, s = 1.29$

The bootstrap method uses the original random sample (in our case of size ten) to sample ten values with replacement:

Bootstrap sample 1:

Run	2	8	10	2	1	4	9	6	5	4	
# *Top*	10	12	12	10	12	12	11	9	12	12	10 obs.; $\bar{X}_1^* = 11.2, s_1^* = 1.14$

As you can see from the example, some of the original observations appear in the *bootstrap sample* more than once, others only once, or not at all. The number of observations in the bootstrap sample is always equal to the number of observations in the original random sample.

The bootstrap method utilizes hundreds of bootstrap samples obtained in the same manner from the original random sample, and for each sample it evaluates the estimator of interest. Here is another such sample:

Bootstrap sample n:

Run	3	4	7	1	1	6	8	6	2	7	
# *Top*	9	12	10	12	12	9	12	9	10	10	10 obs.; $\bar{X}_n^* = 10.5, s_n^* = 1.35$

The sample mean and standard deviation (of any estimator of interest) of these hundreds of bootstrap samples are then used to estimate the population mean and the population standard deviation of the estimator. The bootstrap method uses the entire empirical distribution function of these many values of the estimator as an estimator of the true population distribution function of the estimator.

Imagine we have 100 bootstrap samples, and therefore 100 values for s^*. To find the lower and the upper bounds of the 95 percent confidence interval for the population standard deviation of the number of subjects choosing *Top*, we just have to find the 0.025 and 0.975 sample quantile of the s^*. The lower endpoint is going to be the $100(0.025) = 2.5$, rounded up to 3, order statistic. The upper bound is going to be the $100(0.975) = 97.5$, rounded up to 98, order statistic. So order your 100 values of s^* from the smallest to the largest, and select the third and ninety-eighth:

$$1.03, 1.07, \boxed{1.14}, \ldots, \boxed{1.32}, 1.35, 1.45$$

Your approximate confidence interval is 1.14–1.32.

You have probably already noticed how everything in the bootstrap procedure depends on the original sample values. A different set of sample values would give you a different set of estimates. So make sure you are starting with a "good" random sample!

The BOOTSTRAP option in the PROC MULTTEST and a few other SAS procedures use this method. Experienced SAS users can write macros to perform bootstrap analysis to compute approximate standard errors, bias-corrected estimates, confidence intervals, etc.

Logit and OLS with treatment dummies

You probably are already familiar with linear regression models, written compactly as $y_i = X_i\beta + u_i$. A simple way of testing whether your treatments are significant is to include a dummy variable for each two-level treatment in the list of explanatory variables X. When the coefficient estimate (e.g. from OLS) for a dummy is significant, you can conclude that the treatment actually did affect the observed performance y.

When the dependent variable can take only two values $y = 0$ or 1, however, a linear regression model has two problems. First, it does not constrain the predicted value to lie between 0 and 1; second, it is heteroscedastic since the residuals can take on only one of two values: either $1 - X_i\beta$ or $X_i\beta$.

One solution is to transform $X\beta$ into a probability. You can do this with a function F (e.g. a cumulative density function) that maps $X\beta$ in $(-\infty, \infty)$ into a number between 0 and 1. The transformed model is $\Pr(y_i = 1) = F(X_i\beta)$.

Choosing F to be the standard normal gives us the *probit* model. Choosing F to be the logistic distribution gives us the *logit* model. The main difference between the two is that the logistic distribution has more weight in the extreme tails, but we do not know any actual data analyses for which logit and probit led to different conclusions. Both models are widely used for testing alternative hypotheses on individual behavior and are included in many computer programs. The logit is a little more popular and easier to generalize to more than two bins; however, see the ordered probit regression in Chapter 22. SAS estimates basic logit models using the command PROC LOGIT.

Let us see how things work on data from Prisoner's Dilemma games (for more details see Cassar, 2003). Here, twelve subjects, located on a circle, played under three different treatments: NONE (subjects could not see neighbors' payoffs), PARTIAL (subjects did see neighbors' payoffs), FULL (in addition to neighbors' payoffs subjects knew the average action selected by the entire group the previous period). We want to test hypotheses regarding agent behavior. For example, we could check whether an agent reciprocated neighbors' actions or, instead, imitated the most successful among the actions observed in their neighborhoods, and whether their strategies changed with the treatments.

We will use a logit fixed effects model because (as is often the case with lab data) the general tendency of a subject to favor one sort of action might carry over from one period to another, and possibly even across games. We will estimate the model:

$$\text{Prob(Cooperation)} = \frac{1}{1 + e^{-X'\beta}}.$$

The dependent variable (action) is 1 if the player chose to cooperate, 0 if she chose to defect. The explanatory variables X includes group (identify) (the fixed effects), lagacton (action chosen by the player the previous period), lagacts (number of neighbors who played Cooperate the previous period), and several interactions with dummy variables for treatments, for example, lagactsp = lagacts × {partial information dummy}, lagactsf = lagacts × {full information dummy}, lhigapar = {action that last period gave the highest payoff} × {partial information dummy}, lhigaful = {action that last period gave the highest payoff} × {full information dummy}, and lmeanful = {lag of the average group action} × {full information dummy}.

SAS does not yet have a convenient way of including fixed effects, so the following box shows the program and results using STATA.

```
STATA PROGRAM AND OUTPUT:
. clogit action lagacton lagacts lagactsp lagactsf lhigapar lhigaful
   lmeanful, group(identify)
Note: multiple positive outcomes within groups encountered.
Note: 12 groups (975 obs) dropped due to all positive or negative outcomes.
Iteration 0: log likelihood = -3610.5079
Iteration 1: log likelihood = -3287.2814
Iteration 2: log likelihood = -3284.6875
Iteration 3: log likelihood = -3284.6861
Conditional (fixed-effects) logistic regression  Number of obs = 8877
                                                      LR chi2(7)  = 1179.58
                                                      Prob > chi2 = 0.0000
Log likelihood = -3284.6861                           Pseudo R2   = 0.1522

--------------------------------------------------------------------------
action    |     Coef.  Std. Err.      z    P>|z|   [95% Conf. Interval]
--------------------------------------------------------------------------
lagacton  |   1.591944   .0632239   25.179  0.000    1.468028   1.715861
lagacts   |   .6735348   .0739109    9.113  0.000    .5286722   .8183974
lagactsp  |   .4972711   .1409962    3.527  0.000    .2209235   .7736187
lagactsf  |   .2489872   .1547154    1.609  0.108   -.0542493   .5522238
lhigapar  |  -.2598496   .1920493   -1.353  0.176   -.6362594   .1165601
lhigaful  |  -.6583504   .2167942   -3.037  0.002  -1.083259  -.2334415
lmeanful  |   1.760916   .5649874    3.117  0.002    .653561    2.868271
--------------------------------------------------------------------------
```

This model is estimated by maximum likelihood and the output includes the values of the log-likelihood function as it iterates to its maximum. It also includes the χ^2 test of the model against the null that the appropriate model contains only a constant. In our case, this test allows us to decisively reject the null.

The output gives evidence of inertia (the significant positive coefficient on lagacts), reciprocity to local conditions, especially under the partial information treatment, and positive reaction to the global variable. However, we do not find significant evidence of imitation of the most successful action in one's neighborhood, actually the opposite: when information was full, our model shows that observing that last period cooperation was the action with the highest payoff decreases significantly the probability that the agent will cooperate the next.

Bayesian techniques

Classical hypothesis tests as described above summarize the evidence by rejecting (or failing to reject) at some conventional significance level the null hypothesis of no difference in favor of a one- or two-sided alternative hypothesis. This style is what most economists are familiar with and it is best for a beginner to use it. However, its philosophical foundations are weaker than those of Bayesian techniques, which report revised beliefs that combine prior beliefs with the evidence provided by the data. With increasing computer power and reader sophistication, the Bayesian techniques are becoming more practical. We urge you to learn them and use them when you can.

Practical advice

This is a long chapter, so a short list of practical points might be helpful:

1   Before beginning your experiment, think about how you will analyze the data.
2   Use good design to avoid collinearity, omitted variables, etc.
3   Choose your laboratory protocols to reduce measurement errors.
4   Choose your treatments to produce good, representative samples.
5   Choose a design that allows you to use efficient statistics (e.g. matched-pairs).
6   Search the literature and your imagination to find effective graphical displays and summary statistics.
7   Look for irregularities and outliers in your data.
8   Use standard parametric and nonparametric hypothesis tests to draw your conclusions.

References

Box, G.E.P., Hunter, W.G., and Hunter, J.S. (1978) *Statistics for Experimenters*, New York: John Wiley and Sons.

Cassar, A. (2003) "From local interactions to global cooperation and coordination? Experimental evidence on local interactions and imitation," Working paper, UCSC.

Conover, W.J. (1998) *Practical Nonparametric Statistics*, 3rd edn, New York: John Wiley & Sons.

Friedman, D. and Sunder S. (1994) *Experimental Methods: A Primer for Economists*, Cambridge: Cambridge University Press.

Rogers, C. (1995) *On Becoming a Person: A Therapist's View of Psychotherapy*, Mariner Books.

Tufte, E. (1983) *The Visual Display of Quantitative Information*, Cheshire, Conn.: Graphics Press.

6 Do it

Running a laboratory session

Daniel Friedman and Alessandra Cassar

OK, you have sharpened the economic question to investigate, created an appropriate laboratory economy, worked out an experimental design, and planned how to analyze the data. It is time to actually conduct an experiment. How to proceed?

This chapter will walk you through the process of choosing and recruiting human subjects, bringing them to your lab facility, conducting a lab session, and paying them.

The subject pool

Permissions

The first step is to recruit human subjects. In US universities and perhaps elsewhere, you need approval from the Human Subjects Committee (or Institutional Review Board, as it is sometimes known) to comply with national law. The purpose of the legislation is to prevent any moral, physical, psychological, or financial harm to your subjects. Such risks are virtually nonexistent in most economics experiments, and many experimental economists routinely get exemptions under category 2 ("survey procedures, interview procedures, or observation of public behavior") or sometimes category 4 ("collection of existing data") of the relevant government document, 45 CFR 46.101. None of these is a perfect description of what we do, but the intent of the law seems entirely consistent with claiming an exemption for anonymous interactions as in market-like experiments. We believe that, had it been necessary, all the Trento Summer School student projects would have qualified for exemption.

Approvals take about 2 weeks to process at most US universities, but do not count on a rapid turnaround on your first project. Some Human Subjects Committees need to be educated about the nature of economics experiments.

Who?

With any necessary approvals in hand, you can recruit your human subjects. Who should you go after? Occasionally, the subject pool is a focus variable and your

choice will be determined by the hypotheses, for example, men are more generous than women. Usually, you are investigating economic hypotheses that say
nothing about the subjects' characteristics. In that case, you want subjects who are
convenient to recruit and schedule, and who can quickly understand the economy
you created, and who will not become bored too quickly.

The usual solution is to recruit undergraduate or MBA student subjects, and
perhaps check robustness by running a few sessions with children or professionals. Students are a good choice for several reasons. First, if you are doing your
experiment at a university facility, your subject pool is readily accessible, making
it convenient to recruit and to participate. Second, most students have a low
opportunity cost. Third, students tend to have a steep learning curve. Fourth, they
seldom know much about your hypotheses.

> By contrast, PhD students and faculty members are unreliable subjects.
> Often they get interested in what you are doing, and respond to their under-
> standing of your topic rather than to the incentives you have constructed.
> The results can be disastrous; see Friedman *et al*. (1984: 395–396, agent 5)
> for an understated example. Since then we have used such subjects only in
> early pilot runs, to help us debug our procedures.

It is a good rule not to use the students from a class you teach, or your friends
and acquaintances. Dominance and salience are at risk. Your relationship with
your subjects outside the lab creates internal and external validity problems in the
lab. Moreover, your goals as a teacher (e.g. to impart a full understanding and to
give a fair grade) may conflict with the scientific goals (e.g. to maintain privacy
and to provide economic incentives). An exception: such subjects can be helpful
in early pilots or exploratory sessions. The incentives and privacy do not matter
so much at this stage, and your friends and students might give you some useful
suggestions on adjusting the laboratory economy or clarifying the instructions.

Some economists have argued that students are a narrow, unrepresentative
segment of the population, and that may compromise external validity. On the
other hand, as noted in the box below, there can be problems in using professionals,
like businessmen or policy makers. Salience is more difficult to establish with
such subjects.

> Burns (1985) compared the results of professional wool buyers versus
> student buyers. Students proved to be far more adept than the professionals
> at maximizing their profits in the laboratory economy. The professionals'
> key skill was in detecting quality, and in the laboratory this was missing.
> They concentrated at maximizing their quantities and were slower than the
> students in learning from prices in the laboratory.

For most markets and many other economic institutions, years of experiments have shown that the results are insensitive to the choice of subject pool. You need not worry about your choice of subject pool if your experiment closely resembles such previous work. However, if time and budget permit, it is good practice in other cases to try two or more different subject pools. You can be more confident of the results when they are consistent across pools.

A team from the Trento Summer School ran a bargaining experiment, reported in Chapter 21. Bargaining outcomes can be sensitive to many details and certainly could be affected by the choice of subject pool. Fortunately, one of the team members had access to a group of professional negotiators. Although behavior of the professionals differed in some ways from the usual student subjects, the main effect (a "zone of agreement bias") seemed the same in both subject pools.

Sex

The observable characteristics of subjects – gender, age, etc. – deserve a brief discussion. While economic theory is genderless, popular theories in social psychology suggest that men are more individually oriented and women are more socially oriented. Several recent studies in experimental economics focus on this question, finding mixed results; for a survey, see Eckel and Grossman (forthcoming). Market experiments show hardly any gender effects. Gender differences are often found in Prisoner's Dilemma, Ultimatum, Public Goods, and Dictator experiments, but they do not seem consistent across studies. Eckel and Grossman argue that there is an underlying regularity. When subjects are exposed to risks, the results seem to depend on the experimental procedure and payoff structure but not much on gender. However, when little risk is involved (e.g. as respondent in Ultimatum experiments or Dictator games), gender differences become significant and systematic: women are more socially oriented than men.

Overall, until we understand this phenomenon more, you should be careful about gender, if the task involves face-to-face adversarial interactions as in the bargaining experiments. Also, you should be careful if you work as a waiter: Conlin *et al*. (forthcoming) found that for smaller bill (up to $27) men tip better than women, after that the reverse is true!

Age

Again, economic theory predicts no effect unless subjects are too young or too old to understand the instructions. Harbaugh *et al*. (2002) developed instructions accessible to elementary school children, and have documented some interesting effects. For example, younger children come closer than older children to the predictions of economic models of bargaining; older children and adults seem to factor more "fairness" into their behavior. Intriguingly, height within age group is strongly associated with toughness in bargaining, more so than gender or other characteristics.

This research is ongoing, but generally it encourages you to seek subjects with diverse personal characteristics when investigating "weak" economic institutions.

Risk attitudes

By contrast, risk attitudes are not directly observable but are considered crucial in standard economic models. Experimental economists have three different approaches to subjects' risk attitudes. First, the subjects can be left free to use their own innate risk preferences in making their decisions. The advantage of this approach is that it tests whether a proposition holds with more general assumptions. The disadvantage of losing control on the risk attitudes is that a particular theory of risk preference then cannot be tested.

A second approach is to measure the risk attitudes of the participants at the beginning, and to screen out those who do not have the required attitudes. (They can participate as monitors, or pay the show-up fee and be asked to come back for another experiment.) A problem is that measured risk attitudes are not very stable over time or measure (e.g. Isaac and James, 2000).

The third approach is to induce in your subjects any desired risk attitudes toward experimental points, using the binary lottery procedure (Smith, 1961; Roth and Malouf, 1979). The project in Chapter 17 uses a similar procedure. There is good evidence that the procedure induces the desired comparative statics, but evidence on levels is mixed at best; see, for example, Cox and Oaxaca (1995), Selten *et al.* (1999).

Rabin (2000) added to the controversy by pointing out that stable personal risk attitudes as in standard models are an implausible explanation for behavior in small-stakes lab experiments. Someone whose utility function is so concave that he would reject a 50–50 bet to win \$110 or lose \$100 at any wealth level would reject a 50–50 bet to win \$1,000,000,000 or lose \$1,000. It seems unlikely that anyone is so risk averse. Cox and Sadiraj (2003), however, dispute Rabin's interpretation of the theory. They argue that the utility function can be defined on changes in wealth rather than the level of terminal wealth, and therefore risk aversion is a legitimate explanation of the lab data.

So what should you do? Personally, we are inclined to assume that subjects are approximately risk neutral for small-stakes lab experiments, and we would use the binary lottery procedure to induce specified risk preferences only when risk preferences are a treatment variable. But not everyone agrees. Being aware of the ongoing controversies will help you avoid unpleasant surprises when referees and readers react to your work.

Experience

As we saw in Chapter 5, it is important to control for learning within sessions and across sessions. Many subjects will want to come back and will just show up at the right time. You do not want to discourage that, but neither do you want to lose control over the subject pool. Keep an updated file with you, so you can always check in real time whether a subject has already participated in the experiment. See one of our students' projects (Chapter 16) for an example of an artful mix of experienced and inexperienced subjects.

Number of subjects

How many subjects should you draw from the chosen pool? The relevant theory, the laboratory facilities, and your budget will help you decide. A frightening thought is that perfect competition seems to call for an infinite (indeed an uncountable) number of agents! Of course, even the global economy is finite, and the question really is how many people are needed so that the competitive (price taking) assumption is a good approximation. Laboratory work and some theory suggest that as few as three people of each type (e.g. sellers) suffice for many strong economic institutions, and six to eight people suffice for most games (e.g. Smith, 1982; Friedman, 1996; Cason and Friedman, 1997).

Larger groups sometimes are necessary. For example, one of us investigated the effect of three different networks (local, random, and small-world) for coordination and cooperation. In order to have networks with sufficiently different characteristics, it was necessary to use at least eighteen subjects. With a bottomless budget, twice as many subjects would have been even better.

To summarize, small groups usually suffice. Budget and facilities permitting, use larger groups or vary the group size when theory suggests that it might matter.

Laboratory facilities and setup

Until the mid-1970s, all economic experiments were run manually. Paper and pencil, a chalkboard, a watch, and a classroom were all you needed to run an experiment. In the 1980s, computers were introduced into economics labs. Computers permit tighter control of communications with and between subjects, often speed up the execution and allow more periods, and reduce the cost and error rate of recording data. They also open the door to a wide range of new experiments. For example, one author's current experiments with Internet congestion, and another author's experiments with networks would be simply infeasible without computers.

Manual experiments still have advantages. They are cheap and easy to get started, and easier to modify. Even if you have a generous budget and lots of time, manual is usually the best choice for early pilot experiments and for teaching in the classroom. Many of our students' projects started as manual experiments: see Chapter 17 for a special sort of noncomputerized market and Chapter 16 for a simple oral double auction.

If you are running a lot of sessions and need sharp control to ensure replicability, however, computerized experiments regain the advantage. Once the software is properly tuned, it minimizes marginal cost in terms of experimenter time and cost per observation. It also greatly reduces some possible nuisances, such as information conveyed by subjects' body language, or the experimenter's attitude or mood.

The fixed costs of computerized experiments have declined in recent years. Some general-purpose software are now available (e.g. ztree <http://www.iew. unizh.ch/ztree/index.php>, or the suite of programs at <http://www.people. virginia.edu/~cah2k/programs.html>). The web and e-mail now permit automated recruitment, reminders, instructions, and updates of the subject database, further reducing costs.

Conducting a session

Like learning to swim or bike, the best way is to try it! The first time it seems that there are too many things to keep track of, but it becomes routine after a while. Here is our list of tricks for conducting a successful session.

Scheduling. Reserve the room or laboratory and notify the subjects of the time and place 1–3 days in advance. Have them RSVP. You should overbook, because usually there are a few no-shows. The no-show rate rises on exam week and near long weekends, and usually declines when sessions are regular and subjects are experienced. We typically assume a 30 percent rate, but it varies from 0 to 50 percent.

Logbook. It is good practice to keep a laboratory logbook on which you record each experiment you conduct. Memory fades fast! You can start with the date, the number, and type of subjects who participate, the experiment parameters, and the number of periods completed. Be sure to note for future reference any unexpected event. Occasionally, these notes will help you spot a bug in the program, or understand data that turns out to be anomalous, or get some great new ideas for new experiments.

Checklist. Have handy a checklist of what to bring to the lab, and what to do. This way you will not forget, and even with different conductors each experiment can be run the same way. Our checklist is attached at the end of the chapter.

Setup. It is important that you arrive in the laboratory before your subjects arrive, so you can prepare the terminals or desks, assign a number to them, and arrange packets with instructions, payment sheet, and final questionnaire. You may want to set up your computer in the front facing the subjects.

Check-in. Have a sign-up sheet at the entrance, and keep track of no-shows and last-minute replacements. Be sure that the actual subject pool is close enough to the one you intended! Keep subjects from talking about the experiment and do not say anything about it until you are ready to give formal instructions to everyone. If too many people show up, send the extras home with the cash show-up fee (or, if it works better for scheduling a later session and the subjects do not mind, a larger IOU to be redeemed next time).

Randomized seats assignment. If the number of subjects is small, you can wait until all your subjects are present and hand out a numbered card corresponding to their assigned seat. If you have lots of subjects, let them pick cards as they arrive to reduce the dead time.

Conductors and monitors. You are probably the best person to run pilots and exploratory sessions to develop improvements. Once you have finalized the design, however, it is actually better if someone unaware of the purpose of the experiment conducts it. This is a standard part of medical experiments, and helps ensure an aspect of privacy, especially in manual experiments. For manual experiments, you may need monitors to help gather subjects' responses, write down results for each subject, etc. Monitors can be selected randomly from the subject pool, or by vote, or can be hired in advance. Monitors selected from the subject pool can ensure the credibility of your instructions or random devices by verifying the information you provide to subjects. See Chapter 19 for an example of randomization devices.

Oral and written instructions. Experimental economists rely on written instructions. Subjects read these instructions when they arrive, and the instructions usually are repeated orally. Consistency in the instructions is often crucial for replicability.

Answering questions. In most cases you want to respond publicly to all questions. Of course, you must not reveal a subject's private information. Subjects often ask you what actions they should take, but of course you do not want to tell them. With diplomacy, deflect questions that you cannot answer.

Quiz and dry-run periods. It is a good practice (for salience) to give a 2-min quiz and some practice periods. This way you make sure that the subjects understood the rules, and that they know that the other subjects understand the rules.

Termination. Usually you do not tell your subjects the number of periods in advance. You simply say that the experiment is completed when they finish the last scheduled period. That way you minimize (although perhaps do not eliminate) possible end-period effects and unwanted issues concerning backward induction. Overall, you should try to finish at least 10 min earlier than the announced end. This will give you more time to pay and debrief subjects, and still allow them to leave at the promised time.

Bankruptcy. Subjects know that you cannot ask them to pay you money, so if their cumulative earnings become negative they have a one-way bet. Further losses will cost them nothing, but gains may increase take home pay. Hence, you must deal with uncontrolled endogenous risk-seeking incentives as a subject approaches bankruptcy. The best policy usually is to let your subjects know in advance that if their payment goes close to zero they will be asked to leave immediately.

Bailout. Sometimes things will go wrong – not enough of the right kind of subjects show up, the software has a glitch, or there is a power failure. You should have a bailout plan, and know when to use it. Subjects should be paid even if the data are useless to you; they should get the show-up fee plus something appropriate for their time and trouble.

Exit procedures. Have each subject fill out a receipt for their earnings, and pay them one at a time, privately, in cash. Avoid checks or vouchers if possible, and avoid public indications of earnings amounts or ranks. Debriefing is routine in experimental psychology but not in economics. Economists are concerned that debriefings may compromise experimenter privacy in for later sessions. We usually debrief only by asking subjects waiting for payment to fill out an optional and neutral questionnaire that asks whether the instructions were clear, payments were sufficient to keep motivation high, etc., with space for any extra comments.

Most experiments run many periods. Usually the experimenter adds up each subject's earnings and pays the sum (or a positive linear transformation of the sum, using a pre-announced exchange rate and an initial balance and/or show-up fee). However, sometimes subjects are paid only for a single period, selected at random. Chapter 20 explains the rationale and reports a project comparing the two payoff procedures.

Backup data. Do not forget to back up your data on another machine right after the experiment is over. Have a directory where you can store all of your raw data, and do your work on a copy.

Checklist

Here is a copy of the routine for conducting experiments that we have refined over the years.
   Before the experiment:

1   prepare directories on the computer for storing input and output data and lab notes;
2   prepare the input data ("control file"), and determine the number of human subjects needed;
3   e-mail or phone people in the subject pool, overbook 10–50 percent as history dictates;
4   get adequate cash in useful denominations from the bank;
5   prepare instructions and photocopy enough for each of the subjects and a few extras;
6   check visual materials: powerpoint files and projector, transparencies and overheads projector, etc.;
7   check that there are enough receipt forms, highlight the parts they must complete, and write in the date;
8   check that there are enough quiz forms;
9   figure out the conversion rate ($/point) and place the appropriate notes file in the directory.

Bring to the experiment:

1   cash;
2   instructions;
3   forms for getting paid (receipts);
4   overheads (and disk w/overheads);
5   pens (for them to sign their receipts with);
6   a calculator to do the final payoff calculations (in case script fails);
7   numbers to assign seating and a hat or bag from which they can be drawn;
8   the script.

Right before the experiment:

1   arrive early, make sure that the computer screens are visually isolated;
2   setup the overhead projector and make sure there are white-board markers;
3   place instruction sheet at each computer and make sure that the back of the instructions is up and says that they should not turn them over until they are told to do so;
4   set up the computers that will be used.

As subjects arrive:

1   have them sign in as they arrive;
2   assign seats randomly using the numbered instructions;
3   give them time to read the instructions;
4   go over the instructions;
5   write the conversion rate (and other parameters as appropriate) on the board;
6   give the quiz;
7   start the server (or other computer program for the experiment);
8   log in the subjects;
9   play the practice rounds;
10   reset program (zero-out the earnings);
11   conduct experiment meanwhile: begin lab notes file in directory, outline design, note date, place, and unusual circumstances.

When the experiment ends:

1   hand out surveys and receipts and ask subjects to fill them out;
2   make a backup directory and copy all files into it;
3   print pay list from output file;
4   pay subjects, privately, one at a time; check that the receipt form is properly filled out, has the correct payment, and subject's signature;
5   copy pay list data into the lab notes file;
6   back up all data on to a different machine or medium.

After the experiment:

1   copy the receipts and keep one copy; originals will go to accounting and two copies stay with you;
2   update the subject pool file for no-shows and unused substitutes;
3   for participants, update the file to show payments received, type of experiment, and date.

References

Burns, P. (1985) "Experience and decision-making; a comparison of students and businessmen in a simulated progressive auction," in V.L. Smith, ed., *Research in Experimental Economics*, vol. 3, Greenwich, CT: JAI Press, pp. 139–157.

Cason, T. and Friedman D. (1997) "Price formation in single call markets," *Econometrica*, 65(2): 311–345.

Conlin, M., Lynn, M., and O'Donoghue, T. "The norm of restaurant tipping," *Journal of Economic Behavior and Organization*, forthcoming.

Cox, J. and Sadiraj, V. (2003) "Risk aversion and expected utility theory: coherence for small- and large-stakes gambles," University of Arizona manuscript, March.

Cox, J.C. and Oaxaca, R.L. (1995) "Inducing risk neutral preferences: further analysis of the data," *Journal of Risk and Uncertainty*, 11: 65–79.

Eckel, C.C. and Grossman, P.J. "Sex and risk: experimental evidence," in C. Plott, V.L. Smith, eds, *Handbook of Experimental Economics Results*, Amsterdam: Elsevier Science, forthcoming.

Friedman, D. (1996) "Equilibrium in evolutionary games: some experimental results," *Economic Journal*, 106(434): 1–25.

Friedman, D., Harrison G.W., and Salmon, J.W. (1984) "The informational efficiency of experimental asset markets," *Journal of Political Economy*, 92(3): 349–408.

Harbaugh, W.T., Krause, K., and Vesterlund, L. (2002) "Risk attitudes of children and adults: choices over small and large probability gains and losses," *Experimental Economics*, 5(1): 53–84.

Isaac, R.M. and Duncan, J. (2000) "Just who are you calling risk averse?" *Journal of Risk and Uncertainty*, 20: 177–187.

Rabin, M. (2000) "Risk aversion and expected-utility theory: a calibration theorem," *Econometrica*, 68(5): 1281–1292.

Roth, A.E. and Malouf, M.K. (1979) "Game-theoretic models and the role of information in bargaining," *Psychological Review*, 86: 574–594.

Selten, R., Sadrieh, A., and Abbink, K. (1999) "Money does not induce risk neutral behavior, but binary lotteries do even worse," *Theory and Decision*, 46: 211–249.

Smith, C.A.B. (1961) "Consistency in statistical inference and decisions," *Journal of the Royal Statistical Society*, Series B, 23: 1–25.

Smith, V.L. (1982) "Markets as economizers of information: experimental examination of the Hayek hypothesis," *Economic Inquiry*, 20(2): 165–179.

7   Finish what you started

Project management

Daniel Friedman and Alessandra Cassar

There is something deceptive about a well-written research paper. The introduction highlights an important issue (often one that somehow had previously escaped your attention!) and makes it seem obvious how to think about it. A theoretical section explains lucidly what is already known and/or can be deduced about the issue. If the paper is empirical, it lays out experimental or data collection procedures that seem obvious and appropriate. Then new conclusions are derived in a compelling manner. It all seems to flow logically.

But the research process behind the paper typically is quite different. It probably involves false starts, backtracking, surprises, and rethinking. Usually, the logical flow becomes clear only at the end of the project. You will miss many research opportunities if you do not understand the very different processes of running a research project and writing up the results. This chapter will try to help you with both processes.

Conceptual

Your research project starts with an issue that interests you and some idea about how to examine it in the lab. But how do you move from a vague idea to a sound laboratory protocol? How do you come up with the best laboratory economy, treatments, design, and statistics? In brief, our answer is: try it out, learn from your experience, iterate, and refine!

Where does the initial idea come from? Sometimes the issue comes from a theoretical model that guides you pretty closely. For example, bargaining or auction theory will be fairly explicit about the basic protocol (e.g. sealed or open bidding), the treatments (e.g. the number of bidders, the distribution of values, and the information available to bidders).

At other times you need a clever idea. No physicist before Galileo, it seems, thought about measuring how the length and mass of a pendulum affected the duration of its arc. The sociologist Stanley Milgram sent a package to several hundred people in the Midwest who were asked to pass it to someone they knew personally who might move it toward a target person in Boston. The results gave Milgram important new data on personal networks in America, leading to the famous "six degrees of separation" rule (Milgram, 1967).

There are many similar examples in economics. For example, in Chapter 11, Rosemarie Nagel explains a clever protocol for finding the "depth of reasoning" or steps of backward induction that people undertake. In Chapter 19, one of the students develops an experiment by artfully simplifying a macro-model to a two player, two state, 2×2 coordination game.

Unfortunately, nobody has an infallible recipe for generating clever ideas. Our best suggestion is to read what others have done, think about it, and try some things out. Inspiration seems to strike more often people who are already immersed in a problem.

OK, suppose you have an idea, fiendishly clever or perhaps more routine. How do you develop it into a good protocol? We recommend a little backward induction: think about the data analysis from the outset. For example, if you want to test two competing theories about individual behavior (say, best reply versus imitation of those with higher payoff), think about statistical tests and data that would distinguish them. This in turn leads you to think of treatments that would clearly separate the two kinds of behavior. Thinking this through from the beginning can help you get cleaner results at the end.

Pre-pilots and pilots

Backward induction is only a start. Do not expect to figure it all out right away! You have an initial protocol (aided by backward induction) but it probably needs a lot of refinement before it will really work.

Begin with some pre-pilot sessions. You can ask your friends or students to help you check out your instructions, software (if any), and procedures. Collect the data, even though it is not reportable, to check your data capture, data verification, and data processing ideas. Probably you will see some problems or maybe notice an opportunity you overlooked, perhaps even get a seriously clever idea. Make the changes and do another pre-pilot until you think it is ready for testing with real subjects. In Chapter 16, you can find an example of how our students' pilot experiment glitches to improve later design. Chapter 22 is another example of learning from pilots.

Pilot experiments use paid subjects. Run a few to see whether your treatments are separated enough, which parameter values to use, whether the instructions are clear, how long will a session last, and so on. Once you feel you are done with dress rehearsals, you can enter in full production.

Production runs

This phase actually requires less from you. The design decisions have been made, and ideally you will have somebody else conduct the sessions who does not know too much about your research goals. You should monitor a few sessions to make sure that the proper protocols are used, however. At this stage, your most active task is to look over the data as they arrive.

Follow-ups

Chances are something unexpected and interesting will come up as you analyze the data from production runs. We can hardly think of an experiment that came out exactly as expected, and we have learned a lot by investigating the reasons behind the surprises. So…save some of your budget for some follow-up experiments!

Actually, one of us is currently running a project that consists mainly of follow-up experiments. The project investigates treatments that promote the sunk cost fallacy. It is turning out to be an elusive quarry; treatments that we initially thought would encourage the fallacy turned out to encourage rather rational decisions. So we are now working with several new treatments developed long after the project began.

Write-up

Writing is crucial for two reasons. You may think you understand your project and the data, but when you write it up you usually find gaps and new puzzles. Writing helps you think everything through. Equally important, your work has value only to the extent that it affects the thinking of other people in your field. You must communicate with them, and writing is the primary vehicle.

Your first challenge in the write-up is to decide what material to cover and at what depth. Of course, you want to keep a sharp focus and not lose your readers' attention. But you also want to explain each detail that you painstakingly worked out. How do you manage the conflict between these goals?

Modern technologies can help you find the right balance. Your web-page can accommodate all the details of your experiment. You can write up appendices that lay out all the details needed to replicate your work, and post them on a website. Point the interested reader to the website, and spare the more casual readers. If you feel some material is necessary part of the paper, but somehow off-point, you can always relegate it to an appendix attached to the paper. For example, instructions, data cleaning, and statistical procedures belong in an appendix, probably on the web. Sample instructions from the Trento Summer School projects appear as an appendix to this chapter.

Empirical papers usually are organized as follows: introduction (which states the main question, motivates the research, surveys the literature, and gives an overview of the paper and the main results), relevant theory, laboratory procedures, results and discussion. Depending on the focus of your paper, you can move the theory to, or the literature survey from, the introduction. Avoid footnotes whenever possible.

Two books that might inspire you to write well:

- *Economical Writing* by Deirdre McCloskey.
- *A Guide for the Young Economist* by William Thomson.

For pictures and tables:

- *The Visual Display of Quantitative Information* by Edward R. Tufte.

Save all raw data! Once you have published your first paper, you should make your data available upon request. As yet there is no centralized databank for economics experiments, but eventually there may be. The US National Science foundation's Digital Library initiatives are encouraging such developments. Information may eventually appear on sites like http://dlc.dlib.indiana.edu/.

Seminar

Do not be shy! After your first write-up (and before your lab budget is exhausted!), present your results at a seminar. The reactions of seminar audiences create excellent opportunities to improve the write-up and often give you ideas for follow-up experiments. Seminars also are an important vehicle for communicating your results to the world.

Polish and publish

Keep the polishing for the final step. Concentrate your attention not only at the prose, but also at making clear tables and graphs. What format should you use? You might want to keep your paper double-spaced with the tables and pictures at the end; this is the style required for submission by most journals. But the main principle is to make it as easy as possible for the reader to understand what you did and what you discovered.

Appendix

Instructions for animal-spirits cycles – Chapter 19

You are about to participate in an economics experiment in which you will play a game with an unknown participant for thirty rounds.

In each round, you have to choose A or B. The other participant will also choose A or B. Your profit for that round depends on three things: *your choice*, the *other participant's choice*, and *a random event*. The table below shows how your profits are calculated:

	Your choice	*Other participant's choice*	*Your profit*
Random event X	A	A	p
	A	B	q
	B	A	r
	B	B	s
Random event Y	A	A	t
	A	B	u
	B	A	v
	B	B	w

Each round, either one of two *random events* occurs: X or Y. If random event X occurs, for example, and you choose A and the other participant chooses B, then you will get q number of points. If random event Y occurs and both you and the other participant choose B, then you will receive w points for that round.

Some combinations of choices by you and the other participant will yield more profits than other choices, although you will not know in advance which choices are more profitable.

Finally, for each round before you make your choice, the overhead will show one of the following two pictures:

Picture 1

Picture 2

These pictures may or may not be related to anything relevant in the game (e.g. which random event occurred). You may choose to ignore the pictures or to use them in some way.

On the *record sheet*, please fill out the first two columns each round. In the first column, "Pictures," write in which picture is shown on the overhead for that round.

In the second column, "Your Choice," write in your choice for that round: A or B.

Do not fill out the rest of the form. When you have filled out the first two columns, we will take the sheet and fill out the other participant's choice, the random event and your profit for the round.

Remember that your profits depend only on three things: your choice, the other participant's choice, and the random event.

Instructions for professional subjects[1] for integrative negotiation – Chapter 21

You are about to participate in an experimental study in decision-making and negotiation. The experiment will last for about half an hour. The instructions of the experiment are simple, and if you follow them carefully, you may win a lot of unique gifts and typical products from our region [money for students]. Please, do not speak with the other player until the experiment starts.

According to how you perform the gifts [money] will be delivered to you tomorrow. Please, write your name and the letter assigned to you for each period of experiment on the record sheet.

Decisions and earnings

Everyone of you will be randomly matched with another participant. You have almost 10 min to gain as many points as you can. The number of gifts [the amount of money] will be directly proportional to the total number of points you will score in the experiment. *Note that the amount of gifts [money] you will receive will be proportional to your own performance and not to the performance of the couple.* At the beginning we assign you fifty points.

What to do

As you see, you have a sheet with two tables, each made of two columns: in the left column you have a scale of numbers from 0 to 10. In the right column you have the number of points associated with each number in the left column. The tables of the other player might be different from yours. Your table and the points you get for each number of the left column is not known to the other player. *Please, keep your tables secret.*

You have to negotiate with the other player in order to choose a number in the left column. You have to negotiate for one number in the first table (called "first number") and one number in the second table (called "second number"). If you both agree, write it in the record sheet and call a laboratory assistant. *The total points you gain are the sum of the points you get from the agreement in each table.* If you do not agree, you remain with your initial points.

Please, note that you can agree with the other player on the "first number" and not on the "second number" and vice versa. In this case you will get the points corresponding to the number on which you agreed and you will get zero points for the number on which you did not agree. Of course you can agree on both or neither.

During the negotiations you can speak freely with the other player but you can not show your table to the other player.

Note

1 Changes for student subjects are shown in square brackets.

References

McCloskey, D. (1999) *Economical Writing*, Prospect Hts, IL: Waveland Press.
Milgram, S. (1967) "The small world problem," *Psychology Today*, 2: 60–67.
Thomson, W. (2001) *A Guide for the Young Economist*, Boston, MA: MIT Press.
Tufte, E.R. (2001) *The Visual Display of Quantitative Information*, Cheshire, Conn.: Graphics Press.

Part III

Applications

8 Markets

Daniel Friedman and Alessandra Cassar

Market experiments deserve an entire course; this chapter is mainly an invitation to read more. It presents some classic experiments prior to 1980 and one strand of work in the 1990s. The common thread is the Hayek hypothesis: somehow the market combines dispersed private information held by individual buyers and sellers, and finds a competitive equilibrium price that maximizes social gains. Applied to field data, the hypothesis is a bit mystical because the private information (willingness to buy or to sell) is not observable. Laboratory markets allow us to penetrate the mystery, check the truth of the hypothesis, and start to identify the underlying forces.

The last section of the chapter lists some currently active research areas. See Chapters 3 and 4 of Davis and Holt (1993) and Chapters 1 and 2 of Friedman and Rust (1993) for useful surveys; and see the other chapters in Friedman and Rust (1993) for related original research.

Some classic experiments

Most economists know of Edward Hastings Chamberlin for his pioneering work on monopolistic competition as an alternative to competitive equilibrium. Experimental economists, however, know him mainly for his 1948 paper summarizing the results of a decade of classroom experiments.

> What else was happening about that time? Thurstone (1931) had already completed a series of experiments to estimate indifference curves, starting experimentation in individual choice, and Flood (1952) reports early experiments in game theory, beginning in the 1940s.

Using Harvard PhD students attending his class, Chamberlin created a market with a large number of traders, very imperfect information, and no auctioneer to coordinate trade. He privately assigned single unit values to buyers and costs to sellers. Sellers and buyers then wandered around the room searching for counterparties, and sometimes agreed on transaction prices in bilateral negotiations. Prices were not publicly reported during trade.

Chamberlin found considerable price dispersion, some bias in transaction prices, and significant inefficiency, mostly due to extramarginal trade. Beyond these findings, his experiments are important because they foreshadow induced values and market institutions, two crucial innovations for experimental economics.

Chamberlin's motive apparently was polemical and pedagogical: he wanted to shake his students' faith in competitive equilibrium so that they might take monopolistic competition more seriously. 2002 Nobel laureate Vernon Smith was among his students in the 1940s, and thought that competitive equilibrium might have a better chance if he changed some of the procedures a bit.

Smith (1962) reports classroom experiments run between 1956 and 1961 at Purdue University. In Smith's experiments, buyers and sellers could transact by making and accepting public bids and asks; this market institution later became standard and known as the Oral Double Auction (ODA). At the same time, Smith introduced two other now-standard procedures: stationary repetition, in which the values for the buyers and the costs for the sellers were held constant across several trading periods; and (in some sessions) salient cash payments.

Smith's results were very different than Chamberlin's. The transaction prices converged reliably and fairly quickly to the competitive equilibrium values. The slight inefficiencies came mostly from missed intramarginal trades. Since then, thousands of experiments have corroborated Smith's results with only few buyers and sellers. Over the next decade or so, experiments showed that the competitive equilibrium (CE) model predicts double auction market outcomes well even with large asymmetries in buyer and seller surplus.

Two other classic experiments deserve separate mention. Plott and Smith (1978) report an experiment contrasting the ODA with the posted offer (PO) commonly used in retail markets. (In seller PO, the sellers simultaneously choose posted price and then buyers choose purchase quantities.) This landmark study shows how to compare market institutions (or other economic institutions) in the lab. While both institutions were relatively efficient, convergence was much faster with the ODA, which approached 100 percent efficiency. Many later experiments with the PO market institution are discussed in Davis and Holt (1993).

Williams (1980) implemented the first Continuous (or Computerized) Double Auction (CDA). He used an early network protocol called PLATO; by now laboratory versions of the CDA runs on most major network protocols. Perhaps the most striking result is that convergence in the CDA is slower than in the ODA!

Given Williams' result, and the lower cost of getting an ODA experiment started, you might wonder why the CDA now is so popular among experimentalists. We can think of four reasons. First, the CDA allows tighter control over communication among traders. In an ODA, it is virtually impossible to control the snickers and groans that may speed up learning but are hard to quantify or model. Second, using standard software, previous results are more easily replicated in the CDA. Third, computerization lowers the cost of recording and checking the data; ODA sessions are labor intensive and error prone. Fourth, the CDA allows much greater flexibility for automated agents, private information flows during trade, etc. Indeed, it is possible to create market variants and information conditions that are infeasible in the ODA. Often experimentalists run ODA pilot sessions, and then (after settling on the main treatments) switch to CDA for full production.

The Hayek hypothesis in the 1990s

Classic surveys of the early market results can be found in Smith (1982b) and Plott (1982). Smith (1982a) takes a subset of the results and documents a "scientific mystery," which he calls the Hayek hypothesis. Participants apparently need to know very little to take the right action to achieve competitive equilibrium. The hypothesis is that the market institution somehow forces traders to reveal their private information (their willingness to transact) even when only a few traders are present.

Since Marshall, most economists have thought that stringent conditions are required for the invisible hand to work properly. In particular, it was often said that necessary conditions to achieve competitive equilibrium include a large number of buyers and sellers, each one of them small relative to the market, and each with perfect information about the demand and the supply schedules. Hayek was among the minority of economists who believed that buyers and sellers need no public information other than current prices. Hardly anyone believed that competitive equilibrium could be approximated well with as few as three or four buyers and three or four sellers. Yet, this is precisely what the classic market experiments demonstrated. How did the double auction perform this magic? That was the mystery.

Gode and Sunder (1992, 1993) argue that the magic is in the market institution, not the traders. They present computer simulations of zero-intelligence (ZI) traders, who bid randomly below their reservation values or ask randomly above their costs. The outcomes typically are highly efficient and average prices closely approximate competitive equilibrium. The authors attribute this result to the CDA and the usual downward sloping demand and upward sloping supply curves. We would also point to two other features of the ZI algorithm: the no-loss constraint (e.g. sellers never ask below cost) and the convention that nobody waits or gives up, but tirelessly generates new random bids or asks as long as potential gains remain.

Of course, this is not the whole story. ZI simulations do not allow traders to hoard their private information, as humans might. The only inefficiency the simulations allow in a CDA is extramarginal trading, but failure to trade intramarginal units is the more common form of inefficiency for human traders. Unlike humans, ZI traders under stationary repetition are just as efficient in the first period of trade as in the last, and they are far less efficient than humans in some other market institutions. ZI traders are now a standard benchmark, but by themselves they do not dispel the mystery about the high efficiency humans achieve in markets.

Friedman and Ostroy (1995) provide a different insight, on how stationary repetition allows small numbers of humans with private information to achieve near-competitive outcomes.

The paper started with an argument between the coauthors. Ostroy pointed out that the essence of the traditional view of competitive equilibrium is that each individual buyer (or seller) faces perfectly elastic supply (or demand). A large number of buyers and sellers guarantees this, but is not actually necessary. It suffices that demand and supply functions are flat and close to each other in the region of the competitive equilibrium, or (for a wider range of parameter configurations) that each trader demands or supplies only a few indivisible units. In such cases, traders cannot profitably underreveal willingness to transact (see Figure 8.1). Ostroy's clincher was that most lab experiments used approximations of these special cases.

Friedman thought that the competitive outcomes arose from the market institution, not from special demand and supply parameters. The CDA, he argued, created a dynamic form Bertrand competition that forced traders to reveal their willingness to transact. By contrast, a static market institution, such as the Call market (a two-sided sealed auction, also known as the clearinghouse) would produce less competitive outcomes. The authors agreed on an experiment that would resolve their dispute.

The experiment featured box-like parameter configurations for demand and supply that would maximize the gains to non-competitive behavior (see Figure 8.2), and a new procedure (called odd-lot trading) that permits almost perfectly divisible units to be traded. Now a single trader could have had a large influence on price just by withholding a small quantity. To the delight of one author, this CDA experiment produced highly competitive outcomes.

The next step was to run a Call market experiment using the same box-like parameters and odd-lot procedure. To the surprise of both authors, the experiment produced outcomes almost as efficient and competitive as those in the CDA! A

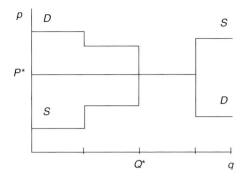

Figure 8.1 Traditional view of competitive equilibrium: demand and supply functions flat and close to each other at the margin.

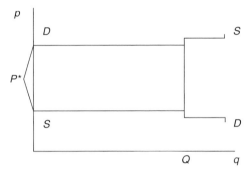

Figure 8.2 Experiment (CDA): box-like parameter configurations for demand and supply.

closer look at the data revealed something quite interesting. Although true demand and supply were box-like, in later periods of the Call market the *revealed* demand D' and supply S' typically were very competitive: very elastic at the market clearing price, as in Figure 8.3.

The authors then formulated a theory, dubbed the as-if complete information Nash equilibrium approach. Traders' equilibrium strategies fully reveal quantity, but misrepresent prices as completely elastic at the market clearing price. The idea is that stationary repetition suffices for traders to learn the market clearing price, the only additional piece of information the strategy requires. Previous authors had also discovered that competitive equilibrium outcomes correspond precisely with complete information Nash equilibrium (Dubey, 1982; Simon, 1984, 1987; Benassy, 1986) and Smith himself (private communication) had similar intuitions on resolving the mystery.

To complete the scientific investigation, the paper shows that the new theory predicts that some market institutions will produce inefficient outcomes given odd-lot trading and box-like parameters, and a final experiment verifies that prediction.

The ZI approach and the as-if complete information approach do not resolve a very important part of the mystery: when markets are not repeated (or in the first period with stationary repetition), how do humans achieve fairly efficient outcomes?

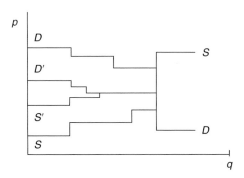

Figure 8.3 Behavior in Call market/odd-lot experiments. Given the box-like demand
and supply parameters *D* and *S*, subjects reveal only the elastic demand
and supply *D'* and *S'* in later periods.

A new incomplete information theory, surveyed in Satterthwaite and Williams
(1993), seems relevant. It assumes that each trader is fully aware of the strategic
value of his/her own private information and knows the structure of other traders'
strategies but not their private values for single, indivisible units. The theory derives
fairly efficient Bayesian Nash equilibria (BNE) for Call market trading.

Cason and Friedman (1997) conducted an experiment to investigate this BNE
approach. Single unit values for four buyers, and costs for four sellers, were identically and independently drawn each period from a uniform distribution.
Typically, there is a range of clearing prices, and the authors investigated three
cases: $k = 1$ (high end of the range), $k = 1/2$ (middle), and $k = 0$ (low end). The
other treatment involved traders' experience: with other humans, or with robots
playing the BNE strategies, or inexperienced.

The observed price and market efficiency were closer to the BNE predictions
than to the competitive equilibrium or to the ZI predictions. (ZI predicts very
inefficient outcomes in Call markets and, of course, competitive equilibrium
predicts 100 percent efficiency.) Equally interesting were several systematic deviations from BNE predictions. Subjects' observed bids and asks were not respon-
sive to changes in the pricing rule (k), and they revealed more willingness to
transact than predicted. Another interesting clue was that overall the BNE predictions did not improve with greater experience.

A closer examination of the data lead to an explanation. As demonstrated in
Cason and Friedman (1999), traders respond much more strongly to "missed"
trades due to underrevelation than to adverse pricing due to overrevelation. This
learning bias pushes traders to reveal more than they would in BNE. Indeed, the
median inexperienced trader in early trading periods revealed about 90 percent of
true willingness to buy or sell (roughly as predicted in BNE for $k = 1/2$) while the
median experienced trader in late trading periods revealed about 99 percent. Of
course, such overrevelation promotes efficient outcomes and thereby helps
explain the success of the Hayek hypothesis.

To summarize, our account of laboratory markets points to three reasons for the "mysterious" efficiency of markets:

1   Market institutions, especially the CDA, push even zero-intelligence traders towards a market clearing price.
2   When traders know a market clearing price, they can use as-if complete information strategies that underreveal willingness to pay in the price dimension but fully reveal in the quantity dimension. All non-trivial Nash equilibrium strategies take this form, and support efficient market outcomes.
3   When they do not know a market clearing price, human traders seem to use a biased learning process that pushes them toward full revelation and hence efficiency. The bias is that missing a profitable trade provokes a disproportionately large adjustment.

> Did you notice that this narrative switched from double auctions, the original objects of the Hayek hypothesis, to the simpler Call market? More complex theories are needed to explain how traders achieve efficiency in a continuous market. Several of the more complex theories (and also ZI) are explained and tested on double auction data in Cason and Friedman (1996).

Other market experiments

Are there settings where the CDA performs badly? Van Boening and Wilcox (1996) show that large sunk costs (and perhaps other indivisibilities) undermine its absolute and even relative performance. Is there some learning process that explains both within-period and across-period learning in Call markets, or in other market institutions? What happens when buyers and sellers enter and exit while trade is taking place? These are still open topics, suitable for dissertation research.

Asset market experiments allow a single trader to buy and to resell financial claims that pay dividends over many periods. Do asset prices aggregate diverse private information? Can there be bubbles, where asset price far exceeds intrinsic value? There is a rich laboratory literature beginning in the early 1980s; Sunder (1995) surveys about 200 of the articles and Charles Holt's website <http://www.people.virginia.edu/~cah2k/assety2k.htm> lists many more recent articles.

Contributions to the asset market literature continue, including two chapters of this volume! Chapter 16 reports a two-sided ODA experiment with common values. The students used an artful mix of experienced and inexperienced subjects to test how the entry of inexperienced subjects affects asset prices. They ran one session where inexperienced subjects in the fourth round replaced 25 percent of the experienced subjects. In Chapter 17, our students studied nonlinear price dynamics in a unique laboratory asset market.

All markets discussed so far are auctions, where buyers and sellers seek the best possible price and do not care with whom they transact. At the other extreme are matching markets, where price is not an issue and the whole point is with whom you transact. Examples include placement of medical internships in hospitals, and marriage. See Roth (2002) for an introduction to the theoretical, field, and laboratory literature. An emerging research area concerns markets where price and counterparty both are important. Examples include non-auction market institutions for ordinary goods (e.g. Rich and Friedman, 1998), market institutions of various sorts when buyers and sellers form attachments that are costly to break (e.g. Cason *et al.*, 2003), and matching markets with endogenous price determination (e.g. Kamecke, 1998).

Posted offer markets predominate in retail transactions, and have a rich laboratory literature. See Davis and Holt (1993, Chapter 4) for a survey of the classic work. Comparisons of market institutions continue in various settings, and new market institutions are being invented and tested (e.g. McCabe *et al.*, 1993).

Of particular interest are the so-called smart or computer-assisted markets, for example McCabe *et al.* (1993, 1997). Delivered electric power, airport takeoff and landing rights, natural gas delivery, and computer resource packages traditionally are transacted via bilateral negotiation and contracting (or by government agencies). Thanks to computers and telecommunications networks, it now is practical to create competitive markets for such complex combinations of goods or composite goods. Laboratory tests so far are very encouraging. The main idea (sometimes called a Smith auction, after its application to public goods in Smith, 1980) is that human buyers and sellers make bids for the packages they desire, partially revealing the true demand. The computer program then computes prices and allocations that maximize the social value revealed in the bids. Over time, humans tend to reveal enough to achieve surprisingly high efficiency. The underlying process may be similar to the biased learning that leads to very efficient outcomes in the simple random Call markets.

References

Benassy, J.P. (1986) "On competitive market mechanisms," *Econometrica*, 54(1): 95–108.

Cason, T. and Friedman, D. (1996) "Price formation in double auction markets," *Journal of Economic Dynamics and Control*, 20(8): 1307–1337.

Cason, T. and Friedman, D. (1997) "Price formation in single call markets," *Econometrica*, 65(2): 311–345.

Cason, T. and Friedman, D. (1999) "Learning in a laboratory market with random supply and demand," *Experimental Economics*, 2(1): 77–98.

Cason, T., Friedman, D., and Milam, G.H. (2003) "Bargaining versus posted price competition in customer markets," *International Journal of Industrial Organization*, 21(2): 223–251.

Davis, D.D. and Holt, C.A. (1993) *Experimental Economics*, Princeton: Princeton University Press.

Dubey, P. (1982) "Price–quantity strategic market games," *Econometrica*, 50(1): 111–126.

Flood, M.M. (1952) "Some experimental games," Research Memorandum RM-789, RAND Corporation, Santa Monica.

Friedman, D. and Ostroy, J. (1995) "Competitivity in auction markets: an experimental and theoretical investigation," *Economic Journal*, 105(428): 22–53.

Friedman, D. and Rust, J. (1993) *The Double Auction Market Institutions, Theories, and Evidence*, Reading, MA: Addison-Wesley.

Gode, D.K. and Sunder, S. (1992) "Lower bounds for efficiency of surplus extraction in double auctions," Carnegie-Mellon Graduate School of Industrial Administration (GSIA) Working Paper, February 17, 1992.

Gode, D.K. and Sunder, S. (1993) "Allocative efficiency of markets with zero-intelligence traders: market as a partial substitute for individual rationality," *Journal of Political Economy*, 101(1): 119–137.

Kamecke, U. (1988) "Wage formation in a centralized matching market," *International Economic Review*, 39(1): 33–53.

McCabe, K.A, Rassenti, S. and Smith, V. (1993) "Designing a uniform price double auction: an experimental evaluation," in D. Friedman and J. Rust, eds, *The Double Auction Market: Institutions, Theories, and Evidence,* Santa Fe Institute Series in the Science of the Complexity, *Proceedings*, vol. 15, Reading, MA: Addison-Wesley.

Plott, C.R. (1982) "Industrial organization theory and experimental economics," *Journal of Economic Literature*, 20: 1485–1527.

Plott, C.R. and Smith, V.L. (1978) "An experimental examination of two exchange institutions," *Review of Economic Studies*, 45(1): 133–153.

Rich, C.S. and Friedman, D. (1998) "The matching market institution: a laboratory investigation", *American Economic Review*, 88(5): 1311–1322.

Roth, A.E. (2002) "The economist as engineer: Game theory, experimentation, and computation as tools for design economics," Fisher-Schultz Lecture, *Econometrica*, 70(4): 1341–1378.

Satterthwaite, M. and Williams, S. (1993) "The bayesian theory of the *k*-double auction," in D. Friedman and J. Rust, eds, *The Double Auction Market: Institutions, Theories, and Evidence,* Santa Fe Institute Series in the Science of the Complexity, *Proceedings*, vol. 15, Reading, MA: Addison-Wesley.

Simon, L. (1984) "Bertrand, the Cournot paradigm, and the theory of perfect competition," *Review of Economic Studies*, 51: 209–230.

Simon, L. (1987) "Bertrand price competition with differentiated commodities," *Journal of Economic Theory*, 41: 304–332.

Smith, V.L. (1962) "An experimental study of competitive market behavior," *Journal of Political Economy*, 70(2): 111–137.

Smith, V.L. (1980) "Experiments with a decentralized mechanism for public good decisions," *American Economic Review*, 70(4): 584–599.

Smith, V.L. (1982a) "Markets as economizers of information: experimental examination of the Hayek hypothesis," *Economic Inquiry*, 20(2): 165–179.

Smith, V.L. (1982b) "Microeconomic systems as experimental science," *American Economic Review*, 72: 923:55.

Sunder, S. (1995) "Experimental asset markets: a survey," in J.H. Kagel and A.E. Roth, eds, *Handbook of Experimental Economics*, Princeton: Princeton University Press.

Thurstone, L.L. (1931) "The measurement of social attitudes," *Journal of Abnormal and Social Psychology*, 26: 249–269.

Van Boening, M. and Wilcox, N. (1996) "Avoidable cost: ride a double auction roller coaster," *American Economic Review*, 86: 461–477.

Williams, A.W. (1980) "Computerized double-auction markets: some initial experimental results," *Journal of Business*, 53: 235–258.

9 Auctions

Daniel Friedman and Alessandra Cassar

Auctions are a showcase for economic science. It would take several thick volumes to properly describe the advances in recent decades in auction theory, auction empirics and auction practice; or how innovations in theory spurred innovations in empirics and practice, and vice versa. This chapter will just touch on the process, highlighting the interplay of laboratory experiments with theory and other empirical work.

Laboratory experiments on auctions work especially well with other empirical studies using field data. The advantage of field data is that it reports the outcomes when experienced and skilled professionals bid in full-scale auctions for high stakes. The disadvantage is that key variables are uncontrolled or unobservable, so conclusions are hard to draw. For example, if revenue is higher for flower auctions in the Netherlands than in Brazil, is it because of environmental differences such as buyers' values, or is it because of the different auction formats? Laboratory experiments allow control of theoretically relevant variables, including buyer values and the auction format, and provide matched comparisons that allow sharp inferences. Bidders' experience is less in most laboratory experiments and stakes are usually smaller, but the results listed below come from subjects who have mastered the laboratory environment and who have enough at stake (usually \$5–30) to do their best. Hence, laboratory experiments compensate for the weaknesses of field data and vice versa.

Auction formats and environments

Commerce in every era consists of sellers finding buyers at mutually beneficial prices. The task is difficult because buyers and sellers typically understate their willingness to transact in order to achieve a better bargain, and so potential transactions are lost. To solve this fundamental problem of commerce, many different market formats have evolved, ranging from random search and haggling, to posted price, to auctions. In Chapter 8, we looked at a few of the more prominent market institutions or formats, but now it will help to take a broader perspective, as outlined in Figure 9.1.

An auction is a market format in which a seller (and/or a buyer) receives price offers (buyers' bids and/or sellers' asks) and awards the objects to those who offered the highest bids (and/or lowest asks). Auctions have many different

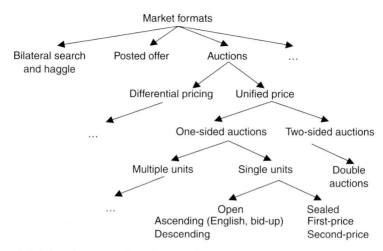

Figure 9.1 A broader perspective of market formats.

formats but all have the same basic rule: transaction priority goes to those who make the best offers, the highest bids and/or lowest asks (McAfee and McMillan, 1987a; Friedman and Rust, 1993). Thus, auctions use the principle of competition to overcome the fundamental problem of commerce. A buyer (and/or seller) must offer a better price than rivals in order to transact, and so reveals much about his willingness to transact.

Before discussing auction formats in detail, we outline some key distinctions regarding the environment in which an auction is conducted.

> Environment = All circumstances relevant to traders' choices and payoffs in a particular market format, including the nature of the good, the buyer values and seller costs, the participation costs, and the available information.
> Format = Set of rules for making bids and transactions, for example ascending or descending, etc.

The goods or services being transacted can consist of *single* or *multiple units*, divisible or indivisible. Buyers' per unit value and sellers' per unit cost may depend on the number of units bought or sold, or on holdings of substitute or complement goods. Unless otherwise noted, we assume values and costs are independent across units.

Buyers may know their own value exactly but only know the distribution of other buyers' values. This is the *independent private values* (IPV) environment, which we assume unless otherwise noted. It is a reasonable description for most merchandise. Alternatively, buyers may all share the same value, but each has only his own imprecise estimate of what that value is (the *common values* or CV environment). Offshore oil leases are a classic example: each lease buyer (oil company) makes its own estimate of the amount of oil that can be recovered, but the actual costs and revenues would turn out to be about the same for all buyers. Intermediate cases are also possible, and similar distinctions can be made with regard to sellers' costs.

The set of potential sellers and the set of potential buyers may not be known in advance. Buyers and sellers may have significant *costs of participating* in an auction, and on top of this they may have *costs of waiting* for the auction to conclude. The sale at auction may not be final, but rather lead to post-auction bargaining between buyer and seller or other agents. Unless otherwise noted, we ignore these complications.

Now, we are ready to discuss auction formats; see Figure 9.1. An auction is *one sided* if only bids or only asks are permitted, and *two-sided* if several buyers and several sellers submit bids simultaneously, as in the double auctions (ODA and CDA) discussed in Chapter 8. Here, we focus on one-sided auctions. For simplicity we assume that the seller chooses the auction format and buyers submit bids, but with suitable modifications all results apply to auctions in which the buyer chooses the format and sellers submit asks, for example, for government procurement contracts.

An auction can be *open* (sometimes called oral or continuous), allowing all bidders to see earlier bids, or *closed* (sometimes called sealed-bid) allowing each bidder a single bid that is not observed until all bids are collected.

An open auction can be *ascending* (also known as English or bid-up), recognizing only bids that are higher than earlier bids, or *descending* (called Dutch in the academic literature), with the auctioneer (human or automated) decreasing the price over time until some buyer accepts the current price. The Roman auctions presumably were ascending,[1] and ascending is still the most prevalent format. Descending auctions are traditionally used to sell cut flowers in the Netherlands, fish in Israel, and tobacco in Canada, among other instances.

A closed auction can be *first-price* (the highest bidder buys the object at her bid price) or *second-price* (the highest bidder buys the object, but the price is the second highest bid). Governments usually sell mineral rights and award procurement contracts via first-price closed auctions. Second-price closed auctions are historically rare but have become more popular in recent times (Vickrey, 1961; Lucking-Reiley, 1999).

Other variants to the basic auction rules include a *reserve price*, below which the seller rejects bids, and an explicit *entry fee* for the right to participate in the auction. Some bidders may differ in observable ways and be given *privileges* in terms of bid priority (e.g. minority-owned firms in some government run auctions) or access to information (e.g. specialists in the New York Stock exchange).

Classic theoretical and experimental results

Modern auction theory goes back to Vickrey (1961) and has been very active since Milgrom and Weber (1982).[2] The theory compares auction formats in various environments, assuming that every buyer fully understands the environment, does not try to collude, and otherwise acts in his own best interest. The classic results listed in Table 9.1 further assume that the seller is auctioning a single item,

Table 9.1 Summary of theoretical and empirical results

	Theory	*Empirical results*	
		Laboratory	*Field*
IPV and risk neutrality	Avg. revenue is equal in descending, first-price, ascending, second-price	Avg. revenue in first-price is higher than in descending Avg. revenue in second-price is higher than ascending	Avg. revenue in descending is higher than in first-price Avg. revenue in ascending is similar to second-price
	Increasing number of bidders increases avg. revenue	Increasing number of bidders increases avg. revenue	Increasing number of bidders increases avg. revenue
IPV and risk aversion	Avg. revenue is equal in descending and first-price, but greater than ascending and second-price		Bidders with higher value submit higher bids
	Uncertainty about number of bidders increases avg. revenue	Uncertainty about number of bidders increases avg. revenue	
Affiliated values	Avg. revenue in ascending is higher than second-price which is higher than first-price which is equal to descending	Winner's curse is found in first-price, second-price, and ascending	
	Increasing number of bidders drives price to item's true value		
	Public info about other bidders' estimates increases avg. revenue for seller	Public info about other bidders' estimates has an uncertain effect on avg. revenue for seller	Public info about other bidders' estimates increases avg. profit for bidder

that all buyers are present at no participation or waiting cost, and that none have special privileges. The results consider the impact of buyers' risk attitudes and value correlations (e.g. IPV versus CV environments). Recent surveys of auction theory and empirical tests can be found in McAfee and McMillan (1987a), Kagel (1995), and Klemperer (1999, 2000).

Result 1 (Vickrey, 1961)

The descending auction yields the same outcome as the first-price auction regardless of buyers' risk attitudes and value correlations. The intuition is worth explaining. A buyer in a first-price closed auction chooses his bid by trading off the probability of winning (by placing the highest bid) against the profitability if he does win (higher bid means higher price and lower profit). The tradeoff calculation is exactly the same in a descending auction; the only difference is that he is choosing when to accept the current price rather than writing down a bid. Either way, Vickrey showed that the equilibrium is for all buyers to bid at some discount from their own estimated value, for example, bid 75 percent of value when there are three other bidders in an IPV environment with uniformly distributed values (McAfee and McMillan, 1987b).

Laboratory evidence

Contrary to theory, classical laboratory experiments by Coppinger *et al.* (1980) and Cox *et al.* (1982) show that average revenue in descending auctions is 5 percent lower than in first-price auctions. In follow-up work, Cox *et al.* (1982, 1983) test two possible explanations. They find little support for the explanation that bidders enjoy playing the "waiting game" in the descending auction. Their results support the alternative explanation that in a descending auction lasting only a few minutes or seconds, the bidders mistakenly revise downward their estimates of rivals' values as time passes with nobody stopping the clock to win the item.

Result 2 (Vickrey, 1961)

The ascending auction yields the same outcome as the second-price auction in the IPV environment, regardless of risk attitudes: the item is purchased by the highest value buyer at a price equal to the second highest buyer value. The intuition here is simple. In both auction formats it is optimal for every buyer to fully reveal his value, no matter what other buyers do. This means staying in the ascending auction until the bid rises above his value, and bidding his actual value in the second-price auction. Bidding higher than one's value (or staying in longer) can never give a positive profit, and bidding lower (or dropping out early) means passing up profitable opportunities. As a result, when everyone bids optimally, the highest value buyer wins the auction and pays the price set by the next highest value buyer.

Laboratory evidence

Kagel *et al.* (1987) find that theory predicts well the outcomes in ascending auctions, but that prices are 11 percent higher than predicted in second-price auctions. Later work, for example, Harstad and Rothkopf (2000), shows that with enough experience bidding in second-price auctions eventually converges to the theoretical prediction. It seems that many subjects are slow to realize that bidding above one's true value is never profitable in second-price auctions; you do win the auction more often but only when winning is unprofitable. But losses from overbidding are infrequent and usually small, so learning is weak compared to the ascending auction where the futility of bidding above value is immediately apparent.

The first two theoretical results together show that, compared to the descending (or first-price) format, buyers in the ascending (or second-price) format bid higher, but the auction price is lower for given bids. So which effect is more important? Vickrey showed, to the surprise of many, that on average the effects exactly cancel, so all four formats produce the same revenue.

Result 3: Revenue-equivalence theorem (Vickrey, 1961)

Assume IPV with risk neutral buyers. Then the descending, ascending, first-price, and second-price auctions all are efficient with respect to the participating buyers and all produce the same average revenue for sellers. Increasing the number of bidders increases the seller's average revenue. The last part is clear enough: the revenue is equal to the second highest buyer value, which tends to be higher when there are more buyers. Efficiency is also clear: in each format, the highest value buyer wins the auction.

Laboratory evidence

In the laboratory, prices are higher in the first-price and second-price auctions, where buyers explicitly state prices, than in open auctions where the decision is whether or not to accept the price announced by the auctioneer. Why? Kagel (1995) suggests that the reason is psychological. In sealed auctions the attention is focused on price, while open auctions focus on profitability, generating somewhat lower prices.

Risk aversion

Note that revenue equivalence holds only on average. Depending on the particular alignment of buyer values, the descending/first-price auction could produce higher or lower revenues than the ascending/second-price. It can be shown that revenue has higher variance (depends more sensitively on the alignment of buyer values) in the descending/first-price formats. Thus, if the sellers were risk averse and the buyers were risk neutral, then the sellers would prefer the ascending or second-price auction. However, risk-averse buyers will bid higher than risk-neutral buyers in the descending or first-price auction; bidding closer to true value is a form of insurance against losing the auction.

This insight leads to:

Result 4

When bidders are risk averse, the descending or the first-price auction on average produces higher revenues than the ascending or the second-price auction. What if buyers do not know how many other buyers are present? It does not matter if they are risk neutral, but it does matter if they are risk averse.

Result 5

When bidders are risk averse[3] in a descending or first-price auction, the average revenue is higher when the bidders do not know how many other bidders there are.

Laboratory evidence

Cox *et al.* (1988) and Kagel and Levin (1993) found that, consistent with theoretical predictions, increasing the number of rivals almost always resulted in higher (more aggressive) bidding in first-price auctions. Dyer *et al.* (1989) showed that concealing the exact number of bidders raises average revenue, as predicted for risk-averse bidders.

Most of the theory analyzes one-shot auctions, so it has been left to experiments to understand the effect of how price information feeds back on bidding in repeated auctions. Cox *et al.* (1984) and Battalio *et al.* (1990) studied the effects of price information following bid submission, and found no effect on bidding. Isaac and Walker (1985) reported that prices were consistently higher under limited feedback information.

Ockenfels and Selten (2002) find that reporting all submitted bids at the end of each period in first-price auctions leads to lower bids and lower revenues than the usual practice of reporting only the winning bid. Standard auction theory predicts no effect, but the authors show that the observed effect can be explained by the impulse balance equilibrium theory. See Chapter 12 for a presentation of this new theory.

Common values: winner's curse

Now consider the CV environment, in which the uncertainty is not due to different actual buyer values, but instead is due to buyers' different estimates of the item's true value. For example, all buyers might have the same plan to resell the good but might have access to different information about the resale price. Here, an important phenomenon called *winner's curse* can arise. The basic idea is that, since the bidder who has the highest estimate wins the auction, the very act of winning conveys the bad news that everyone else had a lower estimate of the item's value. Unless the bidder had already taken this into account, he will find that he overestimated the true value and paid too much.

A rational bidder will escape the winner's curse by presuming that her or his own estimate of the item's value is the highest and discount it accordingly. This strategy is rational because when some other buyer with equally precise information has a higher estimate she or he should not try to outbid him or her. With rational bidders, the auction price is equal on average to the true value even though no individual in the economy knows what this true value is and no communication among the bidders takes place. The "on average" qualification can be dropped as the number of buyers increases.

Kagel and Levin (2002) present a general overview of CV auction theory and survey the laboratory results. Here we offer a only brief summary.

Result 6

If information is sufficiently dispersed among the bidders in a CV environment, then the selling price converges to the item's true value as the number of bidders becomes arbitrarily large.

Laboratory evidence

Kagel and Levin (1986) and Kagel *et al.* (1989) showed in their laboratory experiments that inexperienced bidders are quite susceptible to the winner's curse in first- and second-price auctions: they bid too high and earn much lower profits than fully rational buyers in equilibrium. The winner's curse declines slowly with experience, and is smaller (but still present) in ascending auctions. Cox and Smith (1992) find that the winner's curse disappears much more quickly when buyers choose whether to participate.

Experiments with skilled individuals from the construction industry show that professional bidders also incur the winner's curse in laboratory auctions (Kagel and Levine, 2002). Cox and Hayne (2002) examine the winner's curse in common value situations where committees prepare bids instead of individuals, and also compare committees and individuals on their rational use of information, with mixed results.

Affiliated values

Let us now consider cases between IPV and CV. Here the bidders' estimates of the item's value are *affiliated* in the sense that one buyer's perception that the item's value is high makes it more likely that other bidders also perceive it to be high. In this case, bidders in an ascending auction have more information than in the other formats because they can observe at which prices the other bidders drop out. This information dispels the winner's curse, allows bidders to be more aggressive, and increases the seller's average revenue.

Result 7 (Milgrom and Weber, 1982)

When bidders' estimates are affiliated, the average revenues can be ranked as follows: ascending > second-price > first-price = descending auction.

Result 8 (Milgrom and Weber, 1982)

When bidders' estimates are affiliated, the seller can increase average revenue by having a policy of publicizing any information he has about the item's true value. The reason is that the new information tends to increase the value estimates of those bidders who perceive the item's true value to be relatively low, causing them to bid more aggressively.

Laboratory evidence

Kagel *et al.* (1987) found that in first-price auctions with affiliated private values, public information about others' estimates increases average market prices but by only about 30 percent of the increase predicted by theory and often not significantly different from zero.

Field evidence

Three predictions of auction theory, supported by experimental data, have been confirmed using a variety of field data. See Kagel (1995) for a summary and Porter (1995) for more perspectives:

1   a bidder with a higher value will submit a higher bid;
2   as the number of bidders increases, so does average seller revenue;
3   in common value auctions, better-informed bidders make a higher rate of return than less-informed bidders.

But we will see in the next section that some field evidence differs from the corresponding laboratory evidence, and from theory.

New directions

The classic results are a wonderful mix of empirical confirmation and empirical contradiction of theory, ideal for creative ferment. The mix has kept auction theory, empirics, and practice bubbling vigorously to the present day.

Much of the recent work moves beyond the classic assumptions that only a single item is available, that bidders are rational and know the distributions and environment, have no participation or waiting cost or special privileges, and do not collude. Recent meetings of the Economic Science Association usually feature several sessions on auctions, with topics including multiple unit auctions, Internet auctions, hybrid auction formats, and ambiguity regarding the number and/or valuations of other bidders. The work begins to overlap with behavioral economics, institutional engineering, market experiments, and other fields once quite separate. We will be able to touch on only a few of these topics, but see Chakravarti *et al.* (2002) for a recent survey aimed at a general audience.

Internet auctions

Lucking-Reiley (1999) reports a small-stakes field experiment run on the Internet. Beginning in 1994 he purchased over $2,000 of Magic game cards and resold them via auctions over the Internet. The basic procedure was to auction two copies of the same card in two different auction formats to obtain a matched comparison across formats. The ascending and descending auctions lasted days or weeks, rather than the seconds or minutes as in most laboratory experiments. The results show that, contrary to theory and laboratory results, *the descending auction produces 30 percent higher revenues than the first-price sealed-bid auction*, while the ascending and second-price sealed-bid auctions produce roughly equivalent revenues.

Several issues arise when comparing auctions on the Internet to those done "Brick and Mortar" or done in the lab: synchronous versus asynchronous participation, access to bidder identity and to verbal and non-verbal communication clues, re-auctioning opportunities, and more. These are just some of the exciting new directions (see Chakravarti *et al.*, 2002). Our own conjecture is that participation costs explain the Lucking-Reiley result: a winner in his descending Internet auction could use the card a week or more before a winner in the sealed auction, while there is no difference in participation costs in the lab.

Internet auction results appear to be sensitive to the closing rule. The end of the auction may be determined randomly (drawn from a distribution that is common knowledge), may involve a "soft close" (e.g. Amazon.com automatically extends the auction a few minutes after each new bid) or a "hard close" (as in eBay auctions). These different rules influence bidding behaviors, for example, "sniping" (bidders entering in the closing minutes of an Internet auction), as well as prices and revenue outcomes (Roth and Ockenfels, 2002).

Multiple units and interrelated goods

Ausubel (1997) and Ausubel and Cramton (1998) studied the problem of multiple-unit auctions. When the seller has more than one unit of the same good or many related goods to sell, and bidders may demand more than one unit, most of the classic results listed above are no longer valid. In particular, even the second-price auction is generally inefficient with multiple units. Buyers who value several units have an incentive to reduce demand for the last few units in order to reduce the price paid on the first units. As a result, sometimes they lose the last few units to buyers with lower values for those units.

Ausubel (1997, 2002) proposes a different ascending format that might avoid inefficiency in auctioning multiple identical units when values are affiliated. The auction organizer announces a current price, the bidders report back the quantity demanded at that price, and the auctioneer raises the price. Objects are awarded to bidders at the current price whenever they are "clinched,"[4] and the process continues until the market clears. With private values, this design yields the same efficient outcome as a second-price sealed-bid private auction, but might be easier for the bidder to understand. See Milgrom (2000) for efficiency limitations on any auction format in environments with interrelated goods.

Participation cost and uncertainty

Dooley *et al.* (1993) study the failure of privatization auctions for state-owned enterprises in Eastern Europe. They show that a combination of participation cost (e.g. for inspecting the item to estimate its value) and post-auction bargaining over use of the item (e.g. with labor unions) can discourage buyers from bidding realistically or even participating. The idea is that once the buyer has revealed his value by winning the auction he is subject to aggressive post-auction bargaining and may not be able to recover the sunk cost of participation. The revenue losses are likely to increase more than proportionally with the value of the item at stake.

To get the latest on auction experiments, look at recent and upcoming conference programs on the ESA homepage: http://economicscience.org.

Notes

1 The word auction is derived from the Latin "augere," to increase.
2 William Vickrey shared the 1996 Economics Nobel Prize for this and other work. He died of a heart attack a few weeks after the prize was announced, and Paul Milgrom gave the Nobel Lecture that year on Vickrey's behalf.
3 This result holds under constant or decreasing absolute risk-aversion, but not necessarily for arbitrary specifications of risk aversion.
4 A bidder's unit is clinched at a price p when the total demand by other bidders falls below total supply for the first time.

References

Ausubel, L.M. (1997) "An efficient ascending-bid auction for multiple objects," University of Maryland, Working Paper No. 97-06.
Ausubel, L.M. (2002) "An efficient ascending-bid auction for multiple objects," University of Maryland manuscript.
Ausubel, L.M. and Cramton P. (1998) "Demand reduction and inefficiency in multi-unit auctions," University of Maryland Working Paper.
Battalio, R.C., Kogut, C.A., and Meyer, D.J. (1990) "The effect of varying number of bidders in first-price private value auctions: an application of a dual market bidding technique," in L. Green and J.H. Kagel, eds, *Advances in Behavioral Economics*, vol. 2, Norwood, NJ: Ablex Publishing.

Chakravarti, D. *et al.* (2002) "Auctions: research opportunities in marketing," *Marketing Letters*, 13(3): 281–296.

Coppinger, V.M., Smith, V.L., and Titus, J.A. (1980) "Incentives and behavior in English, Dutch and sealed-bid auctions," *Economic Inquiry*, 43: 1–22.

Cox, J.C. and Hayne, S.C. (2002) "Barking up the right tree: are small groups rational agents?" University of Arizona, Working Paper.

Cox, J.C. and Smith V.L. (1992) "Endogenous entry and exit in common value auctions," University of Arizona, Mimeograph.

Cox, J.C., Roberson, B., and Smith, V.L. (1982) "Theory and behavior of single object auctions," in V.L. Smith, ed., *Research in Experimental Economics*, Greenwich, CN: JAI Press.

Cox, J.C., Smith, V.L., and Walker J.M. (1983) "A test that discriminates between two models of the Dutch-first auction non-isomorphism," *Journal of Economic Behavior and Organization*, 14: 205–219.

Cox, J.C., Smith, V.L., and Walker, J.M. (1984) "Theory and behavior of multiple unit discriminative auctions," *Journal of Finance*, 39: 983–1010.

Cox, J.C., Smith, V.L., and Walker, J.M. (1988) "Theory and individual behavior of first-price auctions," *Journal of Risk and Uncertainty*, 1: 61–99.

Dooley M., Friedman, D., and Melese-d'Hospital, S.H. (1993) "Good and bad explanations for the failure of privatization," Paper for Conference: The Transition of Centrally-Planned Economies in Pacific Asia, May 7 and 8.

Dyer, D., Kagel, J.H., and Levin, D. (1989) "Resolving uncertainty about the number of bidders in independent private-value auctions: an experimental analysis," *Rand Journal of Economics* 20: 268–279.

Friedman, D. and Rust, J., eds (1993) *The Double Auction Market Institutions, Theories, and Evidence*, Reading, MA: Addison-Wesley.

Harstad, R. and Rothkopf, M.H. (2000) "An 'alternating recognition' model of English auctions," *Management Science*, 46(1): 1–12.

Isaac, R.M. and Walker, J.M. (1985) "Information and conspiracy in sealed bid auctions," *Journal of Economic Behavior and Organization* 6: 139–159.

Kagel, J.H. (1995) "Auctions: a survey of experimental research," in J.H. Kagel and A.E. Roth, eds, *Handbook of Experimental Economics*, Princeton: Princeton University Press, pp. 501–585.

Kagel J.H. and Levin, D. (1986) "The winner's curse and public information in common value auctions," *American Economic Review*, 76: 894–920.

Kagel J.H. and Levin, D. (1993) "Independent private value auctions: bidder behavior in first-, second-, and third-price auctions with varying numbers of bidders," *Economic Journal*, 103: 868–879.

Kagel J.H. and Levin, D. (2002) *Common Value Auctions and the Winner's Curse*, Princeton: Princeton University Press.

Kagel J.H., Harstad, R.M., and Levin, D. (1987) "Information impact and allocation rules in auctions with affiliated private values: a laboratory study," *Econometrica*, 55(6): 1275–1304.

Kagel J.H., Levin, D., Battalio, R., and Meyer, D.J. (1989) "First-price common value auctions: bidder behavior and the winner's curse," *Economic Inquiry*, 27: 241–258.

Klemperer, P. (1999) "Auction theory: a guide to the literature," *Microeconomics* 9903002, Economics Working Paper Archive at WUSTL.

Klemperer, P. (2000) "What really matters in auction design," CEPR Discussion Papers 2581, CEPR Discussion Papers.

Lucking-Reiley, D. (1999) "Using field experiments to test equivalence between auction formats: Magic on the Internet," *American Economic Review*, 89(5): 1063–1080.

McAfee, R.P. and McMillan, J. (1987a) "Auctions and bidding," *Journal of Economic Literature*, 25: 699–738.

McAfee, R.P. and McMillan, J. (1987b) "Auctions with a stochastic number of bidders," *Journal of Economic Theory*, 43: 1–19.

Milgrom, P. (2000) "Putting auction theory to work: the simultaneous ascending auction," *Journal of Political Economy*, 108(2): 245–272.

Milgrom, P. and Weber, R.J. (1982) "A theory of auctions and competitive bidding," *Econometrica*, 50: 1485–1527.

Ockenfels A. and Selten, R. (2002) "Impulse balance equilibrium and feedback in first price auctions," Working Paper, Max-Planck-Institute for Research into Economic System.

Porter, D. and Smith, V.L. (1995) "Futures contracting and dividend uncertainty in experimental asset markets," *Journal of Business*, 68(4): 509–541.

Roth, A.E. and Ockenfels, A. (2002) "Last-minute bidding and the rules for ending second-price auctions: evidence from eBay and Amazon auctions on the Internet," *American Economic Review*, 92(4): 1093–1103.

Vickrey, W. (1961) "Counterspeculation, auctions, and competitive sealed tenders," *Journal of Finance*, 16: 8–37.

10 Oligopoly

Steffen Huck[1]

In simple oligopoly experiments, subjects act as sellers while buyers are simulated by demand functions. The godfather of such models is Cournot (1838) and I will first focus on experimental evidence on "Cournot games." I will outline the most important facts experimental research has delivered up to now and I will sketch what I think are important omissions and, hence, avenues for future research.

In the second part of this chapter I will look beyond Cournot. Here, I will almost exclusively focus on research I have been involved in myself (which is only partly due to vanity). There is simply not too much out there. Accordingly, the possibilities for future research are even greater.

Cournot

What we know

In the standard Cournot model, there are n sellers deciding simultaneously about their output. Their products are perfect substitutes and (inverse) demand only depends on aggregate output. The market is always assumed to be cleared. Firms' profits result from revenue (quantity times price) minus cost.

Often demand and cost functions are assumed to be linear, in which case one can choose price and quantity units in order to "normalize" inverse demand to

$$p(X) = 1 - X \tag{10.1}$$

and costs to zero. In (10.1), $X = \Sigma_i x_i$, where x_i is the output of firm $i = 1, 2, \ldots, n$. The resulting price is denoted by $p(X)$. Profit of firm i is simply given by $x_i p(X)$ and first-order conditions can be written as

$$x_i = 1 - X \tag{10.2}$$

Solving this system of simultaneous equations,[2] the equilibrium quantities are derived as

$$x_i^* = \frac{1}{n+1} \tag{10.3}$$

Intuitively, individual output falls in the number of competitors n, while total output increases in n. As a consequence, the price falls in n and total welfare increases in n.

From a theoretical point of view, this is all that matters. All we need to know in order to predict market outcomes are cost and demand functions. In experiments, however, it might be possible that other details of the environment matter – such as the verbal description of the environment or the possibility of communication before the actual game. Both features would be irrelevant in the theoretical model.

In the following, I will try to summarize the existing experimental evidence on Cournot games by making a claim about behaviour under *standard conditions*. I will describe what is meant by standard conditions and will further proceed by briefly describing what happens in experiments that deviate from these conditions. So, here is the claim.

Claim Under standard conditions the Cournot equilibrium, as derived in (10.3), predicts behavior well for $n > 2$. For $n = 2$ there is a considerable amount of collusion.

The claim seems to support the theoretical model, but how well is "well?" Clearly, "well" does not mean "exactly." Rather, outputs are very close to equilibrium outputs, typically much less than one standard deviation. However, there is always some volatility around the equilibrium (even after many rounds) and, typically, quantities are slightly above the equilibrium level (see, e.g. Huck *et al.*, 2002c). Davis *et al.* (2002) suggest that both facts have the same reason and allude to "complicated gaming behavior." How this gaming behavior works exactly remains, however, an open question.[3]

For the duopoly case the prediction is more ambiguous. Typically, there are some subjects who play according to the equilibrium solution, but there are also others who manage to collude[4] – provided that interaction takes place in fixed pairs, the first part of standard conditions.

Standard conditions

a   Interaction takes place in fixed groups.
b   Interaction is repeated over a fixed number of periods.
c   Products are perfect substitutes.
d   Costs are symmetric.
e   There is no communication between subjects.
f   Subjects have complete information about their own payoff functions.
g   Subjects receive feedback about aggregate supply, the resulting price, and band their own individual profits.
h   The experimental instructions use an economic frame.

So, let us now discuss what happens if experiments deviate from these conditions.

a   *Random matching between rounds*. With random matching, behavior is driven closer to the equilibrium. This is most important in the duopoly case where collusion is no longer prevalent. See, for example, Holt (1985) or Huck *et al.* (2001a).

b1 *One-shot experiments.* In games as complex as Cournot games, one would typically be not too interested in totally inexperienced behavior. Hence, there are hardly any Cournot experiments where subjects play just once. One exception is a recent note by Huck and Wallace (2002), who find behavior in duopolies very close to equilibrium.

b2 *Randomized stopping.* Sometimes it is argued that randomized stopping rules, where a throw of the dice decides, for example, whether the experiment continues for another period or not, can be used to create environments where folk theorems are applicable.[5] Continuation probabilities can then also be interpreted as discount factors. Randomized stopping has been used by Holt (1985) and different continuation probabilities have been investigated by Feinberg and Husted (1993). They find that low probabilities decrease collusion.

c *Differentiated products.* Huck *et al.* (2000b) study price and quantity competition for the same four-firm market with differentiated products (close but not perfect substitutes). For quantity competition, they get a picture that is very similar to the case with homogenous products. The equilibrium predicts behavior equally well and there is the same volatility around it. See also Davis and Wilson (2000).

d *Asymmetric costs.* There are two main effects of cost asymmetries that are documented in the literature. For duopolies, Mason and Phillips (1997) show that collusion is harder to achieve, that is, competition becomes tougher, which is beneficial for consumers. A different effect is documented in Rassenti *et al.* (2000) who run five-firm oligopolies. They show that behavior becomes much more unstable with cost asymmetries. Volatility is increased and the equilibrium prediction loses descriptive power on the individual level.

e *Communication.* Unsurprisingly, communication increases collusion (see Binger *et al.*, 1990; Harstad *et al.*, 1998).

f *Subjects do not know their own payoff function.* Huck *et al.* (1999) have studied an extreme version of this case where subjects have virtually *zero* information about the market. Amazingly, they find that as long as subjects receive only feedback about their own profits aggregate outcomes converge to equilibrium levels.

g *Subjects receive additional feedback about other's actions and profits.* As predicted by imitation models (Vega-Redondo, 1997), competition becomes more intense when subjects can also observe others' actions and profits. This is documented in Huck *et al.* (1999, 2000b) as well as in Offerman *et al.* (2002). Key to understanding this finding is the observation that, as long as prices are positive, the firm with the greatest output is also the most successful firm in a market. Hence, imitation of successful behavior should lead to increases in (others' and total) outputs. Even though a similar theoretical prediction can be made for price competition, it does not hold empirically as shown in Huck *et al.* (2000b), who study the same demand system – once with quantity and once with price competition. Similar increases in competition can be explained by concerns for relative market performance, which can only be computed if subjects have information about their own and others' profits.

h   *Abstract framing.* Somewhat surprisingly, removing the (competitive) market frame and replacing it by an abstract frame, where subjects simply choose some numbers that are fed into an abstract payoff function, leads to less collusion in duopolies. With more firms, outputs are slightly reduced. Both effects are reported in Huck *et al.* (2002c). They are only seemingly contradictory because in both instances the abstract frame pushes behavior closer to the equilibrium.

What we do not know

The most important shortcoming of the literature as of today is its dependence on symmetric setups. Take, for example, the effects of additional feedback on others' actions and profits that might be of some relevance for competition policy. If increased competition is really caused by imitative behavior, the question arises whether subjects would still imitate if they knew that others are different from themselves.[6] Why imitate somebody who faces a different problem than yourself? Of course, imitation might still be reasonable if others are not too different…

With respect to imitation, or, more generally, learning dynamics in markets, it would also be interesting to see what happens if some firms had better information about the market than others. In that case, imitation might be totally rational for uninformed firms (provided they know that others are informed). As asymmetries are known to reduce collusion, it would also be important to know whether in the presence of asymmetries communication would still increase price–cost margins.

Beyond Cournot

Stackelberg

The second workhorse model in Industrial Organization is the Stackelberg model where some of the firms in a market have strategic (commitment) power. Let us just consider the case of $n = 2$ with the same demand and cost structure as above. The key difference to the Cournot model is that here firms are assumed to move sequentially. The firm that moves first is typically called the (Stackelberg) leader, the second mover is called (Stackelberg) follower. A central assumption is that the follower can observe the leader's action before taking his own. The ensuing game can be solved by backward induction. The follower's optimal response to some output of the leader, x_L, is $x_F = (1 - x_L)/2$. This is anticipated by the leader who, therefore, maximizes $x_L(1 - x_L - (1 - x_L)/2)$. In the unique subgame perfect equilibrium, the leader produces $x_L = 1/2$ and the follower $x_F(x_L) = 1/4$.[7] Thus, total output is greater than in a Cournot duopoly with identical demand and cost functions, which benefits consumers and increases overall welfare.

The first experimental test of the Stackelberg model is reported in Huck *et al.* (2001a)[8] who run Stackelberg duopolies with fixed and random matching. Total market output is roughly in line with the subgame perfect equilibrium[9] prediction but individual outputs are not. Market shares are far less unequal than predicted. This is mainly driven by followers' deviations from the theoretical best-reply function. With random matching the empirical reply function is much less steep, and with fixed-pairs it is even upward sloping – crossing the money-maximizing response function at the Cournot outcome.[10] These deviations by followers are in line with models of inequality aversion (see, e.g. Fehr and Schmidt, 1999; Bolton and Ockenfels, 2000).[11]

Endogenous timing models

While Stackelberg markets (in theory as well as in the laboratory) nicely illustrate that consumers can benefit from increases in market concentration, the question arises where the differences in strategic (commitment) power comes from. One possible answer is provided by endogenous timing models where firms choose when to produce. Hamilton and Slutsky (1990) study a game with two firms and two periods. In the first period, both firms decide independently from each other whether to produce some output, or to wait. If they decide to produce, this decision is irreversible. On the other hand, a firm that decides to wait has to decide about its final output in the second period, knowing the other firm's first-period decision.

This game has three subgame perfect equilibria: one symmetric equilibrium where both firms choose Cournot outputs in the first period and two asymmetric ones where one of the firms produces the Stackelberg leader output in the first period and the other, waiting in the first period, produces the Stackelberg follower quantity in the second. Only these asymmetric equilibria are in undominated strategies.[12] Hence, Hamilton and Slutsky (1990) argue they should be selected as the solution.

In Huck *et al.* (2002b) we test a symmetric version of Hamilton and Slutsky's game. Our main finding is that Stackelberg equilibria do *not* arise. Rather, subjects tend to play Cournot. But, of course, symmetry makes coordination on an asymmetric equilibrium extremely hard. Therefore, we test Hamilton and Slutsky again in Fonseca *et al.* (2002), this time with asymmetric firms. Van Damme and Hurkens (1999) predict for this case that the low-cost firm should emerge as Stackelberg leader.[13] However, Stackelberg outcomes again are extremely rare.[14]

Separation of ownership and management

Another potential source for (strategic) market power is delegation. As originally pointed out by Schelling (1960), delegation can be entirely motivated by strategic considerations. Essentially, delegation can be used as a commitment device. This idea has been applied to oligopolies by Vickers (1985) and Fershtman and Judd

(1987). If just one firm can hire a delegate, it can ensure for itself the Stackelberg leader profit.[15] If two firms can hire delegates, they face essentially a dilemma problem. Regardless of what the other owner does, each owner always has an incentive to make his manager more aggressive than the owner himself would be in the quantity game.[16]

Huck *et al.* (2000a) test a duopoly model along these lines. In their (symmetric) setup, quantities are chosen from a rather coarse grid and there are only two types of contracts, a low-powered contract that does not pay a sales bonus and the equilibrium contract entailing a sales bonus. The data show that the aggressive equilibrium contracts are rarely chosen. The main reason for this seems to be the fact that managers who have been endowed with contracts that depend only on profits and do not entail a sales bonus are very aggressive in asymmetric sub-games where their opponents have more market power because they were endowed with the equilibrium contract: They punish those who try to exploit their market power. In fact, manager behavior is so extreme that, given their reactions to contract choices, owners no longer face a dilemma game. Offering the low-powered nonequilibrium contract becomes a dominant action.

As most firms and, in fact, industries are characterized by separation of owner-ship and management, further investigations seem worthwhile. Again, it would be interesting to see what happens if firms have different cost functions. In ultimatum games, there is, for example, some evidence that weaker players become more yielding if *all* outcomes favor the stronger player (see Guth *et al.*, 2001). Along these lines, one could expect that managers of high-cost firms might behave less aggressively in asymmetric subgames where they have been endowed with the low-powered contract. But this is, of course, speculation and needs testing.

Mergers

So far, we have looked at oligopoly games where theory predicts more asymme-try than is observed in the laboratory. In our final example, we examine a case where it is the other way round.

Consider the simple Cournot setup from above. Now suppose that, for what-ever reasons, two out of $n \geq 3$ firms merge. What happens? Due to the linear cost functions the newly merged firm does not differ from all other firms. (It may have two plants but it is irrelevant how production is split amongst them.) Hence, the post-merger market is identical to the pre-merger market with the exception that there is now one firm less. In the post-merger equilibrium, each firm will produce $1/n$ and profits will be $1/n^2$. Total outputs are reduced and so is total welfare. Firms that have not been involved in the merger benefit, as there is less competi-tion. But what about the firms that have been involved in the merger? Prior to the merger, they earned together $2/(n + 1)^2$, after the merger they earn (as everybody else) $1/n^2$. It is easy to see that for $n > 2$ the latter is smaller than the former. Hence, the merger is unprofitable! This result, sometimes called the "merger paradox" or "merger puzzle" was first formulated by Salant *et al.* (1983), and Huck *et al.* (2002b) have tested it for the first time in the laboratory.

Four (three) subjects start playing a symmetric Cournot market, knowing that the experiment will last for 2×25 periods but only knowing the rules for the first half. After period 25, two subjects are randomly drawn and forced to merge. One of the subjects becomes the sole manager of the new firm; the other subject becomes, more or less, inactive.[17] Profits are equally shared between them.

Theory predicts that play moves from the Nash equilibrium with four (three) players to the Nash equilibrium with three (two) players, and, just looking at total output, one gets the impression that this is really the case. However, examining individual outputs, a different picture emerges. The merged firm produces consistently more than its competitors, and this difference does not disappear over time. In the case of initially four firms, this renders the merger even (weakly) profitable. (There are some considerable short-run gains and no long-run losses.)

Interestingly, the unmerged firms learn to play Cournot equilibria with respect to the residual demand given the merged firm's output (while merged firms are perfectly stubborn and continue to produce more than predicted). This pattern looks almost like Stackelberg play – only that it does not stem from a sequence of moves.[18]

The pattern is explained by players having aspiration levels that are induced during the first twenty-five periods. The merged firm does not want to lose; the unmerged firms do not bother because they earn more than before anyway. This explanation is tested against two alternative explanations by two extra treatments and receives strong support from the data. Given the frequency of mergers, the ambiguous predictions of theory and the extremely messy field evidence, experiments seem the ideal vehicle to study mergers. The linear setup studied in Huck *et al.* (2002a) can only serve as a benchmark. Numerous more (and more exciting) experimental designs can be easily envisaged.[19]

Bertrand

The vast majority of studies mentioned so far examine quantity competition. A number of related studies examine price competition in markets with differentiated products. But, of course, price competition takes on a more extreme form when products are perfect substitutes. In that case, competition of only two firms leads already to perfectly competitive outcomes where price equals marginal costs. This extreme setup has been studied in a very neat paper by Dufwenberg and Gneezy (2000). Using an abstract frame, they examine two-, three-, and four-firm markets. Their findings can be easily summarized. As with standard Cournot markets, the equilibrium prediction works well for Bertrand markets with more than two firms, while there is a considerable amount of collusion when there are just two firms. Remarkably, Dufwenberg and Gneezy observe collusion in duopolies despite random matching. One may conjecture that this is driven by the miserable equilibrium profits and the accordingly immense relative benefits from collusion. Moreover, subjects received feedback not only about price decisions in their market, but about all chosen prices. Thus, subjects could signal their willingness to collude to the entire population of players, and that, in fact, happened.

It would, therefore, be interesting to see whether collusion was robust in a treatment with individual feedback only.

Notes

1 The author acknowledges financial support from the Economic and Social Research Council (UK) via the Centre for Economic Learning and Social Evolution (ELSE).
2 Taking (10.2) one can use symmetry to get $x_i = 1 - nx_i$.
3 Huck *et al.* (2001b) show that inequality in earnings helps to predict volatility.
4 The joint-profit maximizing total output in the above model would be 1/2.
5 Although popular, the view is problematic. Folk theorems break down if there is a commonly known upper bound. Hence, if subjects have common knowledge that the experiment they are participating in will not last for, say, the next 17 years, this is sufficient to trigger backward induction and destroy the folk theorem.
6 Also, it would be interesting to resolve the puzzle from note 5. Maybe the imitation effect depends on whether actions are strategic substitutes (as with quantity competition) or strategic complements (as with price competition). An alternative explanation is that the adverse effects of imitation are more obvious in the case of price competition since imitation of successful behavior typically means that subjects have to lower their prices. That this may reduce profits might be more obvious than in the case of quantity competition where imitation typically requires that subjects raise their outputs. One way of testing these two hypotheses would be to implement a heterogeneous market where goods are complements, such that the game with price competition is a game with strategic substitutes and the game with quantity competition a game with strategic complements.
7 Notice that a follower's strategy is a function and that the game has infinitely many Nash equilibria.
8 There is, of course, a large experimental literature on games with first-mover advantages, most notably the literature on the ultimatum game initiated by Guth *et al.* (1982).
9 Accordingly, the experimental Stackelberg market yields higher overall welfare than a Cournot market with similar demand and cost parameters.
10 This implies a clearcut reward-for-cooperation and punishment-for exploitation scheme.
11 While we find support for the Fehr–Schmidt model when analyzing the responder data, we have to reject the model for proposers who seem to enjoy advantageous inequality!
12 Playing Cournot in the first period is weakly dominated by waiting. In fact, the only strategy against which waiting is not a best response is the other player's waiting strategy.
13 Their prediction is based on risk dominance arguments.
14 Both experiments rely on random matching and things might change with repeated interaction where one firm might have incentives to teach the other. We have run a couple of pilot sessions with asymmetric firms and fixed-pairs in which, again, Stackelberg outcomes were rare.
15 An incentive contract for the manager shapes the manager's quantity reaction curve. Hence, if there is only one owner who has a manager he can essentially choose his most preferred point on the other firm's quantity reaction curve. The incentive contract must just be chosen such that the manager's quantity reaction curves intersect with the other owner's reaction curve at the appropriate point.
16 All these results rest on the assumption that contracts between owners and managers can be published and are non-negotiable. Moreover, it is assumed that incentive contracts are simple convex combinations of profits and sales.
17 We allow him to send messages to the manager every five periods.
18 Which in fact is absent in Stackelberg's (1934) book. There the difference between leader and follower is purely behavioral – the outcome of a mind game.

19 See, for example, Davies and van Boening (2000) who study mergers in markets with differentiated products. There the number of products in the market is not reduced by the merger. Rather, firms make joint decisions about prices.

References

Binger, B.R., Hoffman, E., and Libecap, G.D. (1990) "An experimetric study of the Cournot theory of firm behaviour," Mimeo.

Bolton, G.E. and Ockenfels, A. (2000) "ERC: a theory of equity, reciprocity, and competition," *American Economic Review*, 90: 166–193.

Cournot, A. (1838) *"Reserches sur les Principles Mathematiques de la Theorie des Richesses,"* Paris: Hachette. Translated as *Research into the Mathematical Principles of the Theory of Wealth*, New York: Kelley, 1960.

Davis, D.D. and van Boening, M. (2000) "Strategic interactions, market information and mergers in differentiated product markets: an experimental investigation," Mimeo.

Davis, D.D. and Wilson, B.J. (2000) "Differentiated product competition and the antitrust logit model: an experimental analysis," Mimeo.

Davis, D.D., Reilly, R.J., and Wilson, B.J. (2002) "Cost structures and Nash play in repeated Cournot games: an experimental investigation," Mimeo.

Dufwenberg, M. and Gneezy, U. (2000) "Price competition and market concentration: an experimental study," *International Journal of Industrial Organization*, 18: 7–22.

Fehr, E. and Schmidt, K. (1999) "A theory of fairness, competition, and cooperation," *Quarterly Journal of Economics*, 114: 817–868.

Feinberg, R.M. and Husted, T.A. (1993) "An experimental test of discount-rate effects on collusive behaviour in duopoly markets," *Journal of Industrial Economics*, 41: 153–160.

Fershtman, C. and Judd, K.L. (1987) "Equilibrium incentives inoligopoly," *American Economic Review*, 77: 927–940.

Fonseca, M., Huck, S., and Normann, H.T. (2002) "Playing Cournot although they mustn't," Mimeo.

Guth, W., Huck, S., and Muller, W. (2001) "The relevance of equal splits in ultimatum games," *Games and Economic Behaviour*, 37: 161–169.

Guth, W., Schmittberger, R., and Schwarze, B. (1982) "An experimental analysis of ultimatum bargaining," *Journal of Economic Behaviour and Organization*, 3: 367–388.

Hamilton, J.H. and Slutsky, S.M. (1990) "Endogenous timing in duopoly games: Stackelberg or Cournot equilibria," *Games and Economic Behaviour*, 2: 29–46.

Harstad, R., Martin, S., and Normann, H.T. (1998) "Experimental tests of consciously parallel behaviour in oligopoly," in L. Philips, ed., *Applied Industrial Organization*, Cambridge: Cambridge University Press.

Holt, C. (1985) "An experimental test of the consistent-conjectures hypothesis," *American Economic Review*, 75: 315–325.

Huck, S. and Wallace, B. (2002) "Reciprocal strategies and aspiration levels in a Cournot–Stackelberg experiment," *Economics Bulletin* 3(3): 1–7.

Huck, S., Muller, W., and Normann, H.T. (2000a) "Strategic delegation in experimental markets," Mimeo.

Huck, S., Muller, W., and Normann, H.T. (2001a) "Stackelberg beats Cournot: on collusion and efficiency in experimental markets," *Economic Journal*, 111: 749–765.

Huck, S., Muller, W., and Normann, H.T. (2002b) "To commit or not to commit: endogenous timing in experimental duopoly markets," *Games and Economic Behavior*, 38: 240–264.

Huck, S., Normann, H.T., and Oechssler, J. (1999) "Learning in Cournot oligopoly: an experiment," *Economic Journal*, 109: C80–C95.

Huck, S., Normann, H.T., and Oechssler, J. (2000b) "Does information about competitors' actions increase or decrease competition in experimental oligopoly markets?," *International Journal of Industrial Organization*, 18: 39–57.

Huck, S., Normann, H.T., and Oechssler, J. (2001b) "Market volatility and inequality in earnings: Experimental evidence," *Economics Letters*, 70: 363–368.

Huck, S., Normann, H.T., and Oechssler, J. (2002c) "Two are few and four are many: number effects in experimental oligopoly," Mimeo.

Huck, S., Konrad, K.A., Muller, W., and Normann, H.T. (2002a) "Mergers and the perception of market power: An experimental study," Mimeo.

Mason, C.F. and Phillips, O.R. (1997) "Information and cost asymmetry in experimental duopoly markets," *Review of Economics and Statistics*, 79: 290–299.

Offerman, T., Potters, J., and Sonnemans, J. (2002) "Imitation and belief learning in an oligopoly experiment," *Review of Economic Studies*, 69: 973–997.

Rassenti, S., Reynolds, S., Smith, V.L., and Szidarovszky, F. (2000) "Adaption and convergence of behavior in repeated experimental Cournot games," *Journal of Economic Behavior & Organization*, 41: 117–146.

Salant, S.W., Switzer, S., and Reynolds, R.J. (1983) "Losses from horizontal mergers: the effects of an exogenous change in industry structure on Cournot-Nash equilibrium," *Quarterly Journal of Economics*, 98: 185–199.

Schelling, T. (1960) *The Strategy of Conflict*, New York: Oxford University Press.

van Damme, E., and Hurkens, S. (1999) "Endogenous Stackelberg leadership," *Games and Economic Behaviour*, 28: 105–129.

von Stackelberg, H. (1934) *Marktform und Gleichgewicht*, Vienna and Berlin: Springer Verlag.

Vega-Redondo, F. (1997) "The evolution of Walrasian behaviour," *Econometrica*, 65: 375–384.

Vickers, J. (1985) "Delegation and the theory of the firm," *Economic Journal*, 95: 138–147.

11 Games

Rosemarie Nagel

PART A: HOW TO IMPROVE REASONING IN EXPERIMENTAL BEAUTY CONTEST GAMES – A SURVEY

> I dispute the availability, and thus the value, of that reason which is cultivated in any especial form other than the abstractly logical. I dispute, in particular, the reason deduced by mathematical study. The mathematics are the science of form and quantity; mathematical reasoning is merely logic applied to observation upon form and quantity. The great error lies in supposing that even the truths of what is called pure algebra, are abstract or general truths. And this error is so egregious that I am confounded at the universality with which it has been received. Mathematical axioms are not axioms of general truth. What is true of relation – of form and quantity – is often grossly false in regard to morals, for example. In this latter science it is very usually untrue that the aggregated parts are equal to the whole.
>
> Edgar Allen Poe, *The Purloined Letter* (1980: 211)

Introduction

Game theoretical reasoning can often lead to the wrong conclusion when humans interact. In this survey paper, I summarize experimental studies on beauty-contest games, which show the failure of such reasoning when playing with boundedly rational subjects. The name of the game is due to Keynes (1936: 256) where he likens clever investors to those competitors participating in newspaper beauty-contest games who have to guess the most beautiful face selected by the majority. The game has been introduced by Moulin (1986) in a book on game theory for the social sciences.

In a basic beauty-contest game, each of $n \geq 2$ players simultaneously chooses from a given interval, for example, [0,100]. The winner is the person whose number is closest to a fraction p of an order statistic, for example, 2/3 times the mean of all chosen numbers, and the winner gains a fixed prize. If there is a tie, the prize is split amongst those who tie.

The game is dominance solvable. This means that the process of iterated elimination of dominated strategies starts with eliminating numbers greater than

$p * 100$ (for $p < 1$) since they are weakly dominated, then those which are greater than $(p)^2 * 100$, etc., until in the limit, zero is reached. However, neither infinite elimination nor this type of elimination is how people actually are reasoning in this game. Instead, a model of iterated best reply with limited elimination (between zero and three) best describes the majority of behavior. Such a process starts with the midpoint of the interval, supposing that all others choose randomly. According to the model, people either choose randomly (level zero), best reply to it with $50p$ (level 1), best reply to level 1 with $50p^2$ (level 2), or best reply to level 2 with $50p^3$ (level 3).

The beauty-contest game is interesting for several reasons. First, there is a clear distinction between bounded rationality and the game theoretic solution. Second, as in all zero-sum games, there is a separation of strategic factors from motivational factors (as, e.g. fairness, cooperation). Therefore, behavior can be interpreted as "pure bounded rationality." Third, unlike in most zero-sum games as matching pennies or Bertrand games, here different levels of reasoning can be well structured, made visible, and detected either via the number of iterated best reply or the number of iterated elimination of dominated strategies. Fourth, the rules are very simple to explain and the game can be easily extended in many directions, for example, changing the payoff such that it becomes a nonzero sum game. Most important, this game is a nice demonstration experiment to explain how badly one will play, if one presupposes only hyper-rational players and the knowledge about that, but instead is facing bounded rational players.

In a first wave of experiments on the beauty contest, typical treatments were tested as in other experimental settings: many repetitions, many players versus few players, how an outlier can influence results, payoff changes, and interior solutions versus boundary solutions. The main topic was to formulize the reasoning process as mentioned above and model learning over time. Nagel (1998) gives a more extensive survey on these experiments and Camerer (2002a) surveys a large class of dominance solvable games.

In a second wave of experiments, new treatments have been introduced, which have not been studied in many other game contexts. Rather than observing only students, different subject pools have been invited to play the game; thousands of players participated in several newspaper experiments; more time than in the lab was given; games with equilibria in dominant strategies versus many rounds of eliminations are compared; heterogeneity with respect to experience, different parameters, and team versus individual behavior has been tested. The main topic in these new experiments was to introduce experimental designs with which reasoning could be improved. So far there is only one paper that uses the modified game studying questions unrelated to the model of iterated best reply – but instead related to self-serving bias.

The game and its equilibria

In a basic beauty-contest game, each player simultaneously chooses a real number in a given interval, for example, [0,100]. The winner is the person whose number is closest to *p times the mean of all chosen numbers*, where p is a predetermined and known number. The winner gains a fixed prize. If there is a tie, the prize is split amongst those who tie or a random draw decides the winner. If $p < 1$ there is only one Nash equilibrium in which all choose zero. The process of iterated elimination of weakly dominated strategies for $n \geq 2$ leads to zero. For $n = 2$, the equilibrium is in weakly dominant strategies. If $p > 1$, then the upper bound is also an equilibrium, reached by iterated elimination of dominated strategies.

If only integers are allowed there are several equilibria; in the case of $p = 2/3$, in addition to the equilibrium "all choosing 0," there is an equilibrium "all choosing 1." In the case $p = 0.9$, the set of equilibria is all choosing either 0, 1, 2, 3, or 4 (see Rafael López, 2002). If p is sufficiently close to 1 and the number of players is sufficiently large, then any number can form an equilibrium in which all play the same number.

If a constant is added to the average, then there is a unique equilibrium in the interior. Payments according to the distance to the target number instead of the "winner-takes-all-rule" do not change the equilibrium. If p is different for two subgroups who all interact, 0 is the equilibrium and if a constant is added each subgroup chooses one particular number that is different from the other subgroup.

Reasoning processes and descriptive models

The basic reasoning processes for first-period behavior is summarized in detail by Bosch-Domènech *et al.* (2002). They distinguish five types of reasoning processes: (a) the fixed-point argument of the unique equilibrium; (b) the iterated elimination of weakly dominant strategies (see Introduction); (c) the iterated elimination of best reply (see Introduction) as used in Nagel (1995), Stahl (1996), and Ho *et al.* (1998); (d) Stahl (1998) introduced iterated best reply to probability distributions over different types (random, levels 1, 2, etc.); (e) the last type of reasoning includes those players who notice that pure brainwork does not help to find a good choice and therefore run their own experiments to find an empirical target number.

Bosch-Doménech *et al.* (2002) and Camerer and Ho (2002) introduce two new mixture models to quantify the iterated best-reply model. I will briefly describe these two models below.

Crawford and Costa-Gomez (2002) add for their two-person guessing games types of reasoning that allow to eliminate k rounds of iterated dominance and then give best response to the uniform distribution of the strategies remaining after elimination. In the basic game this is equivalent to $50p^k$, but in their study there is a distinction between those two descriptive models. They also include a sophisticated best-response type, which is a best response to a probability distribution of the choices of the other player.

Describing the single treatments, I will also discuss which learning models were developed or applied to describe behavior over time.

The different studies

First wave of experiments

The first experiments on the beauty-contest games tested the usual treatments as in other experimental studies. The most important contributions of these papers were to develop descriptive models as mentioned above, which explain actual behavior in these games. Nagel (1998) gives an extended survey on these experiments and the descriptive models.

REPETITION

The typical way to improve convergence to equilibrium is to give subjects the chance to repeat several rounds of the same game either with the same players or with changing players. Since the basic beauty-contest game is a zero-sum game with one equilibrium, the number of equilibria does not change in supergames. All studies discussed in this section play the game of four to ten rounds with the same group. Most studies use $p = 2/3$ since then the iterated best-reply model is clearly distinguished from the iterated dominance model and the number of iteration steps is fairly large.

VARIATION OF PARAMETERS

Nagel (1993, 1995) and Ho *et al.* (1998) varied the parameters, using $p = 1/2$ (only Nagel, 1995), 2/3 and 4/3. Ho *et al.* (1998) compare sessions of different underlying intervals to choose from to study the effect of convergence when the number of iterated eliminations of dominated strategies are low. The center of Nagel's study (1995) is that first-period behavior conforms to the iterated best-reply model described above with no more than three levels of reasoning and less than 1 percent equilibrium choices. Behavior over time is explained by the so-called learning direction theory (see also Selten and Buchta, 1998). The data are interpreted such that the level of reasoning, using the previous period mean as a new starting point, does not increase over time. The fastest convergence is in games with $p = 4/3$ since the level of reasoning starting at fifty and ending at 100 is the lowest (three levels). Sessions with 1/2 converge faster than those with 2/3, but the number of reasoning levels applied in each period is not different.

Stahl (1996) reanalyzed Nagel's (1995) dataset in the light of various learning theories. A variation of a reinforcement-based model tied with iterated best-reply behavior and elements of learning direction theory explained behavior best. He interpreted the data over time exhibiting increasing depth of reasoning.

Stahl (1998) tested whether more complicated types of players – Bayesian players, which give best responses to probability distributions over different types – rather than iterated best-response types of players could help to explain Nagel's data even better. The result is that adding more complicated types of players does not improve the description of behavior of the beauty contest data set.

NUMBER OF SUBJECTS

Ho *et al.* (1998) varied the number of players (three or seven) to study the effect of different weights on the mean behavior by a single player. An iterated best-response model predicts that the smaller the number of players, the faster the convergence toward equilibrium. However, the data showed the opposite result. They also let people play several periods with one parameter p and then changed the parameter. In the first switching period, behavior is similar to the very first period, but convergence is faster in the second treatment.

Camerer and Ho (1999) reanalyzed the Ho *et al.* (1998) dataset and the datasets of other games to study the learning behavior. They proposed a general learning model called an experienced-weighted attraction (EWA) model, which contains a basic reinforcement model and a belief-based model as special cases.

INFLUENCE OF OUTLIERS

Duffy and Nagel (1997) studied the influence by a single player on aggregated performance. The order statistic *mean* of the basic game is either replaced by the *maximum* or *median*, with $p = 1/2$. The equilibrium is the same, however, in the maximum game it is a weak equilibrium. The most important findings are that iterated reasoning improves the most in median games, where outliers play a negligible role. Convergence to the equilibrium is not observed in the maximum game. Here, a single player can strongly influence the behavior of all others.

INTERIOR SOLUTIONS

Camerer and Ho (1999), which was taken up by Gueth *et al.* (2002, see also below), presented a game with the equilibrium prediction in the interior of the interval of possible choices. Not surprisingly, first periods' behavior is closer is to equilibrium. However, in later rounds there is no difference to treatments with boundary solution in terms of distance to equilibrium.

CHANGING PAYOFFS

Nagel (1998) introduced a treatment called the (p-mean) variable payoff treatment. The winner receives one dollar times his chosen number instead of a fixed prize. This game is related to the Bertrand game with a nonpareto optimal equilibrium. Convergence is significantly slower than in the original beauty contest game.

Second wave of experiments

In the second wave of experiments many of the treatments tested show features not often found in the experimental literature. The main topic (see point (c) given below) is the introduction of heterogeneity into the game through different methods. Two mixture models have been introduced to quantify the iterated best reply model.

INFORMATION AFTER A PERIOD

Weber (2003) (and also Grosskopf and Nagel, 2001, discussed in the next subsection) varied the information given after a period. After each period a player is informed either about (a) all choices, target number (full info); (b) nothing (no info); (c) No info and telling the subject that the experimenter had calculated the target number and determined the winner (no info and low priming); (d) no info, and requiring a guess about the target number (no info and high priming). Weber finds that in all conditions behavior converges to equilibrium, and best in the full information condition. Priming the subject showed no significant effect.

TWO-PERSON GAMES

Three different two-person beauty-contest experiments have been studied.

1. Grosskopf and Nagel (2001) tested behavior in the two-person beauty-contest games with $p = 2/3$. Note that the average of any two numbers is, of course, in the middle of these two numbers and the multiplication by 2/3 makes the lower number always the winner. Thus, this game is equivalent to the simplest strategic game, "the lower number always wins a fixed prize." Hence, theoretically speaking, only one round of elimination of weakly dominated strategies is necessary to reach equilibrium.

Four information treatments are introduced: (a) full info; (b) own payoff (partial info); (c) no info; and (d) no info and high priming as in Weber. After ten rounds of two-person play, all eighteen subjects of a session participated in a eighteen-person guessing game for four periods under the same information condition as before.

In the light of previous experiments, in which subjects exhibited depth of reasoning of levels one to three, one should expect that people choose zero rather quickly. However, only in the full info treatment subjects converge to equilibrium faster than in the large number treatments. This is explained by the possibility of imitation of those who find the dominant strategy in the first few rounds. The convergence is basically nonexisting in the no info treatment, quite contrary to the study of Weber. The causes for slow convergence are that the majority of players do not reason differently in the two-player case than in the large player number case. This means that they typically neglect their own influence on the target number. But at the same time they realize that the other can easily influence the target number. Therefore, the game is psychologically rather similar to the 1/2-maximum game studied in Duffy and Nagel (1997) where choices also did not converge to zero. (Note however, that in a 2/3 max game there are only mixed equilibria.) If subjects get no feedback they cannot learn the optimal strategy by pure cognition, seeing that the lower number always wins. Prompting them with their own guess helps convergence significantly in comparison to no prompting.

2. Costa-Gomes and Crawford (2002) introduce a rich parameter set for two-person guessing games. Here, unlike in all other experiments, a player has to

guess *p* times the other player's guess and was paid according to the distance of that number (same payment scheme as in Gueth *et al.* mentioned above). The key issue is how a person takes into account that he is a significant part of the other individual's environment. The own choice has no influence at all on one's own target number making it similar to games with very large number of players where the own influence plays almost no role.

Choices can be between a predetermined interval and if they are chosen outside the interval the choice is adjusted to the nearest boundary. Each subject has his or her own lower limit, upper limit and target, possibly different across games.

The main interest in this study is to analyze the reasoning process of sophistication of subjects. Instead of asking for comments, a subject had to open boxes in order to receive information about his or her own parameters and those of the partner and then make a choice. The control treatment was a treatment with open boxes. The results show that behavior is not affected by the procedure. In an additional control treatment subjects participated in practice rounds with training and motivation according to a specific type, including equilibrium and various kinds of boundedly rational types mentioned above. They played the entire session against a computer program.

Each subject played sixteen independent games with a random partnering each period and no information of the results were given between the periods. This way one can study behavior in one-shot games and separate learning by experience from sophistication. At the completion of this survey the data had not been analyzed yet.

3. At this point, I also want to mention the study by Gneezy (2001) on two treatments of a two-person Bertrand game framed as auctions. The auctions were first- and second-price auctions in which the person with the lower number wins and gains his own stated price or the price of the opponent, respectively. Numbers were to be chosen either from an interval [1,...,10] or [1,...,100]. The second game is strategically equivalent to the game of Grosskopf and Nagel (2001) with variable payoffs and most important with the easier framing.

Gneezy tests whether the iterated best-reply model by Camerer and Ho (2002) can explain behavior in these games. This model is a one-parameter model that assumes the frequency of players using different levels of reasoning and follows a Poisson distribution with mean τ and players know the absolute frequency of others at lower levels from the Poisson distribution and give the best reply. Camerer and Ho (2002) test these models not only for several dominance solvable games, but also for those that are not dominance solvable as matching pennies and market entry games.

For the first-price auction and the interval [1,...,10), Gneezy finds that the iterated best-reply model is easily confirmed with choices around five. For the same auction and interval [1,...100] choices are not concentrated around fifty as required by the 0–3 level reasoning model by Camerer and Ho (2002). However, a transformation of the interval [1,...,10] to 1 [11,..., 20] to 2, ..., [91,...100] to 10 and the introduction of 5 percent altruistic players who choose high transformed numbers (7–10) the model is confirmed. In the second-price auction level one and higher levels are interpreted as choices at 1 and the model is confirmed for both interval treatments without any transformation and introduction of altruistic players.

HETEROGENEITY

Usually theoretical models suppose homogeneity of behavior and belief (e.g. all people are rational and know that everybody is rational). Furthermore, everybody usually acts in the same underlying situation. Experimental economics has pointed out the heterogeneity of players with respect to actions and beliefs. However, few experiments introduce different fixed parameters for different subgroups (exceptions are experiments with different discount parameters in bargaining, different marginal rates of contributions in public good games, etc.). Four different studies are presented in the heading heterogeneity.

Different subject pools, high rewards, thousands of players, and lots of time to think   Several economists proposed a new way of running experiments, by inviting readers of newspapers to participate in the beauty-contest game. The rules of the game were published in four different newspapers. The original motivation for these experiments was to introduce a general audience to behavioral finance (Thaler, 1997a,b, in *Financial Times*, Fehr and Renninger, 2000, in *DIE ZEIT*) and to experimental economics (Bosch-Domènech and Nagel, 1997a,b, in *Expansión*, Bosch-Domènech and Nagel, 1997c, in *Financial Times*, Selten and Nagel, 1998, in *Spektrum der Wissenschaft*). More than 10,000 people replied to the invitations in these four sessions with rewards of about 500–1,000 Euros in each and between 1 and 3 weeks to respond. In these experiments homogeneity with respect to education, background, age, etc, as within our usual subject pool of students is not warranted at all.

Bosch-Domènech *et al.* (2002) summarize the findings of the newspaper experiments and compare them with other sessions outside the lab. These include a session of a newsgroup experiment conducted by a participant of the newspaper contest to find his optimal choice, sessions with economists in conferences or done by e-mail, with students in classroom or as take-home experiments. A general result is that parallelism is granted when going from the lab to more uncontrolled experiments. The main difference is that theorists and newspaper readers choose zero much more (10–40 percent) while in the lab it is no more 1 percent.

They analyzed about 800 comments received from two newspapers and classified them according to the reasoning processes mentioned above. From those who described the equilibrium more than 80 percent did not choose zero, reasoning that not everybody will find this solution. However, most of them chose numbers below ten while the winning numbers were in the interval between 12 and 17. The best strategy turned out to be to run an experiment with friends, colleagues, or newsgroups and send in the winning number received in those pre-experiments.

Camerer (1997a) ran 2/3-mean games with business executives and found that they did not behave differently from students.

Bosch-Domènech *et al.* (2002) use the data from their independent experiments to construct a mixture distribution model of independent normal distributions and estimate means and variances of the composing distributions as well as proportions of subjects using different types of reasoning. They find that the estimated means are similar across all different experiments and near the theoretical choices according to levels zero to three and infinity (choice zero).

Different parameters for different subgroups   Gueth *et al.* (2002) and (Costa-Gomez and Crawford, 2002, as mentioned above) introduce a treatment in which subjects are faced with different parameters in different subgroups. Gueth *et al.* fix the target number to 1/3 times the average of all chosen numbers for two players and to 2/3 for two other players of the same group who interact with each other. They also study these treatments in games with interior solutions. Their hypothesis was that there is faster convergence to the boundary solution than in homogenous groups supposing that subjects will think deeper about the other subjects' behavior. However, the opposite holds due to the much more complex situation. They pay subjects according to the distance of the target number and find that behavior converges faster than with 0/1 payment structure.

Team behavior   In economics and also in experimental economics a decision-maker is usually modeled as an individual. However, in real life most decisions are discussed with friends or colleagues beforehand or are taken in teams or families. Kocher and Sutter (2002) run experiments with beauty-contest games in which groups compete against each other. Each group sends only one choice. Furthermore, in an additional treatment also individuals have to compete against group decisions.

In the first treatment Kocher and Sutter (2002) find that groups do not reason better than individuals in the first period. However, over time groups converge faster and employ higher levels of reasoning. The authors argue that "according to the information load theory, based on the work by Chalos and Pickard (1985), groups have higher decision consistency and are better able to process high information load than individuals in intellective tasks." This is only possible from the second period onwards when they know the behavior of the first period. Another explanation is that groups put randomly together first need to coordinate their decision and share their understanding of the game.

In the mixed treatment, groups clearly outperform individuals. This better behavior fades away over time as limited information processing of individuals is compensated by experience. Kocher and Sutter (2002) study in detail various learning models and find that EWA and a belief-based model best fit the behavior. The most striking difference between groups and individuals is that the parameter for forgone payoffs is one for groups meaning that they weigh these as much as actual payoffs while for individuals it is only 0.88.

The authors discuss the team literature of experimental economics and conclude that there is still a long way to know in which situations groups are better than individuals.

Experienced versus non-experienced players   Slonim (2002) has introduced to my mind a very original treatment. He introduces two treatments in which three players interact with each other in each round. In the first treatment (called SAME) three parallel groups play separately a three-period supergame and then are randomly re-matched in each of the two following supergames. Thus, in any point in time they have the same experience level, a treatment that has been used in experiments on public goods- and PD-supergames.

In the second treatment (called MIX) 1 out of 9 players plays three supergames of three rounds each while his two opponents play three rounds of one supergame and then are replaced by inexperienced players. Thus, there is one player who has a different experience level than his other co-players from the fourth period onwards. This is common information to all players. Inexperienced players do not play differently against inexperienced players or more experienced players. This supports earlier findings that it is difficult to reason more than a few steps and to reason how the game develops after one period or in other words what kind of experience the experienced player might have gained.

Experienced players outguess the inexperienced players in the first two rounds; however, in the third round the experience level does not give superiority in terms of winning. The declining advantage of experience level is similar as in experiments with individuals versus groups where groups outperformed individuals in the first round.

When playing against inexperienced players in the first round of a subsequent supergame 95 percent of the experienced players choose in the range of levels 2 and 3 starting at 50 contrasted to only 38 percent who choose in the same interval in the very first game. Since new players have entered, the overall average is higher than in the third period of the last supergame. When playing against players with the same experience level in a new supergames the average also increases in the new supergame but far less than in the Mix treatment.

SELF-SERVING BIAS

So far all experiments on the beauty-contest game were related to the question of iterated reasoning. To my knowledge the study by Kaplan and Ruffle (2000) is the only one that relates the beauty-contest game to something different, the self-serving bias. The authors define that "a self-serving bias exists where the individual's preferences affect his beliefs in an optimistic direction, one favoring his own utility. Beliefs may be about one's own ability, the environment, another player's type or what is a fair outcome."

One of the goals of their paper was to test for the self-serving bias in a context unrelated to fairness considerations and to control for other explanations of the data that have confounded previous studies of the bias. To achieve the latter, they selected a relatively context-free environment. For the purpose of the former, they modified the basic beauty contest game by adding to the fixed payoff an additional variable payoff earned by all players. This payoff depended on the guesses of all other players (excluding oneself). Half of the subjects received a variable payment of

100 minus the average guesses of all other players but oneself, while the other half of the subjects received the average guess of all other subjects but oneself. Since one's own guess is excluded, the motivation for strategically manipulating one's guess is eliminated. According to the self-serving bias, the first half of the subjects should guess lower than the second half. The logic is that the first half of the subjects prefers a low average of guesses in order that their variable payoffs will be large. Thus, the bias predicts that they should believe that others will guess low and therefore they will guess low to maximize their chance of winning the fixed prize. Just the opposite logic holds for the second half of the subjects: their self-serving beliefs lead them to believe that others will choose high numbers so that they should guess high.

The experimental results do not support a self-serving bias in the overall data. However, a closer look at the field of study and gender shows that female psychologists only exhibit the bias. The authors interpret this as very limited support for the bias.

Conclusion

The beauty-contest game or guessing game, as it is also called, has gained quite some popularity in experimental economics and outside the field since the first published experimental article on the game.

It has reached a wide audience as it has been discussed in several popular newspapers with experiments in which readers of these newspapers participated or did not (Camerer, 1997b or Varian, 2002), maybe for its simplicity to explain the game in a few words. It is appearing in microeconomic textbooks that include experiments as teaching tools (e.g. Schotter, 2001) in connection with iterated elimination of dominated strategies. It is discussed in undergraduate micro-classes (see Nagel, 1999), PhD classes on experimental economics, game theory, or behavioral finance in many universities for its contribution to hierarchy of beliefs about other players' behavior. It is used as a demonstration experiment in talks to a general audience.

While the first studies concentrated in developing descriptive models using conventional treatments of experimental economics, the studies in recent years introduced imaginative experimental methods or design features, new or not often seen in the field, especially with respect to subject pools and heterogeneity features.

The most important result in all studies is that subject apply only 0–3 levels of reasoning. Not surprisingly, economists exposed to the game show the highest depth of reasoning. Even if subjects can reason until equilibrium the majority of them do not choose the equilibrium arguing that others might not find the solution as well. However, the choices of these are still close to equilibrium.

Several points are still missing within the existing literature: first, it might be interesting to embed the game within other games or with richer (economic) contests. So far it is, for example, related to financial markets as a cover story in the papers but maybe more context rich experiments might give further insight or improve subjects reasoning. Second, the game should be applied as a test-bed for other behavioral questions. The paper by Kaplan and Ruffle is the first step to use the game for other features than just levels of reasoning. Third, Gneezy shows that it is possible to apply the iterated best-reply model for a dominance solvable game where at first sight it does not seem to explain behavior. A little trick of transformation helps to confirm the model. Camerer and Ho (2002) have used the model for games like matching pennies, which from a theoretic point of view does not incorporate iterated thinking to find the equilibrium. This brings to mind a passage from *The Purloined Letter* by Edgar Allen Poe (1980: 208) referring to a variation of a matching pennies game played by a clever schoolboy:

> Of course he had some principle of guessing; and this lay in mere observation and admeasurement of the astuteness of his opponents. For example, an arrant simpleton is his opponent, and, holding up his closed hand, asks, "are they even or odd?" Our schoolboy replies, "odd," and loses; but upon the second trial he wins, for he then says to himself, "the simpleton had them even upon the first trial, and his amount of cunning is just sufficient to make him have them odd upon the second; I will therefore guess odd;" – he guesses odd, and wins. Now, with a simpleton a degree above the first, he would have reasoned thus: "This fellow finds that in the first instance I guessed odd, and, in the second, he will propose to himself upon the first impulse, a simple variation from even to odd, as did the first simpleton; but then a second thought will suggest that this is too simple a variation, and finally he will decide upon putting it even as before. I will therefore guess even" guesses even, and wins. Now this mode of reasoning in the schoolboy, whom his fellows termed "lucky," – what, in its last analysis, is it?
>
> "It is merely," I said, "an identification of the reasoner's intellect with that of his opponent."

A final note to theorists: while many theorists know the experimental studies and behavioral results of the game (and other dominance solvable games), and use it in their classes, it is never reflected in theoretical models involving iterated elimination of dominated strategies. The typical reason for ignoring facts related to bounded rationality is that the results may not be robust. However, in almost all studies related to iterated elimination of dominated strategies, subjects exhibit levels of reasoning between 0 and 3 or equilibrium behavior. Maybe this robust result can be incorporated into the theoretical discussion about dominated strategies.

PART B: THE EFFECT OF INTERGROUP COMPETITION AND INCOMPLETE INFORMATION IN COORDINATION GAMES – A SHORT SUMMARY

Coordination games are games in which typically all players have an incentive to choose the same action. However, some coordinated actions may lead to higher payoffs than others. Thus, there are multiple equilibria that may be Pareto ranked. Which equilibrium is selected is an important question in economics. Four different directions have been undertaken to find answers to this question: (a) refinement concepts since the invention of Selten's subgame perfect equilibrium concept; (b) equilibrium selection, applying, for example, payoff dominance or risk evaluation of actions; (c) evolutionary game theory showing which dynamics converge to which equilibrium and (d) empirical studies.

The literature on experimental coordination games is probably one of the broader attempts in studying which kind of equilibrium will result when subjects – here, of course, bounded rational subjects – interact with each other. Ochs (1995) has written the first survey for the *Handbook of Experimental Economics*, Crawford in (1997) and recently Camerer (2002b) have completed a survey on the same topic. Camerer gives an excellent variety of real world examples of how some coordination problems have developed in history as, for example, rail road width and its effects on size of space shuttles or why we drive on the right side in most countries.

In this section, I will present very briefly three papers on coordination experiments in which I have been involved with several co-authors. The first paper introduces team competition within coordination tasks as a way to improve coordination. The other two papers introduce incomplete information into coordination, which to my knowledge are the first papers of this kind in experimental economics. The reason might be that coordination games already bear strategic uncertainty, difficult enough to solve for the players. However, incomplete information in coordination games has received a lot of attention in economic theory and important applications since the seminal paper by Carlson and Van Damme (1993). The interested reader can find a small selection of papers on the recent development in this field from a theoretical and experimental perspective in the workshop program "Coordination, Incomplete Information, and Iterated dominance: Theory and Empirics" organized by Cabrales *et al.* (2002).

Coordination games with team competition

Bornstein and his collaborators have studied the effect of intergroup competition mainly in prisoner's dilemma and public good experiments. Bornstein *et al.* (2002) wanted to test whether coordination was significantly improved if this kind of competition was introduced. The control treatment is the Minimum effort game (Van Huyck *et al.*, 1990). In this game, the minimum number chosen in a group and the player's difference to that minimum (which presents a cost) determines the payoff for a player. The higher the minimum the higher the payoffs to all and the lower the difference to the minimum the higher the payoff for a single player. All choosing the same number (which can be between one and seven) are the equilibria, with seven being the Pareto optimal choice. In all treatments ten periods were played.

Three kinds of intergroup competition are introduced, which differ in the payment to each member of a single group. In all treatments two groups play independently the minimum effort game and are informed about both minima after each period. The winning group is the one with the higher minimum effort. In the first intergroup treatment the payoff to each member of the winning group is as in the control treatment. The losers receive nothing. In case of a tie the payoffs are divided into half. There are equilibria as in the control treatment with all subjects chosing the same number. Additionally, there are weak equilibria in which all members of one group chose the same number and at least two members of the other group choose a lower number than in the coordinating group. In the second treatment the payoffs are exactly as in the control treatment for both groups. This means that the minimum of the other group has no influence on one's own payoff. The interest here was to test whether coordination increases if one sees a more successful other group. The third treatment gave a fixed bonus to each player of the winning group, additionally to the payoff as in the control treatment. In case of a tie, the bonus was split. In the second and third treatments all members of the same group have to choose the same number that can be different between the two groups.

In the first few periods of all treatments the minimum and the mean are not significantly different. However, over time effort levels decay similarly in the control and in the treatment with no payoff effects of the competition. The reason is that a low minimum in one period cannot be reversed by the group but instead is imitated eventually by all players. The best coordination (around effort four) is reached in the treatment where the losing group earned nothing. Here, a low choice of effort is not imitated. Those who have chosen the lowest number, typically out of frustration because they have previously chosen very high effort levels in comparison to the others, increase their levels in the next period. The bonus treatment shows the second highest coordination. The authors conclude that competition has a positive effect on coordination if payoffs depend on the other group's performance.

Coordination games with incomplete information

The theory of global game developed by Carlson and Van Damme (1993) and Morris and Shin (1998) has provided a convincing solution to the problem of multiplicity in coordination games. Players do not have complete information of the payoffs of some of their strategies. Instead, they get a private signal about the true payoffs. Those coordination games may have unique equilibria and these models have led to many macroeconomic and financial applications to solve problems of equilibrium indeterminacy.

Cabrales *et al.* (2000) ran two treatments, based on a model of Carlson and Van Damme (1993), that are 2×2 games with uncertainty of payoffs for action A. In the first treatment, the uncertain payoffs for action A (which can be 50, 60, 70, 80, or 90 with equal probability) depend only on the same true state of nature for both players and are independent of what the other player does. In the second treatment, inspired by the work of Battalio *et al.* (2001), the payoff for A depends on the choice of the other player [(X, R) can take five possible values, (36, 84), (32, 80), (28, 76), (24, 72), and (20, 68), where X is the payoff, if the other chooses A, and R is the payoff, if the other chooses B). In both treatments, the alternative action B gives a zero payoff, if the partner chooses A and a payoff of eighty, if the partner also chooses B. In every period, each player receives an independent signal about the true state, which is either +10, 0, or −10 of the true payoff. Both games have a unique strategy profile that survives the iterative deletion of strictly dominated strategies (thus a unique Nash equilibrium). The equilibrium outcome coincides, on average, with the risk-dominant equilibrium outcome of the underlying coordination game. Thus, for each signal the players have to choose action A.

The same game is played for fifty periods against changing partners. Both games are also studied under the certainty payoff structures, that is, payoffs for action A are known and in each period a true state is randomly chosen and announced. If the best state is drawn (90) or $(X, R) = (36, 84)$ there exists one equilibrium in dominant strategies and in the games with the other possible four states there exist two equilibria.

In the initial periods, subjects typically choose action A for very good signals and action B for bad signals. In the first treatment with uncertainty, they learn to choose action A for all signals within fifty periods. The better the signal the faster the learning to play action A. In the second treatment, however, there is no convergence to equilibrium for the bad states within the fifty periods. In the two complete information versions there is no clear convergence for the bad states. A simulation which consists of a reinforcement model à la Camerer and Ho (1999) maps rather well the different kinds of convergence to equilibrium in the uncertainty games and of the complete information game of the second treatment. So far we have no dynamic model for the complete information case of the first treatment.

Heinemann *et al.* (2002) run multi-person coordination games with incomplete information based on Morris and Shin (1998). The experiment consists of a 2×2 design: there are complete and incomplete information games and games with high (fifty) or low (twenty) sure payoffs for action A. Action B depends on the state of nature and of how many other players choose this action. If enough players choose B, then those B players receive the payoff according the true state that is uniformly chosen from the interval $[10, \ldots, 90]$. The better the state of nature the lower is the number of players necessary to play B. If not enough players choose B, then B players get nothing. In the complete information case players know the true state of the world. In case of incomplete information players receive signals that are at most ± 10 around the true state. In each session either a complete or incomplete information game is played. A sequence of eight periods of high sure payoffs is followed by eight periods of sure low payoffs or vice versa.

In the complete information game there are multiple equilibria for middle ranges of the state of the world while for low states all players should choose action A and for high state all should select B. Several refinement concepts are proposed to single out unique equilibria, which are all threshold equilibria. This means that until a certain state A should be chosen and from there onwards B. The incomplete information game has a unique equilibrium with a threshold between the payoff-dominant and risk-dominant equilibrium of the underlying complete information game. Thus, theory predicts better stability for the incomplete information game because of uniqueness and instability for the complete information games. However, our subjects coordinate rather fast on lower thresholds and thus produce higher efficiency in complete information games in comparison to the incomplete information games with slower convergence to somewhat higher thresholds. Comparative statics of the different parameter treatments show that the theory of global games is validated. Tests are done to show which equilibrium concepts best describe behavior.

References

Battalio, R., Samuelson, L., and Van Huyck, J. (2001) "Optimization incentives and coordination failure in laboratory stag-hunt games," *Econometrica*, 69: 749–764.

Bornstein, G., Gneezy, U., and Nagel, R. (2002) "The effect of intergroup competition on group coordination: an experimental study," *Games and Economic Behavior*, 41: 1–25.

Bosch-Domènech, A. and Nagel, R. (1997a) "Cómo se le da la Bolsa," *Expansión*, June 4, p. 40.

Bosch-Domènech, A. and Nagel, R. (1997b) "El juego de adivinar el número X: una explicación y la proclamación del vencedor," *Expansión*, June 16, pp. 42–43.

Bosch-Domènech, A. and Nagel, R. (1997c) "Guess the number: comparing the financial times and expansion's results," *Financial Times*, section Mastering Finance 8, June 30, p. 14.

Bosch-Domènech, A., García-Montalvo, J., Nagel, R., and Satorra, A. (2002) "One, two, three, infinity,…: newspaper and lab beauty-contest experiments," *American Economic Review*; 92(5): 1687–1701.

Cabrales, A., Nagel R., and Armenter, R. (2000) "Equilibrium selection through incomplete information in coordination games: an experimental study," Universitat Pompeu Fabra, Barcelona, Working Paper 601.

Cabrales, A., Camerer, C., Morris, S., and Nagel, R. (2002) Workshop on "coordination, incomplete information, and iterated dominance: theory and empirics," http://www.econ.upf.es/~cabrales/confer/global/progros1.htm

Camerer, C. (1997a) "Progress in behavioral game theory," *Journal of Economic Perspective*, 11: 167–188.

Camerer, C. (1997b) "Taxi drivers and beauty contests," *Engineering & Science*, 1: 10–19.

Camerer, C. (2002a) "Iterated reasoning in dominance solvable games," in C. Camerer, ed., *Behavioral Game Theory: Experiments on Strategic Interaction*, Princeton: Princeton University Press, Chapter 5.

Camerer, C. (2002b) "Coordination" in *Behavioral Game Theory: Experiments on Strategic Interaction*, Princeton: Princeton University Press.

Camerer, C. and Ho, T. (1999) "Experienced-weighted attraction learning in normal form games," *Econometrica*, 67: 827–874.

Camerer, C. and Ho, T. (2002) "Behavioral game theory: thinking, learning, and teaching," Mimeo.

Carlsson, H. and van Damme, E. (1993) "Global games and equilibrium selection," *Econometrica*, 61: 989–1018.

Chalos, P. and Pickard, S. (1985) "Information choice and cue use: an experiment on group information processing," *Journal of Applied Psychology*, 70: 634–641.

Costa-Gomes, M. and Crawford, V. (2002) "Cognition and behavior in two-guessing games: an experimental study," Mimeo.

Crawford, V.P. (1997) "Theory and experiment in the analysis of strategic interaction," in D. Kreps and K. Wallis, eds, *Advances in Economics and Econometrics: Theory and Applications*, I, Cambridge: Cambridge University Press, pp. 206–242.

Duffy, J. and Nagel, R. (1997) "On the robustness of behavior in experimental beauty-contest games," *Economic Journal*, 107: 1684–1700.

Fehr E. and Renninger, S.V. (2000) "Gefangen in der Gedankenspirale," DIE ZEIT Nr. 48, November 23, Wirtschaft, p. 31.

Gneezy, U. (2001) "On the relation between guessing games and bidding in auctions," Mimeo.

Grosskopf, B. and Nagel, R. (2001) "Rational reasoning or adaptive behavior? Evidence from two-person beauty contest games," Harvard NOM Research Paper No. 01–09.

Gueth, W., Kocher, M., and Sutter, M. (2002) "Experimental 'beauty contests' with homogeneous and heterogeneous players and with interior and boundary equilibria," *Economics Letters* 74: 219–228.

Heinemann, F., Nagel, R., and Ockenfels, P. (2001) "Speculative attacks and financial architecture: experimental analysis of coordination games with public and private information," London School of Economics Working Paper.

Ho, T., Camerer, C., and Weigelt, K. (1998) "Iterated dominance and iterated best-response in experimental 'P-beauty-contests'," *American Economic Review*, 88(4): 947–969.

Kaplan, T. and Ruffle, B.J. (2000) "Self-serving bias and belief about rationality," Mimeo.

Keynes, J.M. (1936) *The General Theory of Interest, Employment and Money*, London: Macmillan.

Kocher, M.G. and Sutter, M. (2002) "The 'decision maker' matters: individual versus group behavior in experimental 'beauty-contest' games," University of Innsbruck, Mimeo.

López, R. (2002) "On p-beauty contest integer games," UPF Working Paper No. 608.

Morris, S. and Shin, H.S. (1998) "Unique equilibrium in a model of self-fulfilling currency attacks," *American Economic Review*, 88: 587–597.

Moulin, H. (1986) *Game Theory for Social Sciences*, New York: New York Press.

Nagel, R. (1993) "Experimental results on interactive competitive guessing," Discussion Paper No. B-236, University of Bonn.

Nagel, R. (1995) "Unraveling in guessing games: an experimental study," *American Economic Review*, 85(5): 1313–1326.

Nagel, R. (1998) "A survey on experimental 'beauty-contest games': bounded rationality and learning," in D. Budescu, I. Erev, and R. Zwick, eds, *Games and Human Behavior, Essays in Honor of Amnon Rapoport*, Mahwah, NJ: Lawrence Erlbaum Associates, Inc., pp. 105–142.

Nagel, R. (1999) "A keynesian beauty contest in the classroom," in *Classroom Expericomics* (electronic newsletter), Vol. 8 (October).

Ochs, J. (1995) "Coordination problems," in J.H. Kagel and A.E. Roth, eds, *Handbook of Experimental Economics*, Princeton: Princeton University Press.

Poe, Edgar A. (1980) "The Purloined Letter," in the World's Classics *Selected Tales*, Oxford: Oxford University Press.

Schotter, A. (2001) *Microeconomics: A Modern Approach*, New York: Addison-Wesley Longman.

Selten, R. and Buchta, J. (1998) "Experimental sealed bid first price auction with directly observed bid functions," in D. Budescu, I. Erev, and R. Zwick, eds, *Games and Human Behavior, Essays in Honor of Amnon Rapoport*, Hillsdale, NJ: Erlbaum.

Selten, R. and Nagel, R. (1997) "1000DM zu gewinnen," *Spektrum der Wissenschaft*, November, p. 10.

Slonim, R. (2002) "Competing against experienced and inexperienced players in experimental beauty contest games," Discussion Paper.

Stahl, D.O. (1996) "Rule learning in a guessing game," *Games and Economic Behavior*, 16(2): 303–330.

Stahl, D.O. (1998) "Is step-j thinking an arbitrary modelling restriction or a fact of human nature?" *Journal of Economic Behavior and Organization*, 37(1): 33–51.

Thaler, R. (1997a) "Competition," *Financial Times*, section Mastering Finance 1, May 9, p. 29.

Thaler, R. (1997b) "Giving markets a human dimension," *Financial Times*, section Mastering Finance 6, June 16, pp. 2–5.

Van Huyck, L.B., Battaglio, R.C., and Beil, O.R. (1990) "Tacit coordination games, strategic uncertainty, and coordination failure," *American Economic Review*, 80: 234–248.

Varian (2002) *New York Times*. April 11, 2002.

Weber, R. (2003) "'Learning' with no feedback in a competitive guessing game," *Games and Economic Behavior*, 44(1): 134–144.

12 Learning direction theory and impulse balance equilibrium*

Reinhard Selten

Transcribed by Daniel Friedman

Introduction

An archer can learn to hit a target by following a very simple rule. If he misses to the left, he can aim a little more to the right. If he misses to the right, he can aim a little more to the left.

This sort of directional learning applies to a wide range of situations. Only three requirements must be met:

1   As in any learning situation, there must be time to learn, and here we assume discrete time periods $t = 1, \ldots, T$.
2   There must be a parameter p_t chosen in each period t from an ordered set, typically an interval of real numbers.
3   There must be feedback after each period that allows the learner to infer which values of p might have been better than his actual choice.

The basic idea is simple, a qualitative form of *ex post* rationality. The learner chooses parameter $p_t \le p_{t-1}$ in period t if $p \le p_{t-1}$ might have been better in period $t-1$, and chooses $p_t \ge p_{t-1}$ in period t if last period $p \ge p_{t-1}$ might have been better.

For example, in a first-price sealed-bid auction, the bidder who won the auction set the price. It might have been better for her or him to bid a bit lower, still winning the auction but paying a lower price. On the other hand, consider a bidder who did not win the auction but observes that his own value exceeds the winning bid. It might have been better for him to have bid higher.

The specific prediction of learning direction theory is that parameter changes, when they occur, are in the indicated direction more frequently than would be expected with unbiased random choices. Examples of specific applications will be discussed below.

It should be noted that learning direction theory is qualitative, not quantitative. Of course, quantitative theories can be based on it, and some examples will be noted shortly.

Note also the contrast to reinforcement learning. Learning direction theory ignores the realized rewards *per se*, and relies entirely on comparisons with counterfactual payoffs for choices not made. Reinforcement learning, from its origin

Table 12.1 Papers using learning direction theory

1	Selten and Stoecker (1986)	P.D. end effect
2	Mitzkewitz and Nagel (1993)	Ultimatum
3	Kuon (1993)	Bargaining
4	Ryll (1996)	Bargaining
5	Nagel (1996)	Beauty contest
6	Kagel and Levin (1999)	Auction
7	Berninghaus and Ehrhart (1998)	Coordination
8	Nagel and Tang (1995)	Centipede
9	Sadrieh (1998)	Market
10	Selten and Buchta (1999)	Auction
11	Cason and Friedman (1997, 1999)	Market
12	Selten *et al.* (2001)	Winner's curse

in psychology many decades ago through its recent applications to interactive games, ignores counterfactual payoffs and relies entirely on realized payoffs.

Learning direction theory has by now been applied successfully in a variety of laboratory environments. It was first introduced by Selten and Stoecker (1986) to explain later period choices in finitely repeated prisoner's dilemma games. Table 12.1 notes twelve papers applying it to ultimatum games, bargaining, beauty-contest (or guessing) games, centipede and coordination games, auctions and two-sided auction markets. Some of these papers, including Cason and Friedman (1999), use quantitative extensions of the theory.

An application

Here, we will describe an application of learning direction theory to human learning behavior that shows no tendency to converge to the optimum. The laboratory environment is based on the "winner's curse" observed in oil field auctions according to Capen *et al.* (1971) and later authors. The idea is that different bidders have different estimates of the field's economic value, and that the bidder with the most optimistic estimate is likely to be the highest bidder. If he or she does not adequately discount for the over-optimism implied by being the highest bidder, he or she is likely to pay too much and incur an economic loss.

Samuelson and Bazerman (1985) distilled the winner's curse (or the market for lemons) to the individual choice laboratory task we examine here. As the manager of firm B, the subject bids to acquire firm A. The subject knows that the basic value v of firm A is uniformly distributed between 0 and 100, and that (perhaps because of economies of scope) the value to B will be $1.5v$ if his or her bid is accepted. Firm A is simulated by a computer program that accepts only bids $x \geq v$. After each period the subject is told the realized value of v and receives profit (or loss) $1.5v - x$ when the bid is accepted and 0 otherwise. Then a new period begins with a new value of v drawn independently from the same distribution.

The optimal choice in this task is to bid $x = 0$. This counterintuitive result arises from the fact that the conditional expectation of v given that bid x is accepted is

$E(v|x) = \frac{1}{2} x$, because the bid is rejected for values $v \geq x$ so the conditional probability distribution is uniform on the interval from 0 to x. Thus, the subject's expected payoff when bidding x is the probability that the bid is accepted times $1.5E(v|x) - x = -\frac{1}{4} x$, which indeed is maximized at $x = 0$.

Ball *et al.* (1991) present this task to thirty-seven subjects over twenty periods and find no tendency to converge to the optimum. The average bid starts above fifty and remains there, if anything increasing slightly over the last ten periods. Perhaps subjects' initial choices are guided by the unconditional expectation $Ev = 50$ and $1.5Ev = 75$, but they get useful feedback in every period. Reinforcement learning and most other learning theories predict that subjects eventually learn to play optimally. Why do not we see more movement towards $x = 0$? Learning direction theory provides an explanation.

A new experiment by Selten *et al.* (2001) allows longer opportunities for learning. It also provides a stronger test of the theory by moving the optimal bid around the interior of the action set. The experiment features 100 periods, and a lower bound u for the uniform distribution set at the values 1, 11, and 21; the upper bound remains at 100. Direct computation shows that the optimal bid is $x^* = 22$ when $u = 11$ and is $x^* = 42$ when $u = 21$;[1] these are useful contrasts to the extreme optimum $x^* = 0$ when $u = 0$. Subjects are endowed with 250 points and an income of twenty points per period.

Learning direction theory is easily applied to this environment. If a subject bids $x > v$ in a given period, he or she overpaid and will tend to decrease the bid x in the next period. If he or she bids $x < v$ then his or her bid is rejected and he or she will tend to increase the bid in the next period. The test statistic is the fraction r of all bid changes that are in the indicated direction, taken over all subjects and all periods.

One might first consider $r = 0.5$ as the natural null hypothesis, but this might stack the deck in favor of learning direction theory. For example, if subjects chose their bids independently from the same distribution as the values, then we would on average observe $r = 2/3$. The reason is reminiscent of the original "regression to the mean": the case $x < v$ tends to be associated with a low value of x, which by independence tends to be associated with a higher subsequent draw of x. Similarly, the case $x > v$ tends to be associated with a lower subsequent draw. In either case, r tends to rise above 1/2 without any directional learning.

A more appropriate null hypothesis is that bids, whatever their distribution, are chosen without regard to *ex post* error. That is, we should compare the actual value of r to the value that would give rise to a random pairing of the actual bids and actual values. The precise null hypothesis is that $r = p$, the expected value of r when the value draws are randomly permuted, holding constant the actual sequence of chosen bids. This null hypothesis is rejected in favor of the one-sided alternative $r > p$ consistent with directional learning theory. In all three treatments ($u = 1$, 11, and 21) the rejection occurs at least at the 0.5 percent significance level.

Figure 12.1 shows average play over time in each treatment. There is little time trend in any of these cases, and the averages do not much differ by treatment.

Of course, the departures from optimality are smaller in the new treatments, especially the $u = 21$ treatment.

Individual differences in this experiment are noteworthy. Table 12.2 classifies them by their modal bid, allowing where appropriate for rounding one or two points. Of the fifty-four subjects, ten of them are optimizers with bids tracking the optimum. Three are loss avoiders, choosing modal bids that prevent a negative salient payoff, and eight more are asset conservers, choosing modal bids that prevent a negative payoff inclusive of the non-salient 20-point income. Two

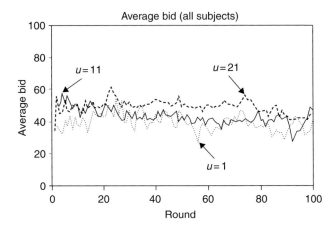

Figure 12.1 Average play over time in each treatments $u = 1$, 11, and 21.

Table 12.2 Categorization of subjects by modal bid

	Lower boundary			No. of subjects
	$u = 1$	$u = 11$	$u = 21$	
Optimizers	0[a], 1, 2	20[a], 21, 22	40[a], 41, 42	10
Loss avoiders	–	15[a], 16	29[a], 30[b], 31	3
Asset conservers	20[a], 21	34[a], 35[b], 36	50[a], 51	8
Gamblers	99	99	99	2
Refusers	–	0	0	2
Adapters				29
Total				54

Notes
a Rounded.
b Intended.
Adapters conform more to learning direction theory.
Significance 1% one-tailed.

choose the maximum allowable modal bids, ensuring that they will always play, and two others opt out by bidding zero. The remaining twenty-nine subjects, more than half, are classified as adapters. The adapters all conform to learning direction theory as evidenced by a 1 percent significance level for rejecting the null hypothesis in favor of $r > p$.

There is an encouraging sidelight for teachers of game theory. Of the fifteen subjects who reported taking a course in game theory, seven were classified as optimizers, versus three of the thirty-six subjects who reported not taking such a course. (Three nonoptimizers did not reply.) The chi-square statistic for the 2×2 contingency table is 7.583, significant at the 1 percent level. We conclude that subjects with game theory knowledge are more likely to be optimizers.

Impulse balance theory

During the 1990s, economists developed several sorts of learning theories that make quantitative predictions for individual and group average behavior. The theories include free parameters that must be fit to data in order to produce specific predictions. By contrast, impulse balance theory is a behavioral equilibrium theory derived from learning direction theory. It makes a point prediction about modal behavior and includes no free parameters.

The idea is simple. Positive impulses to increase the chosen value arise from negative *ex post* errors, and negative impulses to decrease the chosen value arise from positive *ex post* errors. Actual losses create additional impulses. Behavior in many circumstances will tend to cluster around a point where the impulses balance out.

In the context of the application covered in the previous section, we define the realized impulses as follows:

- $a_+(x, v) = v/2$ for $x < v$ and $= 0$ otherwise, the positive impulse from bidding too low (the foregone profit relative to the *ex post* optimal bid);
- $a_-(x, v) = \max \{x - v, 0\}$, the negative impulse from bidding too high (the foregone profit from overpayment); and
- $a_L(x, v) = \max \{x - 1.5v, 0\}$, the incurred loss from bidding too high.

The corresponding *ex ante* expected impulses, given the distribution of value v, are denoted

- $A_+(x) = Ea_+(x, v)$, $A_-(x) = Ea_-(x, v)$, and $A_L(x) = Ea_L(x, v)$.

An impulse balance point is a solution $\tilde{x}$ to the equation $A_+(x) = A_-(x) + A_L(x)$. In the current application the values of $\tilde{x}$ range from 44.5 to 65.2 as the treatment u varies from 1 to 21. Table 12.3 shows that the impulse balance point tracks remarkably well the average bid of the twenty-nine subjects classified as adapters.

Impulse balance points are defined more abstractly on ordered discrete choice sets. Let the ordered choices be denoted $i = 1, \ldots, n$, with $n \geq 2$. Consider a Markov chain with one-step transition probability p_i for a move from i to $i + 1$ and

Table 12.3 Comparison with the data

u	Impulse balance point x	Average bids of adapters		
		Period 10	*Period 90*	*All periods*
1	44.5	43.8	41.2	44.5
11	57.0	62.6	54.8	54.7
21	65.2	65.4	56.2	64.1

probability q_i for a move from $i+1$ to i. The Markov chain is called a *ladder process* if p_i and q_i are positive for all $i = 1, \ldots, n-1$, and if all multi-step transitions (from i to j with $|i-j| > 1$) have probability zero. The ladder process is called *monotonic*, if $p_{i+1} < p_i$ and $q_{i+1} > q_i$ for all $i = 1, \ldots, n-1$. Finally, a choice k is called a (*left*) *impulse balance point* if $p_k/q_k \geq 1 \geq p_{k+1}/q_{k+1}$.

The intuition is simple. The ratios p_i/q_i are well defined in a ladder process and they are decreasing by monotonicity. For $i < k$ the ratio is greater than 1, meaning that upward moves are more likely than downward moves, and the reverse is true for $i > k$. Thus, the choice tends to move toward the balance point k from both sides. The steady state (or stationary) distribution for the Markov process, therefore, should have a mode at the balance point. This intuition is confirmed by the following result.

Theorem *Every monotonic ladder process has a unique left impulse balance point k. This k is a mode of the stationary distribution of the process. There is no other mode unless $p_{k+1}/q_{k+1} = 1$. In this border case, there are exactly two modes, at k and $k+1$.*

Proof Let x_i denote the stationary probability of choice i. By stationarity, $x_1 p_1 = x_2 q_1$ and by induction $x_i p_i = x_{i+1} q_i$ up to $i = n-1$. Hence, $x_{i+1} = (p_i/q_i) x_i$. Thus, we have a sequence $\{x_i\}_{i=1, \ldots, n}$ that (by definition of balance point and by monotonicity) increases until k is reached. If $p_{k+1}/q_{k+1} < 1$ then the sequence decreases after k and otherwise it decreases after $k+1$. Hence, by definition k is a mode. By construction it is unique except in the border case $p_{k+1}/q_{k+1} = 1$, where k and $k+1$ and no other points are modes. □

In the winner's curse task discussed above, bidders can change their bid by more than one step each period, but in other respects the task defines a monotonic ladder process with a balance point. The integer bid values are the ordered choice set, the positive impulses are related to the positive transitions p_i and the negative impulses and loss impulses are related to the negative transitions q_i. The interested reader, no doubt, can think of many other examples of monotonic ladder processes.

In its present form, impulse balance equilibrium differs sharply from aspiration level theories of behavior. In those theories the aspiration level adjusts over time in response to experience. Here, the impulse balance point is defined from the outset and depends, in part, on losses relative to a fixed reference level of zero payoff.

Concluding remarks

Nash equilibrium is scientifically useful in that it provides a benchmark for assessing behavior in a wide variety of situations without the need to estimate free parameters. Since its ability to predict actual behavior is far from perfect, there is a scientific demand for alternative behavioral benchmarks. This chapter presented two such benchmarks and illustrated their use in a simple environment where the traditional benchmark predicts poorly.

Learning direction theory is the more general of the two, and the better known. However, it still is relatively new, and future research will probe the limits of its applicability and forecasting power. As noted earlier, quantitative versions of learning direction theory are currently in development. But what if the direction that "might have been better" is ambiguous, because the counterfactual payoffs are not unimodal? The proper way to extend the theory remains open.

Impulse balance equilibrium emerges naturally from quantitative learning direction theory; the opposing forces balance at a steady state. Like Nash equilibrium, it is parameter free, but has a narrower range of applicability. Research probing that range, and testing its predictive power, is still in its infancy.

Notes

* This chapter was originally delivered as a lecture.
1 The computation proceeds as follows. $E(v|x) = (x + u)/2$ so $1.5E(v|x) - x = (3u - x)/4$. The probability that bid $x \in [u, 100]$ is accepted is $(x - u)/(100 - u)$, and the expected payoff is the product of the last two expressions. The first-order condition for maximizing expected payoff in x simplifies to $x = 2u$.

References

Ball, S.B., Bazerman, H., and Carroll, J.S. (1991) "An evaluation of learning in the bilateral winner's curse," *Organizational Behavior and Human Decision Processes*, 48: 1–22.

Berninghaus, S. and Ehrhart, K.M. (1998) "Time horizon and equilibrium selection in tacit coordination games: experimental results," *Journal of Economic Behavior and Organization*, 37(2): 231–248.

Capen, E.C., Clapp, R.V., and Campbell, W.M. (1971) "Competitive bidding in high-risk situations," *Journal of Petroleum Technology*, 23: 641–653.

Cason, T. and Friedman, D. (1997) "Price formation in single call markets," *Econometrica*, 65(2): 311–345.

Cason, T.N. and Friedman, D. (1999) "Learning in laboratory markets with random supply and demand," *Experimental Economics*, 2(1): 77–98.

Kagel, J.H. and Levin, D. (1999) "Common value auctions with insider information," *Econometrica*, 67(5): 1219–1238.

Kuon, B. (1993) *"Two-Person Bargaining with Incomplete Information,"* Lecture Notes in Economics and Mathematical Systems, vol. 412, Berlin: Springer-Verlag.

Mitzkewitz, M. and Nagel, R. (1993) "Envy, greed, and anticipation in ultimatum games with incomplete information," *International Journal of Game Theory*, 22: 171–198.

Nagel, R. (1996) "Unraveling in guessing games: an experimental study," *American Economic Review*, 85(5): 1313–1326.

Nagel, R. and Tang F.F. (1995) "An experimental study on the centipede game in normal form: an investigation on learning," Mimeo.

Ryll, W. (1996) *"Litigation and Settlement in a Game with Incomplete Information,"* Lecture Notes in Economics and Mathematical Systems, vol. 440, Berlin: Springer-Verlag.

Sadrieh, A. (1998) *"The Alternating Double Auction Market: A Game Theoretic and Experimental Investigation,"* Lecture Notes in Economics and Mathematical Systems, vol. 466, Berlin: Springer-Verlag.

Samuelson, W.F. and Bazerman, M.H. (1985) "The winner's curse in bilateral negotiations," in V.L. Smith, ed., *Research in Experimental Economics*, Greenwich: JAI Press.

Selten, R. and Buchta, J. (1999) "Experimental sealed-bid first price auctions with directly observed bid functions," in D. Budescu, I. Erev, and R. Zwick, eds, *Games and Human Behavior: Essays in the Honor of Amnon Rapoport*, Mahwah, NJ: Lawrenz Associates.

Selten, R. and Stoecker, R. (1986) "End behavior in sequences of finite prisoner's dilemma supergames: a learning theory approach," *Journal of Economic Behavior and Organization*, 7(1): 47–70.

Selten, R., Abbink, K., and Cox, R. (2001) "Learning direction theory and the winner's curse," Bonn Econ. Discussion Papers bgse10_2001, University of Bonn, Germany.

13 Imitation equilibrium*

Reinhard Selten

Transcribed by Daniel Friedman

Introduction

This chapter introduces an equilibrium concept in which players try to copy their more successful peers, and applies the concept to three simple oligopoly models. See Selten and Ostmann (2001) for a more complete formal presentation and proofs of Theorems 1–5.

Laboratory experiments going back to Fouraker and Siegel (1963) provide some support to the Cournot oligopoly model. Deviations from Cournot–Nash equilibrium observed in the classic experiments usually are in the direction of lower output, suggesting cooperation or cartel behavior. Such deviations are larger and more prevalent when the experiment (a) allows verbal communication, (b) has fewer competitors, (c) has symmetric cost and demand, and (d) provides more information about other players' payoff functions. See Sauermann and Selten (1959), Friedman (1967), and a host of later authors mentioned in Chapter 10.

More recently, some experimenters have found deviations in the other direction, toward higher output and more competitive behavior. Huck *et al.* (1999) found such deviations in new, computerized oligopoly experiments. The old experiments were run by hand and provided profit tables that made it easy to find best replies. The new experiments provide less decision time per period and no easy access to best replies, but do provide information on competitors' profits.

Huck *et al.* mention theoretical work by Vega-Redondo (1999) and others showing that if players imitate more successful rivals then the market converges to competitive equilibrium. The intuition is that when price is above marginal cost, the firms with larger output earn higher profits. The authors conjecture that such imitation may account for their results. Earlier empirical evidence for imitation in laboratory oligopoly games can be found in Todt (1970, 1972, 1975).

Imitation equilibrium formalizes the idea and provides a framework for direct empirical testing. The model is free of parameters, but assumes that players observe other players' payoffs. Inspired by the classic writings of Schumpeter, the model features players who imitate a success leader, an individual who experiments to find the most profitable strategy.

Imitation equilibrium

The definition starts with an *n*-player normal form game $G = (S_1, \ldots, S_n; H)$, where player $i \in N = \{1, \ldots, n\}$ has strategy set S_i, and receives payoff $H_i(s)$ at strategy combination $s = (s_1, \ldots, s_n)$. The *model* (G, R) adjoins to the underlying game a *reference structure* R that specifies each player i's reference group $R(i) \subseteq N \setminus \{i\}$.

Players may imitate others in their reference group as follows. Let $C_i(s)$ be player i's *costrategists*, all players k in $R(i)$ who make the same choice $s_k = s_i$ at s. Let $R_i(s)$ be the set of players *comparable* to i, all players k in $R(i)$ who make a different choice $s_k \neq s_i$ at s, but one that is available to him or her, $s_k \in S_i$. Player k is *incomparable* to i at s if her or his choice is not available, $s_k \notin S_i$. A *success example* for i at s is a player j with higher payoff, maximal among comparable players, that is, with $H_j(s) = \max_{\{k \in R_i(s)\}} H_k(s) > \max_{\{k \in C_i(s)\}} H_k(s)$. Say that i has an *imitation opportunity* if i has a success example. Strategy combination s is a *destination* if no player has an imitation opportunity at s.

We will see shortly that an imitation equilibrium is a destination that is stable in the sense that the players return to it following any deviation. Figure 13.1 gives the basic idea, and the next few definitions will sharpen it.

A finite sequence $s^1, \ldots, s^k$ is an *imitation sequence* if each s^j results from s^{j-1} by all players with imitation opportunities adopting strategies of success examples and if s^k, but no earlier s^j, is a destination. A *success leader* at a destination is a player i whose payoff is maximal in $R(i) \cup \{i\}$.

Only success leaders initiate deviations at a destination. The subsequent imitation sequence is called a *deviation path*. It may be worthwhile for a success leader

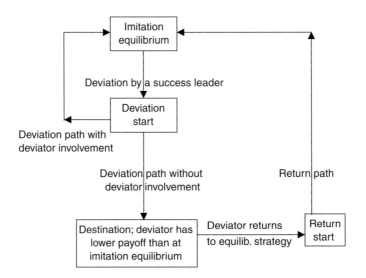

Figure 13.1 Imitation equilibrium.

to deviate at a destination, because other players then may also change their strategies and so the deviation path may lead to a new destination with a higher payoff for the success leader. If the success leader who begins a deviation path takes at least one imitation opportunity along the way, then the path is said to have *deviator involvement*.

Figure 13.1 shows that an imitation equilibrium is a destination where deviations are not worthwhile. The simplest reason, depicted in the small upper loop, is that the deviation path ends up in the same destination where it began. Alternatively, as depicted in the larger loop, the deviation path leads to a new destination less favorable to the original deviator, who deviates again and the return path leads back to the original destination. (A *return path* is an imitation sequence initiated by a deviation back to his original strategy by the original deviator.)

A full formal definition is not necessary to understand the applications, but it will be useful to list the requirements and main distinctions. A destination s is *stable against a deviation* if the following four requirements are met:

1 *Finiteness*. Every deviation path is finite, that is, it reaches a destination in a finite number of steps. This requirement is needed because there can be infinite imitation sequences that never reach a destination.
2 *Involvement*. Every deviation path with deviator involvement returns to the original destination s.
3 *Payoff*. Every deviation path without deviator involvement arrives at a destination t at which the deviator's payoff is lower than at s.
4 *Return*. Every return path beginning at such a destination t ends at s.

A *local imitation equilibrium* is a destination s that is stable against any small deviation by a success leader. Here, "small" means that for some $\epsilon > 0$, the deviation is within an ϵ-neighborhood of the success leader's strategy at s. A *global imitation equilibrium* is a destination s that is stable against any deviation, large or small, by a success leader.

Applications

Symmetric Cournot oligopoly

The n-player normal form game is the standard Cournot model with identical constant unit cost $c \geq 0$ for all players. Each player i chooses output quantity x_i so that total quantity is $x = \sum_{i=1}^{n} x_i$. There is a linear demand curve with slope and intercept parameters $a > 0$ and $b > c$ so that market clearing produces price $p = b - ax$ if $x \leq b/a$, and otherwise produces $p = 0$. Hence, player i's payoff is $H_i = (p - c)x_i$. Well-known calculations give each player's reaction function and their unique intersection point, the Cournot equilibrium $x_i = (b - c)/[(n + 1)a]$, with $p = c + (b - c)/(n + 1)$ and $H_i = (1/a)[(b - c)/(n + 1)]^2$.

The imitation equilibrium is more competitive. Assume, as is natural in the symmetric model, that everyone is in everyone else's reference group, so $R(i) = N \setminus \{i\}$. Then, we have the following:

Theorem 1   *The symmetric Cournot model has a unique local imitation equilibrium $s^* = (x_0, x_0, \ldots, x_0)$ with $x_0 = (b - c)/[na]$. Moreover, s^* is also a global imitation equilibrium.*

The proof (in Selten and Ostmann) is reasonably straightforward, but several cases need to be checked.

The result is quite striking because $x = nx_0 = (b - c)/a$, so $p = c$ and $H_i = 0$. That is, we have a Bertrand outcome with price driven down to cost, and zero profit. The intuition is that at higher price, the success leader is the player with largest output, so the price is driven down when others imitate the larger output.

Asymmetric Cournot duopoly

Now there are only two players. The first has constant unit cost c and the second has constant unit cost $c + h$ with $h \geq 0$. For convenience, normalize demand so that the intercept is $b = c + 1$ and the slope is -1. Let $g = p - c$. Then the demand function can be written $g = 1 - x$ for $x = x_1 + x_2 < 1$ and otherwise $g = 0$. The profit functions now are simply $H_1 = gx_1$ and $H_2 = (g - h)x_2$. It is straightforward to check that the Cournot equilibrium can be written $x_1 = (1 + h)/3$ and $x_2 = (1 - 2h)/3$, with profit margin $g = (1 + h)/3$ and total output $x = (2 - h)/3$. The equilibrium profits are $H_1 = [(1 + h)/3]^2$ and $H_2 = [(1 - 2h)/3]^2$. These expressions and the results below assume that $h < \frac{1}{2}$; otherwise player 2 produces output $x_2 = 0$ and we have a monopoly.

Again, assume that everyone is in everyone else's reference group, so $R(1) = \{2\}$ and $R(2) = \{1\}$. Now we have the following results.

Theorem 2   *The asymmetric Cournot duopoly has a unique local imitation equilibrium $s^* = (\frac{1}{4}, \frac{1}{4})$.*

Theorem 3   *For $h > 1 - \sqrt{(3/4)} \approx 0.134$, the local imitation equilibrium is also a global imitation equilibrium. Otherwise, no global imitation equilibrium exists.*

The proofs are a bit lengthy and again can be found in Selten and Ostmann (2001). Note that the present results stand in sharp contrast to Theorem 1. There the total output (given the current parameter values) is $x = 2/2 = 1$ and profits are 0. Here, the total output is $x = 2/4 = \frac{1}{2}$, the same as it would be in monopoly. Total profit is less than in monopoly (due to the extra cost hx_2 incurred by player 2) but it is positive and larger than in the Cournot equilibrium.

It may be surprising that the case $h = 0$ governed by Theorem 1 is so different from the limiting case $h \downarrow 0$ governed by the present results. The technical reason is that there is only one success leader at the imitation equilibrium when $h > 0$, but two success leaders when $h = 0$. The intuition is that whenever he has even a slight cost advantage, player 1 can lead player 2 to the quasi-monopoly output choice. This is the most profitable strategy for player 1 given that player 2 will imitate his output level.

Mill price competition on the circle

In this application, the n players are competing firms evenly spaced one unit apart along a circle. That is, distance is measured so that the circumference has length n. The distance along the circle between two locations v and w is denoted $|v - w|$; it is a real number between 0 and $n/2$. The location of player (or firm) i is denoted $v = i$. Firms have identical constant unit cost c and choose price at their own locations. Extending the convenient parameterization of the previous application, let $g_i = (\text{price} - c)$ be player i's unit profit. Henceforth, "price" will refer to the unit profit, that is, we will normalize c to 0. However, there are constant marginal transportation costs t, so firm i's delivered price at location v is $g_i + t|v - i|$.

Customers have unit density along the road and each customer purchases a single unit from a lowest price seller as long as that price is below some reservation value g_M. Thus, the effective price at location v is $g(v) = \min \{g_M, \min_{i=1,\dots,n} [g_i + t|v - i|]\}$. To avoid uninteresting complications, we assume that $g_M > 3t$; this ensures that the reservation price will not be a binding constraint in equilibrium.

Firm i has the unique lowest price along some interval of length $I_{i1} \geq 0$, and is tied for lowest price with $m - 1$ other firms on a segment of length $I_{im} \geq 0$. See Figure 13.2. The m firms with lowest price split the demand equally. Hence, firm i's payoff function is its profit $H_i = g_i I_i$, where $I_i = \sum_{m=1}^{n} I_{im}/m$.

The pricing game in Figure 13.2 has a Nash equilibrium in pure strategies, which we will refer to as a Cournot equilibrium. The following known result (e.g. Beckmann, 1968) shows that it is unique and has a very simple structure.

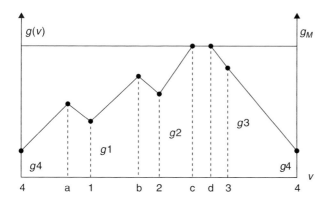

Figure 13.2 Graph showing effective price $g(v)$ as a function of location v. Firm 1 serves territory [a,b], firm 2 serves [b,c], no firm serves (c,d), firm 3 splits [d,3] with firm 4, which serves exclusively the remaining territory.

Theorem 4   *For every n = 2, 3, ... the mill price competition model has a unique Cournot equilibrium, namely (t, t, ... ,t).*

To complete the imitation model, specify the reference structure as the two nearest neighbors, so $R(i) = \{i-1, i+1\}$. Of course, we are working modulo n, so $1-1 = 0 = n$, and $n+1 = 1$. By a symmetric equilibrium, we mean one in which all players choose the same price, call it g_0. The result is as follows:

Theorem 5   *The strategy combination $(g_0, g_0, ..., g_0)$ is a symmetric local imitation equilibrium of the mill price competition model if and only if:*

- $g_0 = t/2$ *for* $n = 2$
- $g_0 = 2t/3$ *for* $n = 3$
- $2t/3 \leq g_0 \leq t$ *for* $n = 4, 5, ...$

Moreover, the symmetric local imitation equilibria are also global imitation equilibria.

The proof is quite lengthy, but some of the intuition may be worth mentioning. Consider first the spatial duopoly $n = 2$. At a symmetric strategy combination, a firm deviating to a higher price will lose share at rate $1/t$ and increase its rival's profits. The deviator will gain share at the same rate when it lowers price, and reduce its rival's profits. A little algebra shows that for moderate deviations from the specified g_o, the deviator reduces his payoff relative to the rival by an amount proportional to the squared deviation. Hence, we get a deviation path with deviator involvement that returns us to the original strategy combination. The argument is quite similar in the triopoly case. With four or more firms, however, the argument is a bit different because a firm that lowers price will reduce its nearest neighbors' profits more than its own. However, the more distant neighbors see no immediate reduction in demand and therefore have higher profits than the deviator, and so they become success leaders for the deviator's nearest neighbors. Thus, there is no imitation opportunity, and the deviation creates a destination with lower payoff for the deviator. Hence, the deviator returns to the equilibrium strategy and the imitation equilibrium is restored.

Concluding remarks

Imitation equilibrium is a new behavioral equilibrium concept that offers an alternative perspective to the standard Nash or Cournot concept. It also has no free parameters to fit, but has a narrower range of applicability than the standard concepts. Its predictions are distinctive and sometimes surprising. For example, in the first and third applications, the imitation equilibria are more competitive than the corresponding Cournot equilibria, but are less competitive in the second application.

The real test of the theory is its ability to predict in novel situations. Theorem 1 was foreshadowed by the motivating discussion, and its predictive success in the new oligopoly experiments may not be very surprising. Ongoing laboratory research examines the predictive content of Theorems 2–5. Clearly, other forces may come into play (e.g. a desire to punish players whose large output drives down price) so success is by no means guaranteed. The new experiments will begin to reveal the importance of imitation relative to other behavioral forces.

Note

* This chapter was originally delivered as a lecture.

References

Beckmann, M.J. (1968) *Location Theory*, New York: Random House.

Fouraker, L.E. and Siegel, S. (1963) *Bargaining Behavior*, New York: McGraw-Hill.

Friedman, J.W. (1967) "An Experimental Study of Cooperative Duopoly," *Econometrica*, 35: 379–387.

Huck, S., Normann, H.T., and Oechssler, J. (1999) "Learning in Cournot oligopoly: an experiment," *Economic Journal*, 109: C80–C95.

Sauermann, H. and Selten, R. (1959) "An experiment in oligopoly," in R. Selten and Reinhard, eds, *Game Theory and Economic Behaviour: Selected Essays*, vol. 2, Cheltenham, UK and Northampton, MA: Elgar. Distributed by American International Distribution Corporation, Williston, VT, 1999; 103–32. Previously published: 1960.

Selten, R. and Ostmann (2001) "Imitation equilibrium," *Homo oeconomicus*, vol. 43, pp. 111–149.

Todt, H. (1970) "Ein Markt mit komplexen Interessenstrukturen. Eine theoretische und experimentelle Untersuchung," Unpublished Habilitation Thesis, Frankfurt.

Todt, H. (1972) "Pragmatic decisions on an experimental market," in H. Sauermann, ed., *Contributions to Experimental Economics*, vol. 3, Tübingen: Mohr, pp. 608–634.

Todt, H. (1975) "Anbieterverhalten bei komplexen Marktstrukturen," in O. Becker and R. Richter, eds, *Dynamische Wirtschaftstheorie. Theorie – Experiment – Entscheidung. Heinz Sauermann zum 70. Geburtstag*, Tübingen: Mohr, pp. 232–246.

Vega-Redondo, F. (1999) "Markets under bounded rationality: from theory to facts," *Investigaciones Económicas*, 23: 3–26.

14 Choice anomalies

Daniel Friedman and Alessandra Cassar

Standard economic models assume that people are rational and selfish, that is, they maximize expected utility arising from own material payoff. The assumption is convenient and often useful, but is it true? Kahneman and Tversky (1979) and subsequent empirical work on choice anomalies undermines belief that the assumption is even approximately correct. The influence of this research program was recognized in the 2002 Nobel Prize in Economics, which was shared by psychologist Daniel Kahneman. (His long time coauthor Amos Tversky unfortunately died several years earlier.)

Choice anomalies research occupies a border region between economics and psychology. Borderlands can be confusing and chaotic, but fascinating and important. So it is with choice anomalies. The literature is difficult to summarize because there is no definitive list of choice anomalies and some are difficult even to classify. Yet, anomalies are the foundation of behavioral economics, currently one of the hottest fields in economics. In this chapter, we will simply describe some of the anomalies that have attracted our attention, and point to further readings. Good general survey articles include Thaler (1992), Camerer (1993), and Rabin (1998).

Most anomalies are first identified in stark laboratory settings, in which isolated individuals make choices unlinked to economic institutions or the choices of other agents, often without economic motivations. It is important for economists to check the robustness of the anomalies and link them to behavior in important economic institutions. In this chapter, we will often tie anomalies to performance in asset markets, drawing on Kelley and Friedman (2002).

An asset market investor must compare the asset price to his estimate of market value. Investor estimates may be distorted by various judgment biases. Investors may neglect some pieces of information and overweigh others; overestimate the resemblance of the future to the immediate past; regard ambiguous news as reinforcing current beliefs; or overrate the precision of their own information relative to other traders' information. They may indulge in the gambler's fallacy or magical thinking, perceiving patterns in random data; over- or under-react to increasing information precision, or switch biases depending on state, for example, overreact to news when asset prices are volatile, but underreact otherwise. Even with a good estimate of market value, an investor may indulge in hyperbolic discounting, and distorting tradeoffs between current income and near future income (Ainslie, 1991). Investors may also make decision errors when they buy and sell assets by overvaluing assets they currently hold or making inconsistent risky choices (Busemeyer and Townsend, 1993).

Thus, we have a long list of possible departures from rationality. Do such departures affect asset prices, and perhaps lead to bubbles and crashes? Before we speculate about the economic impact, let us examine a sample of choice anomalies, one at a time.

Reference levels

Usually, economists put the level of consumption in the agent's utility function. Depending on the context, it could be the current level or the achievable permanent level. However, a considerable body of evidence suggests that people react not to the absolute level of consumption but rather to the difference between their current situation and some reference level (Helson, 1964).

A prime example is *loss aversion*: individuals respond more strongly to decrease in consumption than to an increase (Shea, 1995; Bowman *et al.*, 1997). Tversky and Kahneman (1991) show that individuals are loss averse even at small stakes, and seem to value small losses approximately twice as much as gains of equal size. This is not explainable by the usual theory of risk aversion; it would seem to require a discontinuous change in marginal utility at the reference level.

Another important example is the *endowment effect*: once a person owns a good, that same good suddenly seems more valuable. In the experiment by Kahneman *et al.* (1990), a random group of subjects (sellers) received a mug worth approximately $5.00, while the other group (choosers) did not. The authors then elicited values (see Chapter 3 for the standard methods) and found a median valuation of $7.00 for sellers, but only $3.50 for choosers. Their interpretation is that possessing the mug altered the reference levels of the sellers, who considered it a loss to end up without it.

A related anomaly is the *status quo bias*. In the experiments of Knetsch and Sinden (1984) and Knetsch (1989), the subjects were given either candy bars or mugs upon arrival. Later, each subject was given the opportunity to exchange her or his gift for the other, but 90 percent in both groups decided to keep their gift and passed on the exchange opportunity. (Unbiased preferences suggest that at least half of one of the two groups would prefer to exchange.) An interpretation is that the subjects prefer the status quo to changes that involve losses of something even if they are compensated by other gains. Hartman *et al.* (1991) find empirical evidence of the status quo bias in consumer demand for electricity.

Would you be more likely to walk out of a concert that you were not enjoying if it were free than if you had paid a lot of money for your ticket? A "yes" answer exemplifies the famous *sunk cost fallacy*. Any outcome-oriented decision theory, not just expected utility maximization, would tell you that, once

(continued)

paid and not recoverable (hence "sunk"), the ticket price is irrelevant to your decision. Many introductory economics texts discuss the fallacy at length.

Perhaps some form of loss aversion underlies the fallacy, which is blamed for many bad decisions ("throwing good money after bad") in business and government. On the other hand, the bad decisions might be due to agency problems (e.g. President Johnson escalated the war because he did not want to take the blame for "losing Vietnam") or reputation issues (he might face attacks elsewhere if he were known to back down under pressure). Very few published studies meet contemporary standards of experimental economics; most are unmotivated answers to questionnaires, see for example Arkes and Blumer (1985). Also, the fallacy seems less prevalent in "lower" animals and in human children (Arkes and Ayton, 1999). We currently are trying to isolate the fallacy in our lab, but so far it has been surprisingly elusive.

Diminishing sensitivity means that the marginal effects in perceived well-being are greater for changes close to one's reference level than for changes further away. Kahneman and Tversky (1979) report that 70 percent of their subjects would prefer a [3/4 chance of losing nothing and 1/4 chance of losing $6,000] to a [1/2 chance of losing nothing, 1/4 of losing $4,000 and 1/4 of losing $2,000]. Both choices have the same expected value, so the subjects' responses suggest that the marginal effects in perceived well-being are greater for changes close to one's reference level than for changes further away. Possible causes and consequences of diminishing sensitivity are discussed in Friedman (1989).

Biases in risky choice

Economists traditionally have assumed that, when faced with uncertainty, people correctly form subjective probabilistic assessments. Researchers of anomalies however, have documented many systematic counterexamples. People do not normally compute using the laws of probability, but rather rely on various heuristic shortcuts. These heuristics presumably are useful overall (e.g. Gigerenzer *et al.*, 1999), but sometimes they lead to severe and systematic errors.

Law of small numbers

Tversky and Kahneman (1974) investigate the *representativeness heuristic*, in which people neglect base-rate (or prior) information in forming judgments after observing new information. People do not attend sufficiently to the precision of the new information, and tend to regard even a small sample (possibly biased) as very close to the true population distribution. On the other hand, people often underestimate the resemblance that a large unbiased sample will have to the overall population. A striking example of small sample bias is the *gambler's fallacy*: if a fair coin has not come up tails for a while, then some people expect that tails are more likely on the next flip, because a sequence of flips of a fair coin "ought" to include about as many tails as heads.

A related bias is sometimes called *regression to the mean*. People sometimes read too much into random fluctuations that depart from the norm, and do not expect that further observations will look more normal. So people tend to generate spurious explanations for long streaks that are determined by chance. For example, basketball players and fans generally believe in the *hot hand*: shooters have "on" nights and "off" night that cannot be explained by randomness. However, statistical studies by Gilovich *et al.* (1985), Camerer (1989), and Tversky and Gilovich (1989a,b) indicate that the *hot hand* is just an illusion.

Confirmatory bias

Once individuals devise a strong hypothesis, they will tend to misinterpret or even misread new information unfavorable to the hypotheses (Rabin and Schrag, 1997). Lord *et al.* (1979) provide evidence for this confirmatory bias. They showed the same ambiguous information about the death penalty to subjects previously screened for their initial beliefs on the same topic. Both advocates and opponents of the death penalty felt the new information confirmed their initial beliefs. Darley and Gross (1983) asked subjects to guess how a 9-year-old girl would read. For one group of subjects, the girl was described as coming from a family of college graduates with white-collar jobs and in the video the girl was playing in a playground of a seemingly rich suburban neighborhood. For the other group, the girl was instead coming from a family of high school graduates with a blue-collar job and in the video the playground appeared in a poor inner city neighborhood. The initial estimates of the girl's reading ability were not very different, although, as expected, the group that thought that the girl came from a well off family gave slightly higher estimates. Afterwards, another video was shown, this time identical for both groups, in which the girl was answering some questions sometimes successfully sometimes not. After this second projection, both groups had to re-estimate her reading ability. The subjects in the group that thought the girl was from a poor neighborhood reduced their estimates, while the others corrected them upward. This additional ambiguous information drew the subjects' opinions further apart.

Anchoring and adjustment

Tversky and Kahneman (1974) give the example of subjects trying to estimate different quantities (e.g. the percentage of African countries in the United Nations) by moving upward or downward from a random number obtained by spinning a wheel of fortune in front of them. These initial arbitrary numbers had a significant effects on the subjects' estimates: the median estimates were much lower for subjects who received low starting points than those who received higher starting points.

Hindsight bias

After observing an outcome, people often exaggerate the probability they would have assigned to the outcome before it was observed (Fischhoff, 1975). For example, on Mondays, many sports fans tell everyone who will listen how they would have avoided their teams' weekend blunders. "I just knew it!" is a common, but often unconscious, reaction to unpredictable events.

Salient events

People overweigh salient events even when they have better sources of information. Having had a crush on a French person might make you believe that all French are great lovers. Tversky and Kahneman (1973) report that clinicians whose depressed patients committed suicide are more likely to exaggerate the relation between depression and suicide.

Framing

The choice among logically equivalent ways to phrase a statement ("frames") should not affect decisions, but many studies find that they do. Tversky and Kahneman (1986) ask respondents (including some doctors) to choose a cancer treatment (surgery versus radiation therapy) given statistics in terms of either of mortality rates or equivalent survival rates. They report that 18 percent respondents in the survival frame preferred the radiation therapy, versus 44 percent in the mortality frame. Money illusion may be an important framing effect in macroeconomics and labor relations. For example, Kahneman *et al.* (1986) show that people react less negatively to a 5 percent nominal wage increase with 12 percent inflation than to a 7 percent nominal wage decrease in absence of inflation. Note that heuristics of all sorts are susceptible to framing effects.

Everybody knows that the best day to start a diet is next Monday. *Procrastination* and *succumbing to temptation* undermine the standard economic assumption of time-consistent intertemporal preferences. For the sake of consistency, a given intertemporal trade-off should look the same at every date, but everyday experience and many lab experiments show that we often overweigh immediate gratification relative to delayed costs. For example, Kirby and Herrnstein (1995) gave subjects a series of choices between a smaller earlier reward or a larger later reward, knowing that one of these choices would be implemented. As the delay to both the rewards increased, almost all subjects switched their choices from the smaller earlier reward to the later larger reward, proving striking evidence that preferences might instead be time-variant.

Ainslie (1991) reports earlier studies, and models the inconsistency in terms of a hyperbolic discount factor rather than the standard exponential discount factor. More recent work, for example, Laibson and Harris (2001), models the choice as quasi-hyperbolic, where choices that are not immediate have an extra discount factor applied to the usual exponential factor. The theory and empirics are currently a very active research area. The theory and empirics are currently a very active research area, see for example Rabin and O'Donoghue (2001).

Other-regarding preferences

Even when people are rational, they may have motives other than direct self-interest. Public goods experiments by Dawes and Thaler (1988) find contribution rates between 40 and 60 percent of the socially optimal level in settings where the selfish utility maximizing rate is 0 percent. Such games are explained and further investigated in Chapter 20, with a focus on the increase in contribution rates often seen when the experiment is restarted. Andreoni and Miller (2002) ask subjects to unilaterally allocate money between themselves and an anonymous counterparty at varying exchange rates (the "price of altruism"). In their study more than 50 percent of the subjects violated pure self-interest, but generally responded to price in the usual way.

Similar results are found in bargaining and ultimatum games where subjects (a proposer and a responder) have to split a $1 bill (Guth *et al.*, 1982; Roth and Murnighan, 1982). While self-interest dictates that the responder will always accept the proposer's offer (even a small amount is better than nothing), the laboratory evidence is that a significant fraction of responders reject offers of less than 50 percent (Rabin, 1998; Bolton *et al.*, 1998; Sigmund *et al.*, 2002).

One interpretation is that subjects care about the entire distribution of payoffs, not just their own payoff (Fehr and Schmidt, 1999; Bolton and Ockenfels, 2000; Charness and Rabin, 2002; Cox *et al.*, 2002a). However, there is by now a great deal of evidence that such other-regarding preferences depend also (or perhaps mainly) on the behavior, motivations, and intentions of the other people. Preferences seem to have a *reciprocal* nature: people generally like to help those who have helped others, and like to punish those who have harmed others. For example, people seem more inclined to recycle when their neighbors do.

Laboratory evidence of reciprocal preferences can be found in prisoner's dilemma experiments. Shafir and Tversky (1992) find that reciprocity may be involved also when one sacrifices her or his own benefit to punish someone who behaved selfishly. Rabin (1998) reports that in the case of monopoly a consumer may refuse to buy a product price "unfairly" even if this imposes a cost on the consumer by not enjoying the good. Further, such evidence can be found in many papers including Croson (1999), Offerman (1999), Brandts and Charness (2000), Falk *et al.* (2001), Kagel and Wolfe (2001), and Cassar (2003). In addition to others' actions, reciprocity seems to depend on others' motives. Blount (1995) gave each responder a take-it-or-leave-it offer of splitting $10. One group of responders was told that the proposal came from anonymous other subjects, and the splitting would have been between the proposer and the decider. A second group was told that the offer came from an anonymous third party subject who would not get anything out of it. A third group was told that the offer was randomly generated. Responders rejected less often low offers coming from computers or third parties than low offers coming from persons who would be hurt by the rejections.

We can't resist pointing out that Adam Smith anticipated the laboratory evidence on intentions:

Before any thing, therefore, can be the complete and proper object, either of gratitude or resentment, it must possess three different qualifications. First it must be the cause of pleasure in the one case, and of pain in the other. Secondly, it must be capable of feeling these sensations. And, thirdly, it must not only have produced these sensations, but it must have produced them from design, and from a design that is approved of in the one case and disapproved of in the other.

Adam Smith (1759: 181)

The importance of intentions in workers' efforts depending on wage was explored through experiments by Charness (1996). Akerlof (1982, 1984) and Akerlof and Yellen (1990) proposed that firms pay "efficiency wages" above the market level, to induce workers to work harder. The workers, grateful for this "gift," would reciprocate the firm by putting more effort into their jobs. Fehr *et al.* (1993) tested this hypothesis in the laboratory. Subjects were assigned roles as "firms" or "workers." Firms had to offer a wage and workers had to respond by choosing an "effort level" that was costly to them. Their results exhibit that low wages induced little or no effort by the workers, but high wages were indeed reciprocated by providing high level of effort. Charness (1996) conducted additional experiments to differentiate between the hypothesis that workers reciprocate the volitional generosity of the firm from the hypothesis that instead they choose to share with the firm part of the additional wealth from higher wages. The wages were set either randomly or by a third party. A high wage, therefore, was not the result of a generous firm and a low wage was not an act of selfishness (they were both beyond the firm's control). The results indicate that workers were substantially more likely to reward high wages with high effort and punish low wages with low effort when the wages were the result of the volition of the firm.

Individual learning and institutional evolution

What effect do all these anomalies have on economic outcomes? Some economists argue that the effect is minimal (e.g. Wittman, 1995, Chapter 5). Psychologists generally presume that their impact is direct and strong. Who is right?

Let us begin with evidence favorable to traditional economics. The first part of Friedman (1998) demonstrates one of the strongest of all choice anomalies. In Monty Hall's famous three-door task, a person can double the probability of winning a valuable prize by switching his or her initial choice, but initially only 10–15 percent of subjects do so. However, the paper goes on to show that the majority of subjects eventually learn to choose rationally in an "appropriately structured learning environment" with intense financial incentives, updated performance comparisons of alternative strategies, etc. Subsequent work by Slembeck and Tyran (2002) obtains virtually 100 percent rational switching in a social learning/team competition environment.

Markets can attenuate traders' biases in several ways. First, people can learn to overcome their biases when the market outcomes make them aware of their mistakes. Second, to the extent that biased traders earn lower profits (or make losses), they will lose market share and will have less impact on asset price. Third, institutions evolve to help people overcome cognitive limitations, for example, telephone books mitigate the brain's limited digital storage capacity. Trading procedures such as the oral double auction evolved over many centuries and seem to enhance market efficiency.

Oral double auctions allow all traders to observe other traders' attempts to buy and sell, and might enable them to infer other traders' information. Moreover, the closing price is not set by the most biased trader or even a random trader. The most optimistic traders buy (or already hold) and most pessimistic traders sell (or never held) the asset, so the closing price reflects the moderate expectations of "marginal" traders, the most reluctant sellers and buyers.

Teachers try to improve their students' performance by explaining things carefully. In this spirit, many MBA programs now offer courses, using texts going back to Bazerman (1986), that explain how to avoid biased choices. Likewise, business magazines sometimes include articles on how to avoid the sunk cost fallacy, the status quo bias and so forth; see Roxbaugh (2003) for a recent example. Do such efforts really reduce the economic impact of choice anomalies? We have not seen any evidence either way.

However, it is not safe to assume that people always have adequate learning opportunities. Economic institutions evolve, but they may or may not do so in a way that encourages biased participants to produce the outcomes predicted by standard economic models. Indeed, markets can amplify biases. Several experimental teams (e.g. Camerer and Weigelt, 1991) found that insider information is incorporated into asset price less reliably and less quickly when the number (or presence) of insiders is not publicly known. Some data suggest the following scenario:

Uninformed trader A observes trader B attempting to buy (due to some slight cognitive bias, say) and mistakenly infers that B has favorable inside information. Then A tries to buy. Now trader C infers that A (or B) is an insider and tries to mimic their trades. Other traders follow, creating a price bubble.

Such "information mirages" or "herding" bubbles amplify the biases of individual traders, but they can not be produced consistently, since incurred losses teach traders to be cautious when they suspect the presence of better informed traders. The lesson does not necessarily improve market efficiency, however, since excessive caution impedes information aggregation.

Smith *et al.* (1988) found large positive bubbles and crashes for long-lived assets and inexperienced traders. Their interpretation invokes the *greater fool theory*, another bias amplification process. Traders who themselves have no cognitive bias might be willing to buy at a price above fundamental value because they expect to sell later at even higher prices to other traders dazzled by rising prices. Subsequent studies confirm that such dazzled traders do exist, and that bubbles are more prevalent when traders are less experienced (individually and as a group), have larger cash endowments, and have less conclusive information.

What does history teach us about asset price bubbles? Crises in which asset prices increase and collapse are not new. The South Sea bubble and Tulipmania in the sixteenth century, the Japanese "bubble" in the late 1980s, the 1990s financial crises in Western Europe, Latin America, East Asia, and Russia, and the most recent "dot.com bubble" of 2000 are examples. But it is debatable whether these are true "bubbles," or just unusual movements in fundamental value (Garber, 2000). Since economists cannot observe the private information held by traders in the field, they have no direct measure of fundamental value or bubbles, and the historical evidence remains inconclusive.

Laboratory studies have confirmed two other important market mechanisms that amplify biases. James and Isaac (2000) show that information is not well aggregated when managers have discretion regarding when and how to release it. They also demonstrate that fund managers, whose compensation depends on relative rather than absolute performance, tend to push price away from fundamental value.

See Chapters 16 and 17 for more perspectives and new data on asset market bubbles.

Future directions

Our brief, unsystematic survey at least illustrates the intense recent research along the border of economics and psychology. There is a lot still left to do. Psychologists and neurophysiologists are beginning to identify the brain functions that determine actual choice. Domasio (1994), based mainly on studies of brain-damaged patients, is perhaps the best known to a general audience, but there is also a lot of recent work using brain imaging techniques with normal patients. Gifford (2002) uses such evidence to explain choice anomalies of self-control and procrastination. He argues that evolved cultural "rational" choices (supported largely in the prefrontal cortex brain structures) in some situations will conflict with motivational system choices (supported partly in more primitive brain structures). Economists should monitor this literature as it matures; it seems likely to provide useful new insights and new models of the choice process.

Even more important, the choice anomalies literature opens new avenues of research in economics. We know that institutions mediate individual choice, and economic outcomes depend on both. The emerging field of behavioral economics has only just begun to investigate how choice anomalies fare in economic institutions. An early example is Babcock *et al.* (1997), which uses reference levels to interpret data on taxi cab drivers. A more recent example is Choi *et al.* (2002), which uses behavioral principles to interpret pension choice data. A large number of PhD dissertations (e.g. Kelley, 2000) are starting to spring from this new field, and more can be expected in the future.

References

Ainslie, G. (1991) "Derivation of 'rational' economic behavior from hyperbolic discount curves," *American Economic Review*, 81: 334–340.

Akerlof, G.A. (1982) "Labor contracts as partial gift exchange," *Quarterly Journal of Economics*, 97(4): 543–569.

Akerlof, G.A. (1984) "Gift exchange and efficiency-wage theory: four views," *American Economic Review*, 74(2): 79–83.

Akerlof, G.A. and Yellen, J.L. (1990) "The fair wage-effort hypothesis and unemployment," *Quarterly Journal of Economics*, 105(2): 255–283.

Andreoni, J. and Miller J.H. (2002) "Giving according to GARP: an experimental test of the consistency of preferences for altruism," *Econometrica*, 70(2): 737–753.

Arkes, H.R. and Blumer, C. (1985) "The psychology of sunk cost," *Organizational Behavior and Human Decision Processes*, 35: 124–140.

Arkes, H.R. and Ayton, P. (1999) "The sunk cost and concorde effects: are humans less rational than lower animals?" *Psychological Bulletin*, 125(5): 591–600.

Babcock, L., Camerer, C., Loewenstein, G., and Thaler, R. (1997) "Labor supply of New York city cab drivers: one day at a time," *Quarterly Journal of Economics*, 111: 408–441.

Bazerman, M.M. (1986) *Judgment in Managerial Decision Making*, New York: Wiley.

Blount, S. (1995) "When social outcomes aren't fair: the effect of causal attributions on preferences," *Organizational Behavior and Human Decision Processes*, 63(2): 131–144.

Bolton, G.E. and Ockenfels, A. (2000) "ERC: a theory of equity, reciprocity and competition," *American Economic Review*, 90(1):166–193.

Bolton, G.E., Brandts, J., and Ockenfels, A. (1998) "Measuring motivations for the reciprocal responses observed in a simple dilemma game," *Experimental Economics*, 1(3): 207–219.

Bowman, D., Minehart, D., and Rabin, M. (1997) "Loss aversion in a consumption-savings model," Mimeo, University of California, Berkeley.

Brandts, J. and Charness, G. (2000) "Retribution in a cheap talk experiment," UPF Barcelona Manuscript, September.

Busemeyer, J. and Townsend, J.T. (1993) "Decision field theory: a dynamic cognition approach to decision making," *Psychological Review*, 100: 432–459.

Camerer, C.F. (1989) "Does the basketball market believe in the 'hot hand?'," *American Economic Review*, 79: 1257–1261.

Camerer, C.F. (1993) "Individual decision making," in J. Kagel and A.E. Roth, eds, *Handbook of Experimental Economics*, Princeton, NJ: Princeton University Press.

Camerer, C. and Weigelt, K. (1991) "Information mirages in experimental asset markets," *Journal of Business*, 64: 463–493.

Cassar, A. (2003) "From local interactions to global cooperation and coordination? Experimental evidence on local interactions and imitation," Working Paper, UCSC.

Charness, G. (1996) "Attribution and reciprocity in a simulated labor market: an experimental investigation," Mimeo, University of California, Berkeley.

Charness, G. and Rabin, M. (2002) "Understanding social preferences with simple tests," *Quarterly Journal of Economics*, 117: 817–869.

Choi, J.J., Laibson, D.I., Madrian, B.C., and Metrick, A. (2002) "Defined contribution pensions: plan rules, participant decisions, and the path of least resistance," in J. Poterba, ed., *Tax Policy and the Economy*, vol. 16, Cambridge, MA: MIT Press, pp. 67–113.

Cox, J.C., Sadiraj, K., and Sadiraj, V. (2002a) " Theory of competition and fairness for egocentric altruists," University of Arizona Working Paper.

Croson, R.T. (1999) "Theories of altruism and reciprocity: Evidence from linear public goods games," Wharton Manuscript, July.

Darley, J.M. and Gross, P.H. (1983) "A hypothesis-confirming bias in labeling effects," *Journal of Personality and Social Psychology*, 44(1): 20–33.

Dawes, R.M. and Thaler, R.H. (1988) "Anomalies: cooperation," *Journal of Economic Perspectives*, 2(3): 187–197.

Domasio, A. (1994) "Descartes' error: emotion, rationality and the human brain," New York: Putnam.

Falk, A., Fehr, E., and Fischbacher, U. (2001) "Testing theories of fairness – intentions matter," University of Zurich Discussion Paper, May.

Fehr, E. and Schmidt, K.M. (1999) "A theory of fairness, competition, and cooperation," *Quarterly Journal of Economics*, 114(3): 817–868.

Fehr, E., Kirchsteiger, G., and Riedl, A. (1993) "Does fairness prevent market clearing? An experimental investigation," *Quarterly Journal of Economics*, 108(2): 437–459.

Fischhoff, B. (1975) "Hindsight is not equal to foresight: the effect of outcome knowledge on judgment under uncertainty," *Journal of Experimental Psychology: Human Perception and Performance*, 104(1): 288–299.

Friedman, D. (1989) "The S-shaped value function as a constrained optimum," *American Economic Review*, 79(5): 1243–1248.

Friedman, D. (1998) "Monty Hall's three doors: construction and deconstruction of a choice anomaly," *American Economic Review*, 88(4): 933–946.

Garber, P.M. (2000) *"Famous First Bubbles: The Fundamentals of Early Manias,"* Cambridge and London: MIT Press.

Gifford, A., Jr. (2002) "Emotion and self-control," *Journal of Economic Behavior and Organization*, 49(1): 113–130.

Gigerenzer, G., Todd, P.M., and the ABC Research Group (1999) "*Simple Heuristics That Make Us Smart*," New York: Oxford University Press.

Gilovich, T., Vallone, R., and Tversky, A. (1985) "The hot hand in basketball: on the misperception of random sequences," *Cognitive Psychology*, 17(3): 295–314.

Güth, W., Schmittberger, R., and Schwarze, B. (1982) "An experimental analysis of ultimatum bargaining," *Journal of Economic Behavior Organization*, 3(4): 367–388.

Hartman, R.S., Doane, M., and Woo, C. (1991) "Consumer rationality and the status quo," *Quarterly Journal of Economics*, 106(1): 141–162.

Helson, H. (1964) *Adaptation Level Theory: An Experimental and Systematic Approach to Behavior*, New York: Harper and Row.

James, D. and Isaac, R.M. (2000) "Asset markets: how they are affected by tournament incentives for individuals." *American Economic Review*, 90(4): 995–1004.

Kagel, J.H. and Wolfe, K. (2001) "Tests of fairness models based on equity considerations in a three person ultimatum game," *Experimental Economics*, 4(3): 203–220.

Kahneman, D. and Tversky, A. (1979) "Prospect theory: an analysis of decision under risk," *Econometrica*, 47(2): 263–291.

Kahneman, D., Knetsch, J.L., and Thaler, R.H. (1986) "Fairness as a constraint on profit seeking: entitlements in the market." *American Economic Review*, 76(4): 728–741.

Kahneman, D., Knetsch, J.L., and Thaler, R.H. (1990) "Experimental tests of the endowment effect and the Coase theorem," *Journal of Political Economy*, 98(6): 1325–1348.

Kelley, H. (2000) "Learning to forecast in the laboratory and in financial markets," PhD Thesis, UCSC.

Kelley, H. and Friedman, D. (2002) "Learning to forecast price," *Economic Inquiry*, 40(4): 556–573.

Knetsch, J. (1989) "The endowment effect and evidence of nonreversible indifference curves," *American Economic Review*, 79(5): 1277–1284.

Knetsch, J.L. and Sinden, J.A. (1984) "Willingness to pay and compensation demanded: experimental evidence of an unexpected disparity in measures of value," *Quarterly Journal of Economics*, 99(3): 507–521.

Kirby, K.N. and Herrnstein, R.J. (1995) "Preference reversals due to myopic discounting of delayed reward," *Psychological Science*, 6: 83–89.

Laibson, D. and Harris, C. (2001) "Hyperbolic discounting and consumption," Eighth World Congress of the Econometric Society, February, forthcoming.

Lord, C.G., Ross, L., and Leper, M.R. (1979) "Biased assimilation and attitude polarization: the effects of prior theories on subsequently considered evidence," *Journal of Personality and Social Psychology*, 37(11): 2098–2109.

Offerman, T. (1999) "Hurting hurts more than helping helps: the role of the self-serving bias," Working Paper, University of Amsterdam.

Rabin, M. (1993) "Incorporating fairness into game theory and economics," *American Economic Review*, 83: 1281–1302.

Rabin, M. (1998) "Psychology and economics," *Journal of Economic Literature*, 36: 11–46.

Rabin, M. and O'Donoghue, T. (2001) "Choice and procrastination," *Quarterly Journal of Economics*, 116: 121–160.

Rabin, M. and Schrag, J. (1997) "First impressions matter: a model of confirmatory bias," Working Paper No. 97-250, University of California at Berkeley.

Roth, A.E. and Murnigham, J.K. (1982) "The role of information in bargaining: an experimental study," *Econometrica*, 50(5): 1123–1142.

Roxbaugh, J. (2003) "Hidden flaws in strategy," *McKinsey Quarterly*, number 2.

Shafir E. and Tversky, A. (1992) "Thinking through uncertainty: nonconsequential reasoning and choice," *Cognitive Psychology*, 24(4): 449–474.

Shea, J. (1995) "Union contracts and the life-cycle/permanent-income hypothesis," *American Economic Review*, 85(1): 186–200.

Sigmund, K., Fehr, E., and M.A. Nowak (2002) "The economics of fair play," *Scientific American*, 286: 80–85.

Slembeck, T. and Tyran, Jr. (2002) "Do institutions promote rationality? An experimental study of the three-door anomaly," Department of Economics Working Paper, University of St. Gallen.

Smith, A. (1759) *Theory of Moral Sentiments*. LL.D. Edinburgh.

Smith, V.L., Suchanek, G.L., and Williams, A.W. (1988) "Bubbles, crashes, and endogenous expectations in experimental spot asset markets," *Econometrica*, 56(5): 1119–1151.

Thaler, R.H. (1992) *The Winner's Curse: Paradoxes and Anomalies of Economic Life*, Princeton and Chichester, UK: Princeton University Press.

Tversky, A. and Gilovich, T. (1989a) "The cold facts about the 'hot hand' in basketball," *Chance*, 2(1): 16–21.

Tversky, A. and Gilovich, T. (1989b) "The hot hand: statistical reality or cognitive illusion," *Chance*, 2(4): 31–34.

Tversky, A. and Kahneman, D. (1973) "Availability: a heuristic for judging frequency and probability," *Cognitive Psychology*, 5(2): 207–232.

Tversky, A. and Kahneman, D. (1974) "Judgment under uncertainty: heuristics and biases," *Science*, 185(4157): 1124–1131.

Tversky, A. and Kahneman, D. (1986) "Rational choice and the framing of decisions," *Journal of Business*, 59(4, Part 2): S251–S378.

Tversky, A. and Kahneman, D. (1991) "Loss aversion in riskless choice: a reference-dependent model," *Quarterly Journal of Economics*, 106(4): 1039–1061.

Wittman, D.A. (1995) *The Myth of Democratic Failure: Why Political Institutions Are Efficient*, Chicago: University of Chicago Press.

15 Policy analysis and institutional engineering

Daniel Friedman and Alessandra Cassar

Economic institutions evolve. Many, like the New York Stock Exchange (NYSE), have roots going back to medieval times: princes, merchants, and guild masters would set the rules and adjust them to keep up with rivals, or to help their constituencies. By the twentieth century, the rules were typically adjusted according to committee decision (NYSE, 1988), influenced by lawyers, politicians, and representatives of various constituencies. Economists could only watch from the sidelines.

But times are changing. In the last decade or so, it became routine for committees, lawyers, and politicians to hire an economist for advice. And on occasion, economists were asked to design entirely new market institutions, especially for the Internet.

Policy advice and institutional engineering draw on theory, but are qualitatively different sorts of tasks. The goal is not to refine timeless principles but rather to get the right decision or the right design on time. Experiments are a helpful tool to provide empirical evidence, to assess the performance of different existing institutions *ceteris paribus*, and to finetune a new institution. Economists here have a role similar to architects and engineers, to adapt existing knowledge to the idiosyncrasies of a particular place and time.

Of course, the policy or engineering process does not always turn out well. Perhaps the most spectacular recent failure is electric power deregulation in California in the late 1990s. The state government tried to balance the wishes of power generators (especially those already present), large corporate customers, consumer groups, and taxpayers. Each group hired economists, but the final result was a political compromise. It included a price ceiling for retail customers, very inelastic demand (despite the availability of technologies that enable demand to be contingent on time of day, temperature, etc.), and concentrated supply. The result turned out to be disastrous for everyone: customers suffered blackouts as well as extraordinarily high utility bills, distributors went bankrupt, suppliers (after enjoying huge but brief windfall profits) faced scandal and poor financial prospects, and the politicians can only hope that voters forget the whole mess.

(continued)

For recent analyses, see Smith (2002), Wilson (2002), and Wolak (2002). We cannot resist noting that laboratory experiments with even crude representations of supply and demand conditions would have pointed out the susceptibility to price manipulation (Holt *et al.*, 1986; Friedman and Ostroy, 1995).

A scholarly survey of experiments in policy analysis and institutional engineering is hampered by the fact that most such work is unpublished. The findings usually remain in the hands of the organizations that commissioned the study. Still, some studies are released to the public, and we will discuss just a few of them.

Policy analysis

Experiments to evaluate alternative policies resemble scientific experiments in that the alternative institutions are already defined. The analysis, however, seeks to provide a "good enough" answer to a specific question, rather than general results. The client – usually a governmental agency or a private company – asks the question and decides when the answer is good enough. The experimenter's task is to construct an environment that will provide the most informative results, given the client's time and budget constraints. Usually, there is no opportunity to follow-up on puzzles that emerge during the investigation.

Two classic policy experiments are reported in Hong and Plott (1982) and Grether and Plott (1984). Hong and Plott were hired by the US Department of Transportation and the Interstate Commerce Commission (ICC) to study the possible consequences of a proposal by the barge industry to require advance notice of any changes in posted price. The report was due in one month.

The proposal sounds innocuous to most people: advance notice just seems like common courtesy, and helps clients plan their affairs. But industrial organization theory, controversial at that time, suggested that advance notice might facilitate collusion on higher prices. The ICC wanted to avoid such an outcome.

The barge industry – freight transportation on inland waterways – has many complexities. It is differentiated by start and end points, it has to accommodate a variety of cargo sizes and priorities, it is subject to seasonal fluctuations, it contains large and small buyers and sellers with different short-run and long-run elasticities, etc. The art of policy analysis here (and elsewhere) is to find a simplification that gets to the root of the issue and that satisfies the client.

Hong and Plott chose to take a single representative market, and to re-create an approximate scale replica with and without the proposed change. The design had only one focus variable, the price announcement procedure, which took two values: Posted Price and Telephone. Posted Price included advance notification, while Telephone allowed private bilateral bargaining over phone lines, monitored by the experimenters for data capture and control. The authors also included as a treatment variable the nuisance most likely to be mentioned by adversaries: seasonal fluctuations in cost and demand. That is, some sequences of trading periods used cost and demand parameters representative of the "low" season and other sequences used "high" season parameters. Other control variables, like the number of subjects (eleven buyers, twenty-two sellers), and the other basic parameters were held constant. Two replications required a total of four market sessions held on successive nights using the same group of subjects. Each session included both a low and a high season, and used either Telephone or Posted Price. The authors fit these treatments into an ABBA design that neutralized the effect of experience.

The results were clear. They found that advanced price posting indeed caused higher prices, lower volumes, and reduced efficiency. It hurt the small participants and helped the large sellers (who had backed the proposal). The burden of proof was then shifted back to those advocating the change, and in the end the proposal was not adopted.

Grether and Plott (1984) conducted an experimental study for the Federal Trade Commission (FTC) to assess the claim that four domestic producers of tetraethyl lead (a gasoline additive) were colluding to maintain uncompetitive high prices by using three practices: advanced notification of price change, a guarantee to customers that nobody else could get a lower price, and quotes inclusive of transport costs.

Grether and Plott chose to focus on the first two practices. Even so, they ended up with twenty-four possible treatment combinations: three levels for price publication, two levels for price access, two levels for advanced notice, and two for the guarantee. They held constant other variables such as the exchange institution (telephone bilateral search), supply and demand parameters, but still had to reduce the number of treatments to stay within budget and time. They therefore decided against a factorial design and concentrated on the most interesting combinations: all disputed practices present and all disputed practices absent. They ended up running eight treatment combinations in eleven laboratory sessions of sixteen to twenty-five periods each with an ABBA crossover design.

The results clearly supported the conclusion that prices are near the competitive equilibrium when the disputed practices are absent, but are substantially higher when the practices are present. From an academic point of view, this study needed follow-up work to assess the separate and interactive effects of the disputed practices, but for the authors' purposes it was good enough to convincingly argue that those practices were not innocent. After the experiment, the defendants lost the case to the government in trial, but won on appeal.

These classic studies opened the way for many more, few of which have been published. A recent unpublished study that we conducted illustrates the use of field experiments. At the height of the dot.com bubble, we were contacted by a startup firm that was developing a new electronic auction format. We wrote a white paper based on existing theory and existing data that suggested some possible strengths for the Calendar^{TM} auction, a hybrid

(continued)

descending auction with some ascending features (Cassar and Friedman, 2001). Then we had the opportunity to conduct a field experiment in conjunction with fund raising for the 2001 UCSC Economics Alumni reunion. Local companies had donated items for the event, and we used those that came in pairs.

We put one of each pair in an electronic English auction and the other in an electronic Calendar auction format. To neutralize sequencing effects (the second week of auction turned out to have more traffic than the first), each pair of items was assigned randomly either to Group 1 or to Group 2. Group 1 items were sold the first week under the English (i.e. ascending) format, the second week under the Calendar format. The sequencing was reversed in Group 2. Since the goal for this auction was to raise money, we bid a third of the nominal value of each item not meeting this threshold by the third day of the auction. We considered the items unsold when our bid won the auction. (We then resold those items during the reunion at a silent or an oral ascending auction, not part of the field experiment.)

The results were unambiguous: in our environment, the English format raised higher profits. Four pairs of goods were sold under both formats and in each of these cases the English price was higher than the Calendar price. Eight items were sold only under one format, and in each case the unsold item was in the Calendar format. The remaining six pairs did not sell in either format.

In fairness to our clients, we should say that (as noted in our white paper) the field auction environment (thin trading of once-off items to be delivered later to inexperienced traders) is probably the least favorable to the Calendar auction. Had the Calendar format done well, the field experiment would have given it a tremendous boost, but as it turned out we still do not know the Calendar auction's relative performance in more favorable environments.

Another caveat is appropriate for studies of this sort. Greater revenue or efficiency do not automatically imply that a new market institution will displace a pre-existing alternative. There are at least three obstacles (Friedman, 1993). First, those who profit from the old format may be able to enlist political support to suppress the new rival (Olson, 1982). Second, a buyer or seller might actually prefer trading in an inefficient format if it reveals less of his private information. Third, transaction volume itself is a source of efficiency. Sellers prefer a format where they expect to find more buyers, and likewise buyers prefer a format where they expect to see more sellers. Thus a popular old format has a built-in advantage, called a network effect or an economy of scale. Indeed, a new format with small market share may have lower efficiency than the old format at large share, even though it would surpass it at equal share (David, 1985).

Institutional engineering

Institutional engineering hardly existed 20 years ago, but it already dominates several important areas such as the auctioning of spectrum licenses (revenues in the tens of billions of dollars) and the annual assignment of new medical doctors to US internships. In these and emerging areas such as airline landing rights and the allocation of space station resources, economists have played leading roles in creating new economic institutions.

Roth (2002) highlights three general characteristics of the task: the necessity of fast delivery; the value of existing knowledge from related markets; and the political forces affecting the final choices. Theory is important in the early stage for developing intuitions, but it cannot provide all the necessary details. Field data are not available when you consider something completely new, so laboratory experimentation becomes especially valuable.

The spectrum auctions for wireless communication devices are leading examples of institutional engineering (see Cramton, 1995; McAfee and McMillan, 1996; Plott, 1997; Milgrom, 2000). In the 1980s the Federal Communications Commission (FCC) became disenchanted with allocating spectrum bands by a political process or by lottery, and started a hearing process on auction design. The FCC and some of the larger telecommunications companies, such as Pacific Bell and Airtouch Communications, soon hired academic economists, including several experimental economists, to advise on how to allocate spectrum licenses efficiently.

The FCC initially favored sequential sealed auctions for the licenses, but the economists pointed out that sealed auctions encourage overly cautious bidding due to the winner's curse (see Chapter 9). We recommended simultaneous increasing auctions, and eventually (due in part to the results of new pilot experiments as well as existing theory and evidence) the FCC agreed.

The environment is complex because the value of one license to a particular spectrum band in a particular metropolitan area depends on the allocation of other bands in the same area (substitutes) and the same band in adjoining areas (complements). Existing theory was silent on these matters, but a number of economists (Preston McAfee, Paul Milgrom, and Bob Wilson in particular) recommended a simultaneous soft close. That is, bidding should remain open in all auctions for related licenses as long as new bids appeared in any one of them.

Intuition and pilot experiments suggested that some bidders would prefer to wait until the end to make serious bids, in order to prevent others from learning anything about their valuations. Milgrom and Wilson proposed a fix they called the "activity rule." Bidders had to maintain active bids to keep the right to bid at the end. Designers also had to deal with a variety of other problems such as possible collusion, and the ploy of using a proxy company that can declare bankruptcy right after winning. The US spectrum auction turned out to be quite successful, and economists again played leading roles in later spectrum auctions in Europe. For example, in the United Kingdom, the number of potential bidders barely exceeded the natural number of licenses, and the engineers (guided by pilot experiments in the lab) decided to append a final sealed stage to the auction (Binmore and Klemperer, 2002).

The results were considered a major success at the time. Of course, the crash of telecom stocks in 2001–2002 removed some of the luster, even though the main reasons for the crash were unrelated to the spectrum auctions. More recently, the auction of the spectrum for high-speed Internet access posed several problems due to the large number of possible packages. Economists using simulation and experiments demonstrated that package bidding could achieve higher efficiency than single-item auctions; see Ledyard *et al.* (1997), Plott (1997), Cybernomics (2000), Milgrom (2000), and Ausubel and Milgrom (2001).

The first experiments in institutional design still are instructive. Grether *et al.* (1981) report a classic experiment on the allocation of airplane landing rights in the United States. Landing rights were allocated by committees of airline representatives certified by the Civil Aeronautics Board. With the deregulation of the US airline industry in the late 1970s, this allocation procedure was seen to be a possibly significant barrier to entry by new companies. The experiment examines the impact of various committee and market allocation processes. The authors found under the committee process that there were inefficiencies in handling interdependencies among airports, that the outcome is sensitive to the default option in case of agreement failure, and that the result does not respond to the profitability for the individual airlines. Under market process, they found no significant speculation in landing slots, that the price of landing slots was determined by the marginal value to airlines, and that outcomes were more efficient. Unfortunately, the political process did not lead to actual reform, and airport slots are still not competitively awarded.

Also in the 1980s, the Federal Energy Regulatory Commission funded a series of studies on electric power and natural gas networks. These studies are surveyed by McCabe *et al.* (1991). These goods have important indivisibilities and complementarities. For example, a gas distributor wanting to make a purchase from a gas producer needs to know the availability and price of transmission rights held by pipeline owners. The deregulation process continues its slow and uneven course, with occasional input from the economics laboratory.

New computer technology in the 1980s permitted the creation of "smart" computer-assisted exchange institutions, such as "combinatorial auction" for natural gas, that potentially have higher efficiency than traditional bilateral contracts. The basic idea, sometimes called the Smith auction, is to ask participants to send bids and then to use the computer to compute the allocation and prices that maximize surplus with respect to the bids sent. In theory, participants might not find it in their interest to bid their true values, but in the lab it seems that strategic manipulation is usually unprofitable. As noted in Chapter 8, the efficiency may be due to a biased learning procedure.

Rassenti *et al.* (1982) used a combinatorial auction of this sort to allocate packages of airport takeoff and landing rights in the laboratory. Despite the repeated early attempts by inexperienced subjects to manipulate the system, they achieved overall efficiencies of 98–99 percent. The Arizona team later applied smart computer-assisted markets to a proposal to deregulate the electric power industry (McCabe *et al.*, 1989), and a Caltech team applied the idea to trading pollution permits (Ledyard *et al.*, 1997).

We close our unsystematic survey of institutional engineering with a recent success story about a professional labor market (Roth, 2002). Before the 1950s, the US market for medical internships (entry-level MD positions) had a timing problem. Each hospital found it advantageous to make offers before their rivals, resulting in appointments before medical students could establish clearly their interests and talents. Indeed, the market unraveled to the extent that some appointments were made to students years before graduation! Medical schools tried to prevent this "market failure," for example, by not sending official letters of recommendations before a certain date, but their efforts were not successful. After several attempts, a centralized clearinghouse was introduced and operated successfully until the 1980s. Changes in the medical profession required revisions of the matching system.

Roth led the new design effort. He showed that the historic success of earlier clearinghouses depended on a property called stability: given the submitted preferences, no pair of hospitals or interns would prefer to switch. Kagel and Roth (2000) designed an experiment to examine the effect of different matching algorithms (the stable deferred acceptance market mechanism versus the priority matching mechanism) while holding everything else constant. In the first set of periods, the subjects arranged matches in a decentralized market with enough competition and congestion to create the unraveling problem noted earlier. The subjects had then the opportunity to make early matches at a cost, or to wait and use one of the two centralized mechanisms. The stable mechanism stopped the unraveling and restored efficiency, while the unstable mechanism did not. The similarity of the lab results and the historical field results strengthens confidence that the stability property really is the key to understanding the history of the medical internship market. The Roth–Peranson design was adopted in 1997 as the new algorithm in the entry-level labor market not just by the American physicians, but in many other professions in the United States and Canada.

For further readings, see Unver (2000a,b,c) for follow-up experiments and computational studies extending this analysis to other mechanisms and features of the markets using them. See Roth (2002) for additional analyses showing that even in the presence of complementarities that could undermine stable matching (as couple going together or linked jobs) the departures from simple theory are small and rare in large markets.

References

Ausubel, L.M. and Milgrom, P. (2001) "Ascending auctions with package bidding," Working Paper, University of Maryland.

Binmore, K. and Klemperer, P. (2002) "The biggest auction ever: the sale of the British 3G Telecom Licenses," *Economic Journal*, 112(478): C74.

Cassar, A. and Friedman, D. (2001) "An electronic calendar auction," White Paper commissioned by OneDayFree.

Cramton, P. (1995) "Money out of thin air: the nationwide narrowband PCS auctions," *Journal of Economics and Management Strategy*, 4: 267–343.

Cybernomics (2000) "An experimental comparison of the simultaneous multi-round auction and the CRA combinatorial auction," paper presented at the FCC Combinatorial Conference, May 5–7.

David, P. (1985) "Clio and the economics of QWERTY," *Economic History*, vol. 75, no 2, AEA Papers and Proceedings.

Friedman, D. (1993) "How trading institutions affect financial market performance: some laboratory evidence," *Economic Inquiry*, 31: 410–435.

Friedman, D. and Ostroy, J. (1995) "Competitivity in auction markets: an experimental and theoretical investigation," *Economic Journal*, 105(428): 22–53.

Grether, D.M. and Plott, C.R. (1984) "The effects of market practices in oligopolistic markets: an experimental examination of the ethyl case," *Economic Inquiry*, 22(4): 479–507.

Grether, D.M., Isaac, R.M., and Plott, C.R. (1981) "The allocation of landing rights by unanimity among competitors," *American Economic Review*, 71(2): 166–171.

Holt, C.A., Langan, L.W., and Villamil, A.P. (1986) "Market power in oral double auctions," *Economic Inquiry*, 24(1): 107–123.

Hong, J.T. and Plott, C.R. (1982) "Rate filing policies for inland water transportation: an experimental approach," *Bell Journal of Economics*, 13(1): 1–19.

Kagel, J.H. and Roth, A.E. (2000) "The dynamics of reorganization in matching markets: a laboratory experiment motivated by a natural experiment," *Quarterly Journal of Economics*, 115(1): 201–235.

Ledyard, J.O., Porter, D., and Rangel, A. (1997) "Experiments testing multiobject allocation mechanisms," *Journal of Economics and Management Strategy*, 6(3): 639–675.

McAfee, R.P. and McMillan, J. (1996) "Analyzing the airwaves auction," *Journal of Economic Perspectives*, 10(1): 159–175.

McCabe, K.A., Rassenti, S.J., and Smith, V.L. (1989) "Designing 'smart' computer-assisted markets," in V.L. Smith, ed., *Papers in Experimental Economics*, Cambridge: Cambridge University Press, pp. 678–702.

McCabe, K.A., Rassenti, S.J., and Smith, V.L. (1991) "Experimental research on deregulated markets for natural gas pipeline and electric power transmission networks," *Research in Law and Economics*, 13: 161–189.

Milgrom, P. (2000) "Putting auction theory to work: the simultaneous ascending auction," *Journal of Political Economy*, 10, 105–114.

New York Stock Exchange, Inc. (1988) *Constitution and Rules*, Chicago: Commerce Clearing House.

Olson, M. (1982) *The Rise and Decline of Nations: Economic Growth, Stagflation, and Social Rigidities*, New Haven: Yale University.

Plott, C.R. (1997) "Laboratory experimental testbeds: application to the PCS auctions," *Journal of Economics and Management Strategy*, 6: 605–638.

Rassenti, S.J., Smith, V.L., and Bulfin, R.L. (1982) "A combinatorial auction mechanism for airport time slot allocation," *Rand Journal of Economics*, 13: 402–417.

Roth, A.E. (2002) "The economist as engineer: game theory, experimentation, and computation as tools for design economics," Fisher-Schultz Lecture, *Econometrica*, 70(4): 1341–1378.

Smith, V.L. (2002) "Power to the people," *Wall Street Journal*, editorial 10/16/02, p. A20.

Unver, M.U. (2000a) "Backward unraveling over time: the evolution of strategic behavior in the entry level British medical labor markets," *Journal of Economic Dynamics and Control*, 25(6–7): 1039–1080.

Unver, M.U. (2000b) "Computational and experimental analyses of two-sided matching markets," PhD Thesis, University of Pittsburgh.

Unver, M.U. (2000c) "On the survival of some unstable two-sided matching mechanisms: a laboratory investigation," Mimeo, University of Pittsburgh.

Wilson, R.B. (2002) "Architecture of the power markets," *Econometrica*, 70: 1299–1340.

Wolak, F.A. (2002) Statement before the Senate Committee on Commerce, Science and Technology on Enron's role in the California Electricity Crisis, May 15, Testimony.

Part IV

Student projects

16 An asset market experiment[1]

John Latsis, Tobias Lindqvist, Evan Moore, and Kyu Sang Lee

The purpose of this chapter is to test how the entry of inexperienced subjects affects asset prices in an experimental double-auction asset market. We have run one session where 25 percent of the experienced subjects were replaced by inexperienced subjects in the fourth round. Our experimental data suggest that this replacement does not have a significant influence upon market price dynamics. Hence, we conjecture that a larger portion of inexperienced subjects may be needed for the market to exhibit larger bubbles and crashes than a market consisting of only experienced subjects.

Introduction

Laboratory experimentation has been extensively applied to the study of asset markets.[2] Economists have focused on the double-auction market, which has demonstrated remarkable efficiency in laboratory experiments. This institution is also remarkable for its prevalence in real financial markets.[3] Smith *et al.* (1988) report a series of such experiments.

Sunder (1995)[4] points out that the "risk neutral traders with rational beliefs, and common knowledge of rational beliefs, would have no reason to trade in this environment." Nevertheless, vigorous trading activities were observed in their experiments and the price dynamics revealed a recurrent pattern. Their results are characterized, especially in the experiments with inexperienced subjects, by a period of time where prices exceed fundamental values (bubble), followed by a sudden and rapid drop in price (crash). In Smith *et al.* (1988), King *et al.* (1993), and Peterson (1993), bubbles and crashes were observed for inexperienced subjects, but faded out as the subjects' experience level[5] increased. It was also observed that, when the same participants take part in an experiment for the second time, the bubbles and crashes as well as trading volumes tend to shrink. After a third experiment, bubbles and crashes were often absent altogether. Thus, the conclusions of these studies suggest that only inexperienced subjects will create bubbles and crashes, that is, trade with prices far away from the theoretical price.[6]

Our experiment is concerned with the effect and the importance of *common experience*.[7] The purpose of our experiment is to test how the entry of some inexperienced subjects, who have not acquired common experience, affects asset prices in a double-auction asset market.[8] A mundane observation of the stock market also justifies our focus on the level of experience as a treatment variable. Actual asset markets are not made up of homogeneous groups of inexperienced or experienced investors, varying from year to year. Each year many new investors with little experience enter real markets and trade with experienced investors. The experiment presented in this paper uses inexperienced subjects as treatment variables, mixing them in varying proportions with experienced investors in an oral double-auction asset market. We hope that this will shed some light on the role that inexperienced investors play in the creation and maintenance of bubbles and crashes.

In the next section, the experimental design will be presented. Experimental results and conclusions will follow.

Experimental design and procedure

The experimental design is similar to Smith *et al.* (1988) and Peterson (1993). However, the trading procedure in our experiment is based on an *oral* double-auction asset market mechanism. Each subject receives a balance sheet to keep track of his/her own trading and endowment. By raising a hand, the subjects can call for bids and asks. The experimenter writes down the bids in increasing order, and the asks in decreasing order, on a slide visible to all participants.

The experiment comprises three treatments each composed of four rounds. Each round is made up of four 2-min trading periods. The three treatments require ten, twelve, and fourteen subjects, respectively. The subjects are divided into two equal size classes with different initial cash and asset endowments. At the beginning of a round the four subjects in class 1 each have a cash endowment of 7,000 lire and three assets. The four subjects in class 2 each have a cash endowment of 3,000 lire and seven assets. The assets will pay a dividend at the end of each trading period. Dividend values will be 0, 100, 300, and 600 lire with a uniform underlying probability distribution.

A trader's cash holding at any point may differ from his or her cash endowment by accumulated capital gains or losses via market trading, and accumulated dividend earnings via asset units held in inventory at the end of each trading period. At the experiment's conclusion, participants are paid in cash the amount of their final cash holding in addition to the show-up fee of 5,000 lire.

In our experimental design each session has to be treated as one observation. Therefore, to find reliable results and significance we plan to run six sessions of each treatment. This is justified on the grounds that multiple observations are needed to establish statistical adequacy. The average expected earning in one round is 10,000 lire. Subjects are participating in one, three, or four rounds.

The treatment variable is the introduction of inexperienced subjects in round 4. Rounds 1–3 retain the same eight subject groupings; passing from inexperienced (zero rounds trading), to thrice experienced (three rounds trading). In round 4, randomly selected subjects[9] are removed and replaced by the same number of inexperienced subjects to keep the market size constant. The new subjects are

Table 16.1 Experience level of the subjects

Treatment	Round				
	1	*2*	*3*	*4*	
	0-exp	1-exp	2-exp	3-exp	0-exp
1	8	8	8	6	2
2	8	8	8	4	4
3	8	8	8	2	6

given the same asset/cash endowment as those they replace. Table 16.1 shows the experience level for the subjects in all the rounds and treatments. For example, in the fourth round of treatment 1, there will be six thrice-experienced subjects (3-exp) and two inexperienced subjects (0-exp) trading in the market.

Results[10]

The figures that follow show the relationship between the theoretical asset prices and the actual trading prices for each trade within each of the four rounds. The theoretical prices are based on the expected dividend stream. The expected value of the dividend at the end of each period is 250 lire. Therefore, an asset acquired in the first period has an expected value of 1,000 lire (4 periods $\times$ 250 lire), an asset acquired in the second period has an expected value of 750 lire, and so on. The volume of trade in each period is indicated by the number of points on the theoretical price line at each price. For example, in round 1 there are two points on the theoretical price line with a price of 1,000. This indicates that two trades were made in the first period of round 1.

An initial look at the figures does not indicate that there was any major difference in behavior between the rounds other than increases in the volume of trade. Trade volume increased by one additional trade in round 2 and by two additional trades in rounds 3 and 4. A closer look reveals that the subjects were trading closer to theoretical value as they gained experience.

Table 16.2 presents the mean trading prices and standard deviations for each period in each round. As the subjects gained experience in rounds 1–3 the trading prices moved toward the theoretical price except in the fourth periods of each of these rounds. However, the trading prices are well below the theoretical prices in the first three periods of every round. This indicates that the subjects are either considerably risk averse, or never gained a thorough understanding of the asset's value. The mean price in the fourth periods increases from 267 to 345 lire, which is above the expected value of 250 lire. However, the differential between the mean trading price and the theoretical price is not necessarily evidence of a failure to understand the nature of the asset. Holding assets in the final period is essentially a one-shot gamble, thus subjects purchasing assets at prices above the theoretical price in the fourth periods of every round may be exhibiting risk-seeking behavior.

Table 16.2 Mean trading prices and standard deviations

Period	Theoretical price	Round			
		1	*2*	*3*	*4*
1	1,000	168 (45.96)	267 (57.74)	318 (23.63)	382 (8.37)
2	750	233 (57.74)	307 (37.86)	345 (5.77)	372 (18.93)
3	500	228 (55.60)	308 (15)	360 (17.32)	326 (25.10)
4	250	267 (15.28)	307 (11.55)	345 (5.77)	300 (0.00)

Before the start of round 4 two experienced subjects were replaced with two inexperienced subjects. Comparing rounds 3 and 4, we notice that the trend of trading prices moving toward the theoretical price continues except in the third period. Somewhat surprisingly, the mean trading price in this period falls by almost 10 percent. The trading price falls by 13 percent from a fourth period high of 345 lire in round 3 to 300 lire in round 4. Three of the four trades in the fourth period of round 4 involved the inexperienced players selling assets. This may be evidence of an understanding of the asset's theoretical value as there is an expected profit of 50 lire from each sale. It is further evidence of risk-seeking behavior on the part of the experienced players (as explained above).

Unfortunately, the subjects who participated in the first three rounds did not acquire the traditional notion of experience (i.e. trading close to the theoretical price in each period). Therefore, it is difficult to tell what effect, if any, the introduction of two inexperienced players had on the market. Thus, the introduction of two inexperienced subjects in the last round does not seem to increase the incidence of bubbles and crashes according to our data.

Conclusion

It should be noted, before drawing conclusions, that our experimental design and the actual execution of our experiment were not flawless. The shortcomings of our experiment can be divided into two broad categories: technical and linguistic.

Due to the time constraints and the lack of an adequate computerized double-auction asset market program in Italian, we were obliged to use the *oral* double-auction method. While this functioned relatively well, it reduced the number of periods that could feasibly be carried out in each round. We believe that different results may have been obtained if the subjects were allowed fifteen trading periods rather than four per round. The pen and paper method of trading and profit calculation also contributed to a loss of experimental control. It was, for example, virtually impossible to avert some small level of human error in the profit calculations. In addition, we did not inform subjects of the theoretical value of the dividend stream, nor that it was changing throughout the periods. This was one of the most important components of the experiments designed to test the rational expectations hypothesis. Our data suggest that this feature was not understood among a majority of the subjects.

The language barrier may also have affected our results. None of the authors were able to run the experiment as it had to be conducted in Italian. This posed the extra difficulty of making it harder for us to monitor the questions and responses occurring between the auctioneer and subjects.

The conclusions that can be drawn from our series of laboratory tests are limited due to the number of trading sessions that we were able to conduct given our technical, financial, and time constraints. Our initial findings do not generally confirm the previously established patterns associated with bubbles and crashes in double-auction asset markets. Asset prices were relatively constant for the four trading periods that made up each round of the experiment. The failure of "twice" and "thrice" experienced traders to converge on the theoretical price can be accounted for by two competing hypotheses. First, the trading of assets at significantly below the expected value in periods 1–3 of each round could be interpreted as extreme risk aversion. Having understood that assets held at the end of each period could yield a zero dividend, traders may have preferred to retain their cash to be sure of a positive payment at the end of the experiment. Second, and somewhat more plausibly, the observed undervaluing of assets could be the result of a failure to understand their theoretical value. Having failed to see that their assets were worth a stream of future income, the subjects may have regarded each trading period as a one-off gamble, which would explain the relative stability of prices around 300 lire.

A further interesting aspect of our results was that the mean trading price in the final period of every round was closer to the theoretical price than the trading price of prior periods. It is possible that this change in behavior could be accounted for by a sudden realization of the inherent value of the asset. Furthermore, as noted above, the last period of each round represents a one-off gamble on the expected value of the randomly drawn dividend payment. Given that the expected value of 250 lire was exceeded by the mean trading price in every period, we may infer that subject traders were in fact risk-seekers.[11]

Finally, the manipulation of the treatment variable, namely the number of inexperienced traders in the market, seems to have had no significant effect on the trend in market prices. Given the failure of experienced traders to settle in the region of the theoretical price, very little can be inferred about the effects of an influx of inexperienced subjects. Therefore, it seems that replacing 25 percent of the market with inexperienced subjects is not sufficient to affect the market trade pattern.

Notes

1 We are grateful for comments from Daniel Friedman, Steffen Huck, and Rosemarie Nagel.
2 See Sunder (1995) for a survey.

3 See Domowitz (1993: 28).

4 See also Tirole (1982).

5 An experienced subject is defined as one who has participated in a similar experiment before.

6 See, especially, Lei *et al.* (2001) for the effect of the subjects' experience levels upon the occurrence of bubbles and crashes.

7 See Smith (2000: 412) for the importance of common experience.

8 According to King *et al.* (1993), other treatments than experience level, for example, short selling, different subjects pool than university undergraduates (business executives, and so on), do not change the qualitative results in Smith *et al.* (1988). Nevertheless, it should be noted that the dividend timings were reported to have influence on the stock market price dynamics (Smith *et al.* 2000).

9 The same number of subjects from each class is replaced.

10 The reader should be aware that the results being presented are based on only one experimental session, that is, one session for the first treatment. Further work should include sessions from treatments 2 and 3 also to meet our design.

11 This inference is inconsistent with the above hypothesis that assets are undervalued due to risk aversion.

References

Domowitz, I. (1993) "Automating the continuous double auction in practice: automated trade execution systems in financial markets," in D. Friedman and J. Rust, eds, *The Double Auction Market: Institutions, Theories, and Evidence*, Reading, MA: Addison-Wesley.

King, R.R., Smith, V.L., Williams, A.W., and van Boening, M. (1993) "The robustness of bubbles and crashes in experimental stock markets," in R.H. Day and P. Chen, eds, *Nonlinear Dynamics and Evolutionary Economics*, New York: Oxford University Press.

Lei, V., Noussair, C.N., and Plott, C. R. (2001) "Nonspeculative bubbles in experimental asset markets: lack of common knowledge of rationality vs. actual irrationality," *Econometrica*, 69: 831–859.

Peterson, S. (1993) "Forecasting dynamics and convergence to market fundamentals: evidence from experimental asset markets," *Journal of Economic Behavior and Organization*, 22: 269–284.

Smith, V.L. (2000) *Bargaining and Market Behavior: Essays in Experimental Economics*, New York: Cambridge University Press.

Smith, V.L., Suchanek, G.L., and Williams, A.W. (1988) "Bubbles, crashes and endogenous expectations in experimental spot asset markets," *Econometrica*, 56: 1119–1151.

Smith, V.L., van Boening, M., and Wellford, C.P. (2000) "Dividend timing and behavior in laboratory asset markets," *Economic Theory*, 16: 567–583.

Sunder, S. (1995) "Experimental asset markets: a survey," in J.K. Kagel and A.E. Roth eds, *Handbook of Experimental Economics*, Princeton: Princeton University Press.

Tirole, J. (1982) "On the possibility of speculation under rational expectations," *Econometrica*, 50: 1163–1182.

17 Bifurcation in a stock market experiment

Deborah Lacitignola and Alessandra La Notte

Introduction and the model

Is it possible for an economic mathematical model with bifurcation phenomena to be tested by laboratory experiments? To answer this question, we consider the stock market model of Bischi and Valori (2000). It consists of two different classes of agents, the "dealers" and the "savers," who act sequentially. First the dealers set the stock price as a function of net savings inflows and price from the previous period. Then savers chose their net inflow (negative when they sell more shares than they purchase) given the current price. This behavior is described by the following nonlinear, discrete time dynamical system:

$$S_{t+1} = (1 + ec)\, S_t - aP_t - bS_t^3 - edP_t^3$$

$$P_{t+1} = P_t + cS_t - dP_t^3$$

(17.1)

where $S_t = s_t - s^*$ and $P_t = p_t - p^*$. Here the variable s_t represents the net stock of savings collected by the funds at time t, p_t is the price level at time t, and (s^*, p^*) are "natural levels" that can be deduced as solutions of a system of equations or from some general macroeconomic considerations.

The parameter a measures the capital gain realizing attitude whereas the parameter e represents the reactivity of the savers to the index variation and therefore measures their "speculative" attitude. The parameter c measures how much savings influence index variation whereas the parameters b and d, coefficients of the nonlinear stabilizing terms, give a measure of the strength with which the system tends to approach the equilibrium once it has gone away from it.

The parameters b, c, and d are assumed positive, while different signs of parameters a and e define three regions of the parameters space:

Region 1 = $\{(a,e) \in \Re^2 : a > 0 \wedge a + e < 0\}$
Region 2 = $\{(a,e) \in \Re^2 : a < 0 \wedge a + e > 0\}$
Region 3 = $\{(a,e) \in \Re^2 : a + e > 0 \wedge a > 0\,\}$

The dominant forces, respectively, are savers' desire to cash in capital gains, their desire to speculate, and a balance of both forces.

Bischi and Valori, (2000) show that for $a > 0$, the origin is the unique equilibrium that is stable for $(a,e) \in S = \{(a,e) \in \Re^2: a > 0 \land a < -e \land a > -(4/c) - 2e\}$. For $a < 0$, along with the origin, two new equilibria appear in the system. For $(a,e) \in S$ going through the line $a = -e$ and entering the economically most interesting region, the equilibrium at the origin loses its stability because of a Hopf bifurcation that is supercritical if $-(4/c) < e < 0$ and $e \neq \{2,3\}$. Thus, a and e are bifurcation parameters for the model.

Experimental setup

The experiment automates the role of buyers setting price and uses human subjects to represent sellers. Unfortunately, this choice means that the natural bifurcation parameters a and e are behavioral and hence not directly controllable. The ones we can directly control are instead the parameters c and d: they enter only in the equation controlling the price evolution and thus in the mechanized part of the experiment.

Of course, the price mechanism at time $t + 1$ is influenced by the savings at time t and the savings at time $t + 1$ are influenced by the price at time t. This "coupling" provides an effective mechanism for experimental control: different values of c and d cause different behavioral reactions inducing some of the dynamics present in the three regions of the (a,e) parameter-space.

We run three sessions in 3 days because of the long time required to run every trial by hand (software is unavailable). Each session has three phases. Based on preliminary observations, during the first phase, we use values of the parameters c and d intended to cause periodic behavior in the system. In this phase, the information provided to the subjects consists of both the stock price at the beginning of each period and their own realized profit. These values of c and d also give the participants the chance to quietly learn how to play. The results will indicate whether the subjects have adopted an "adaptive" (they buy more shares when the stock price increases and sell when it decreases) or "capitalizing" attitude (they cash out when prices are high and buy new shares when the price is low) (Table 17.1).

In the second phase, we use values of c and d intended to cause either a steady price trend, or else an oscillatory (or chaotic) price pattern in the following ten periods. In this second phase, we provide our subjects only with the direction of the price change (?) together with their own realized profit. The third phase is like the second except that we return to reporting the stock price as in the first phase.

From the data analysis, the correspondent region in the (a,e) parameter space will be deduced and laboratory results will be compared with the values obtained by the simulations of the mathematical model.

The subject pool is composed of twenty-seven undergraduates, who receive a show-up fee as well as salient payments. The salient payments are computed from price changes and net investment according to the formula

$$\text{payoff} = k^* \, S_i \, (\Delta P)^\alpha;$$

with $k^* = 0.001$ and $\alpha = 1/3$.

Table 17.1 Prospectus of the different phases of the experiment

Period	Phase I	Phases II + III	
	$c = 0.4, d = 0.0001$	$c = 0.1, d = 0.000001$	$c = 0.5, d = 0.000001$
1	●	●	
2	●	●	
3	●	●	
4	●	●	
5	●	●	
6	●	●	
7	●	●	
8	●		●
9	●		●
10	●		●
11	●		●
12	●		●
13	●		●
14	●		●
15	●		●
16	●		●
17	●		●
18	●		●

The data

Session I (Figures 17.1–17.3)

The subject pool is composed of seven subjects; the initial stock price is set at thirty and the initial value of the capital for each subject is fifty.

In Figure 17.1, the savers show initially a strong adaptive behavior, soon replaced by a strong capitalizing one; such oscillating behaviors can be found in part of Region 3. The system seems to be near an unstable equilibrium.

In Figure 17.2, the subjects show mainly a capitalizing attitude during the second phase. Price and the savings trends are qualitatively different: linear prices and strongly oscillatory savings.

In Figure 17.3, even with complete information, the patterns from the previous phase persist.

Session II (Figures 17.4–17.6)

The subject pool is composed of ten subjects; the initial stock price is set at thirty and the initial value of the capital for each subject is fifty.

In Figure 17.4, savers show initially an adaptive attitude that is soon replaced by a capitalizing one. Oscillations of increasing amplitude suggest behavior in Region 3.

In Figure 17.5, the savers exhibit globally an adaptive attitude during this phase; it becomes stronger after the shift. For periods 1–7, prices and savings do not have the same qualitative trend. In periods 8–11, behavior seems to be from part of Region 2. After the shift, both savings and prices have a quite linear trend.

Figure 17.1 Price index and savings – session I, phase I.

Figure 17.2 Price index and savings – session I, phase II.

Figure 17.3 Price index and savings – session I, phase III.

Figure 17.4 Price index and savings – session II, phase I.

Figure 17.5 Price index and savings – session II, phase II.

Figure 17.6 Price index and savings – session II, phase III.

In Figure 17.6, savings and prices both exhibit an oscillatory trend. Before the shift, subjects have a quite adaptive attitude; after the shift they adopt a clear capitalizing behavior. A match with simulations cannot be found for runs 1–7. For runs 8–12 such a behavior could be recognized in part of Region $1\backslash\{S\}$.

Session III (Figures 17.7–17.9)

The subject pool is composed of ten subjects; the initial stock price is set at thirty and the initial value of the capital for each subject is thirty.

In Figure 17.7, savers have initially an adaptive attitude and then adopt a capitalizing one; the last periods are characterized by a routinization phenomenon. Oscillations grow in amplitude Region 3.

In Figure 17.8, the shift apparently causes a change in the savers' attitudes: periods 1–7 are characterized by a capitalizing attitude where in the remaining ones the savers exhibit a strong adaptive attitude. For periods 1–7 no match with model simulations can be done because price and savings do not have the same qualitative trend. Periods 8–11 suggest Region 2.

In Figure 17.9, after the shift both the variables exhibit a kind of large period oscillatory behavior. Both before and after the shift, the savers show coexistence of adaptive and capitalizing attitudes. For periods 7–16, match with simulations can be found for (*a, e*) belonging to Region 3.

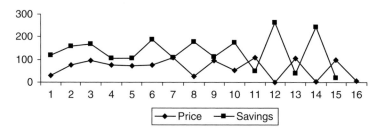

Figure 17.7 Price index and savings – session III, phase I.

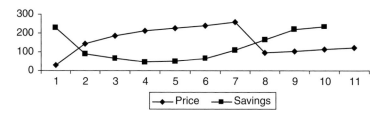

Figure 17.8 Price index and savings – session III, phase II.

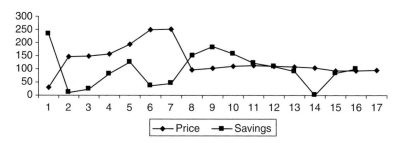

Figure 17.9 Price index and savings – session III, phase III.

Discussion

Of course, the data we have collected so far are not sufficient for a detailed quantitative analysis in statistical sense (although the longer version of the chapter includes regressions of prices and savings on time). Our conclusions, summarized in Table 17.2, therefore, are suggestive and qualitative.

Phase I uses values of the parameters *c* and *d* chosen to induce oscillations; this appears to have worked well in all three sessions. All three groups exhibited initially an adaptive attitude soon replaced by a capitalizing one. In Phase I of Session II, the amplitude of oscillations increased to the point that we were forced to an early closure of the phase. We think that these big fluctuations, not present in Session I, are mainly due to the increased volume of savers' capital because of the increased number of subjects.

Table 17.2 Summary of the different qualitative aspects of the three phases for each session

	Session I / Group I (no shift)	Session II / Group II (shift + no information)	Session III /Group III (shift + information)
Phase I	Oscillatory behavior Initially adaptive, then strongly capitalizing attitude	Oscillatory behavior Initially adaptive, then strongly capitalizing attitude	Oscillatory behavior Initially adaptive, then strongly capitalizing attitude
Phase II	Shift causes no qualitative change • Price linear, savings oscillatory • Global capitalizing attitude	Shift causes qualitative change • Before shift: price linear, savings oscillatory • After shift: prices and savings linear • Except for run 1, adaptive attitude	Shift causes qualitative change • Before shift: price linear, savings oscillatory • After shift: prices and savings linear • Capitalizing attitude (before shift) • Adaptive attitude (after shift)
Phase III	Shift causes no qualitative change • Price linear, savings oscillatory • Global capitalizing attitude	Shift causes qualitative change • Before shift: price linear, savings oscillatory • After shift: prices and savings oscillatory Adaptive attitude (before shift) Capitalizing attitude (after shift)	Shift causes qualitative change • Before shift: price linear, savings oscillatory • After shift: prices and savings oscillatory • Coexistence of both adaptive and capitalizing attitudes in both periods

Phase II is characterized by values of c and d chosen in order to have a quite stationary behavior, and by the lack of price-level information. Only in Group I this shift has caused no qualitative change both in the global behavior of the system and in the savers' attitude that appears to be globally capitalizing. The strong periodicity in the savings curve and the linear price trends are anomalous and may be due to inertia and the lack of price information. Phase III shows little impact from increasing the price information, however.

The first group exhibits a peculiar behavior during all the experiments: neither the parameter shift nor changes in information seem to affect its behavior. We suspect that the smaller number of participants and their mutual understanding before acting have heavily influenced the results. Groups II and III are more heterogeneous and respond more consistently to the treatments.

Table 17.3 lists the data that seem in accord with the theoretical model; we have already noted some data segments that seem inconsistent with the model.

Some caveats: in the experiment, we had to define some theoretical "upper bounds" on the total saving amount in order to avoid crashes. Second, computer

Table 17.3 Summary of the observed behaviors also described by the model

Sessions – phases qualitatively describable	Mathematical region of description	Mathematical phenomenology involved
Session II – phase III (after the shift)	Region $1/\{S\}$	Flip bifurcation or period doubling bifurcation of (s^*, p^*)
Session III – phase II (after the shift)	Region 2	Tendency to one stable equilibria (different from (s^*, p^*))
Session I – phase I Session II – phase I Session III – phase I Session III – phase III (after the shift)	Region 3	Destabilization of (s^*, p^*) through Hopf bifurcation

simulations for the different cases have all exhibited a "transient" time before the dynamics could settle down on the considered specific pattern: the comparison of computer simulations with experimental graphs has to also take into account the question of the "transient estimation" in the experimental data. For this and many other reasons above described, we think that much more periods in each session would produce better data.

A host of open questions remain: is learning able to avoid chaos? Which kind of theoretical "upper bounds" can we put on the total savings in order to avoid crashes? Might our specific choice of k^* and α in the payoff formula have encouraged savers to adopt a certain speculative/adaptive investment policy?

We conclude by recalling our initial question: "Is it possible for a stock-market mathematical model with bifurcation phenomena to be tested in laboratory experiments?" Up to now, our answer is "Yes, but not completely."

Acknowledgments

We would like to thank all those persons who allowed us, with their help, guidance, technical assistance, and financial support, to perform our experiments. We do refer to (in alphabetical order): Prof. Daniel Friedman, Director of the 2001 Summer School in Experimental Economics; Prof. Axel Leijonhufvud, Director of the CEEL program in Adaptive Economic Dynamics; Prof. Luigi Mittone, CEEL Laboratory Director; Mr Marco Tecilla, CEEL Technical Assistant.

Reference

Bischi, G.I. and Valori, V. (2000) "Nonlinear effects in a discrete time dynamic model of a stock market," *Chaos, Solitons and Fractals* 11: 2103–2121.

18 Price instability and search

Miguel Cura-Juri and Sebastian Galiani[1]

Introduction

In this chapter, we report preliminary results of an economic experiment in the field of search theory that we designed at the University of Trento and conducted at Universidad de La Plata, Argentina. The experiment is designed to test the predictions of an intertemporal sequential search problem.

The consumer search problem we evaluate differs from the standard consumer search problem, as described in Sargent (1987), in that consumption takes place at several periods of time and relative prices may vary over time among stores. We assume that real prices follow a first-order Markov stochastic process. Thus, the probability of finding any given store charging the same real price in periods t and $t + 1$ is equal to a constant, ρ, which is the focus variable of our experiment.

There is previous laboratory work testing the theory of sequential search under diverse search environments but our experiment is the first that studies search behavior in a context of repeated purchases where relative prices vary over time.

Schotter and Braunstein (1981, 1982) test the reservation wage hypothesis and find evidence in support of the basic implications of the standard search theory. Cox and Oaxaca (1989) also find evidence in favor of the reservation wage hypothesis. However, Kogut (1990) tests several predictions of the standard search model and finds evidence contrary to the implications of the model. Notably, he reports a high prevalence of recall (see also, Hey, 1982, 1987).

In this chapter, we provide new evidence on the implications of the standard search model. The intertemporal search model we analyze predicts that the first period reservation price is increasing in ρ. We test this prediction. Additionally, we also test if our laboratory consumers pay lower prices when ρ equals one compared to the prices they pay when ρ equals zero, irrespective of whether subjects exhibit a reservation price strategy.

Motivation

There is extensive evidence showing that inflation is positively correlated with the variability of prices across markets and across sellers of the same good (see Domberger, 1987; Lach and Tsiddon, 1992). Tommasi (1993) shows that inflation reduces the level of information that current prices contain about future prices. In a highly inflationary environment, it is hard to establish who are the low-price sellers, since the price observed today is not a good predictor of future prices.

Tommasi (1994) analyzes a market for a homogeneous good under price instability conditions. He assumes that buyers purchase a unit of the good every period. Consumers search in a sequential manner and follow a reservation price strategy. In each period, buyers go from store to store and observe the price tags until they buy the good. Each visit entails a search cost. In such a world, inflation exacerbates the informational problem by depreciating the information that current relative prices convey about future relative prices. Tommasi (1994) shows that buyers react by holding smaller information stocks. This translates into higher reservation prices. However, interestingly enough, the total amount of resources spent on search may either increase or decrease. In this chapter, we study the behavior of consumers in Tommasi's model.

We assume that the cumulative distribution of real prices, $F(p)$, is time-invariant. However, the location of each individual seller on that distribution follows the following first-order Markov stochastic process:

$$p_{t+1} = \begin{cases} p_t & \text{with probability } \rho \\ \text{a drawing from } F(p) & \text{with probability } 1-\rho \end{cases} \tag{18.1}$$

Buyers own free recall from last period's accepted price, that is, buyers can recall without cost the store where they bought the good last period. However, recall is uncertain over time. It is assumed that $\rho = f(\pi)$, where π is the inflation rate and $f_\pi < 0$, even though the results of our experiments hold independently of the reasons why ρ varies. If $\rho = 0$, prices are not related intertemporaly, and each period's search behavior is as described in the standard static search model (see Sargent, 1987). When $\rho = 1$, all searches should be undertaken in the initial period (see Tommasi, 1994). We evaluate this empirical prediction in the experiment we conduct.

The consumers program

In what follows, we match the notation of the model with that of the experiment we conduct. The buyer purchases one unit of the good per period. There are three periods. During a period, a consumer can visit as many stores (i.e. draw prices from the distribution of prices) as he wishes. However, consumers face a real cost per search (i.e. price per drawn) c. Finally, each subject is willing to pay for the good the same amount of money, v. Thus, the objective of a consumer is to minimize his expected expenditure, or

$$\operatorname*{Min}_{p_t} E\left[\sum_{t=1}^{3} p_t + n_t c\right] \tag{18.2}$$

where p_t and n_t are the price paid for the unit of the good purchased and the number of stores visited at period t.

If both $F(p)$ and ρ are known, and satisfy all the conditions for an interior solution (see Tommasi, 1994), the first period reservation price p solves

$$c = \sum_{t=1}^{3} \rho^{t-1} \left(\int_0^p (p-x)\, dF(x) \right) \qquad (18.3)$$

The reservation price is such that the search cost just equals the expected gain from additional search. Notice that ρ affects reservation prices in the same way as the consumers discount factor does. Then, it is straightforward to show that the reservation price is decreasing in the correlation coefficient ρ.

Experimental procedures

The experiment was conducted at Universidad de La Plata in Argentina using undergraduates as subjects. Sixteen subjects were recruited for an "economic experiment"; they were told that they would be paid in cash at the end of the session but were not told the nature of the experiment. A small pilot of this experiment was conducted at the University of Trento.

Each subject was exposed to three levels of the focus variable ρ: 1, 0.5, and 0. Subjects may understand the experiment better (or just change their behavior) over time (trials). To control this nuisance we blocked the treatment variable ρ using a balanced design (see Friedman and Sunder, 1994).

General instructions were read aloud to subjects at the beginning of each session. After the instructions were read, both the experiment and the experimental tasks were exemplified by conducting one experimental sequence for each level of the treatment variable. Before starting the experiment, we verified that subjects understood the meaning of ρ by asking them what price they expect to observe if they recall the store where they bought the good in the previous period for each value of the focus variable.

Each subject was randomly assigned to a different sequence of treatment levels. The four alternative sequences in which subjects were treated are the following: 1, 0.5, and 0; 0, 0.5, and 1; 0.5, 0, and 1; and 0.5, 1, and 0.

During a session, each subject was presented with six search problems, two for each level of the focus variable ρ, in one of the four sequences listed above. Each search problem or search sequence consists of three periods. Prior to these search sequences, each subject had participated in a series of twelve (unpaid) training search problems; four for each of the three levels of the treatment variable ρ presented in the same following order: $\rho = 0$, $\rho = 1$, and $\rho = 0.5$.

Finally, subjects knew in advance the way they were rewarded in the experiment. In each search sequence, they also knew ρ and $F(p)$. Each experiment lasted approximately 30 min. Subjects received \$2 for their participation in the experiment plus

$$s = \sum_{j=1}^{6}\left(\sum_{t=1}^{3}((v-p_t)I_{\{p_t>0\}}-cn_t)\right)$$

where j indexes the six rewarded search sequences, $I_{\{p_t>0\}}$ is an indicator function that equals 1 if the subject buys one unit of the good in period t of sequence j and equals 0 otherwise; v was established at \$1.2, $p \sim$ Uniform(0,2], and c was set equal to \$0.1.

Experimental results

Our results are still explorative. The sample size of our experiment is smaller than the one needed to draw significant conclusions about the behavior of economic agents in the context of our experiment. Nevertheless, the analysis of the results of the experiment allows us to draw important preliminary conclusions.

First, we evaluate whether when ρ equals one subject's only search during the first period as it is predicted by theory. We find that subjects depart from optimal behavior. We find that in 18.7 percent of the search sequences in which ρ is one, subjects search prices during the second period of the sequence departing from predicted optimal behavior. The proportion of search periods in which subjects depart from theoretical optimal behavior is statistically different from zero at the 1 percent level of significance ($t_{31} = 3$). It is worth noting that in this chapter, all the statistics are adjusted for the presence of random groups or cluster effects in the data. They are likely to arise because we have more than one observation by individual.

Interestingly enough, these departures from optimal behavior are positively correlated with both the prices and the number of prices drawn in the first period. This finding is similar to the one reported by Kogut (1990). Thus, it seems that subjects may depart from optimal behavior after they have searched enough without finding a price below the reservation price.

Turning to the analysis of accepted prices, we first evaluate if they are in agreement with theoretical reservation prices and, second, we test if individuals pay lower prices when prices are invariant over time (i.e. $\rho = 1$) in comparison to the case in which prices are extremely unstable over time (i.e. $\rho = 0$).[2]

Table 18.1 summarizes the relevant results. The optimal reservation price is calculated from equation (18.3). It is worth noting that mean accepted prices are close to expected accepted (theoretical) prices. For example, when ρ equals zero the reservation price is 0.632. The first price encountered in a trial that is equal or lower than 0.632 should be accepted. For a uniform distribution, accepted prices would be equally likely anywhere between 0 and 0.632, and, hence, the average expected accepted price is 0.316, which is remarkably close to the mean accepted price during the first period for the search sequences in which $\rho = 0$. We test the hypothesis that the mean accepted prices are equal to the expected accepted prices against a two-tails alternative hypothesis. We do not reject the null

Table 18.1 Prices and search by treatment

	Mean accepted price during the first period	Optimal reservation price	Expected accepted price (Eap)	Test of reservation price hypothesis ($H_0 = p = Eap$)	Number of searches during the first period
$\rho = 1$	0.253	0.365	0.182	1.97**	3.2
$\rho = 0$	0.367	0.632	0.316	0.99	2.2

Notes
t-Statistics are computed using standard errors robust to the precesence of cluster groups in the data.
** Statistically different from zero at the 0.05 level of significance.

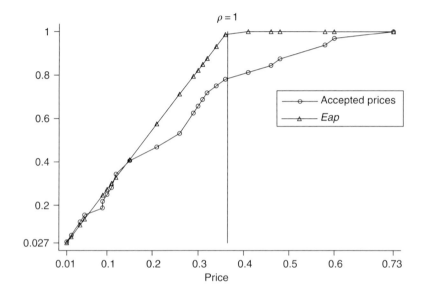

Figure 18.1 Theoretical and observed distribution of accepted prices.

hypothesis when $\rho = 0$ at any conventional level of significance, however, we do reject the null hypothesis when $\rho = 1$ at the 5 percent level of significance although we do not reject it at the 1 percent level of significance.

Figures 18.1 and 18.2 present the cumulative distribution of accepted prices together with the expected theoretical distribution of accepted prices for $\rho = 1$ and $\rho = 0$. Overall, we do not find significant deviations with respect to the optimal price strategy. In both cases, the observed distributions of accepted prices do not depart significantly from the theoretical distributions. Approximately 80 percent of the accepted prices are below the reservation price.

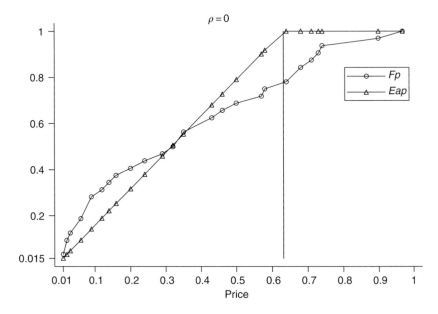

Figure 18.2 Theoretical and observed distribution of accepted prices.

We also test if the mean accepted price when $\rho = 1$ equals the mean accepted price when $\rho = 0$ against the alternative hypothesis that the former price is lower than the latter price, and we reject the null hypothesis at the 10 percent level (but not at the 5 percent level) of significance ($t_{15} = -1.85$). Thus, accepted prices are, on average, lower when $\rho = 1$ than when $\rho = 0$.

Finally, we consider the total search costs associated to price instability. $N(1)$ is equal to 7.2 and $N(0)$ is equal to 9.2, where $N(\rho) = \sum_{t}^{3=1} n_t(\rho)$.[3] Thus, price instability has two costs well identified in our experiment: it increases the average price accepted by consumers and it increases the cost of making transactions.

Preliminary conclusions

In this chapter, we have reported the preliminary results of an economic experiment in the field of search theory conducted at University of La Plata, Argentina. The experiment is designed to test the predictions of a model of sequential search by an individual agent in an intertemporal consumption context.

Our results are still explorative. The sample size of our experiment is smaller than the one needed to draw significant conclusions about the behavior of the economic agents in the context of our experiment. Nevertheless, the analysis of the experiment allows us to draw some preliminary conclusions.

We find that in 18.7 percent of the search sequences in which $\rho = 1$, subjects did not recall the accepted price in the first period during the second period of the search sequence, departing from predicted optimal behavior.

Nevertheless, we do not find significant deviations with respect to the optimal price strategy. In both cases, that is, when $\rho = 1$ and when $\rho = 0$, the observed distributions of accepted prices do not depart significantly from the respective theoretical distributions.

Finally, we also find that the mean accepted price when $\rho = 1$ is lower than the mean accepted price when $\rho = 0$ at conventional levels of significance. In addition, we find that the total cost of search is greater when $\rho = 0$ than when $\rho = 1$. Thus, price instability has two costs well identified in our experiment: on the average, both accepted prices and transaction costs are higher.

Notes

1 We thank Dan Friedman and seminar participants at the summer camp on Experimental Economics, Program in Adaptative Economic Dynamics, University of Trento, Italy; UC at Santa Cruz, UTDT, and Universidad de La Plata for useful comments.
2 Due to sample size considerations, we do not exploit the information for the case in which $\rho = 0.5$ here. We lack statistical power to test differences between the behaviors in the laboratory in this case and any of the other two cases.
3 Note that most of our results only exploits the information of the first period in each search sequence. Thus, we could have had only two periods per sequence instead of three. However, the value of information on prices increase with the number of periods it is worth. Thus, we consider that three periods is a reasonable compromise solution to the trade-off we face.

References

Cox, J. and Oaxaca, R. (1989) "Laboratory experiments with a finite horizon job search model," *Journal of Risk and Uncertainty*, 2: 301–329.
Domberger, S. (1987) "Relative price variability and inflation," *Journal of Political Economy*, 95: 547–566.
Friedman, D. and Sunder, S. (1994) *Experimental Methods: a Primer for Economists*, Cambridge, MA: Cambridge University Press.
Hey, J. (1982) "Search for rules of search," *Journal of Economic Behavior and Organization*, 3: 65–81.
Hey, J. (1987) "Still searching," *Journal of Economic Behavior and Organization*, 8: 137–144.
Kogut, C. (1990) "Consumer search behavior and sunk costs," *Journal of Economic Behavior and Organization*, 14: 381–392.
Lach, S. and Tsiddon, D. (1992) "The behavior of prices and inflation: an empirical analysis of disaggregated price data," *Journal of Political Economy*, 100: 349–389.
Sargent, T. (1987) *Dynamic Macroeconomic Theory*, Cambridge: Harvard University Press.
Schotter, A. and Braunstein, Y. (1981) "Economic search: an experimental study," *Economic Inquiry*, 19: 1–25.
Schotter, A. and Braunstein, Y. (1982) "Labor market search: an experimental study," *Economic Inquiry*, 20: 133–144.

Tommasi, M. (1993) "Inflation and relative prices: evidence from Argentina," in E. Sheshinski and Y. Weiss, eds, *Optimal Pricing, Inflation, and Cost of Price Adjustment*, Cambridge: MIT Press.

Tommasi, M. (1994) "The consequences of price instability on search markets: towards understanding the effects of inflation," *American Economic Review*, 84: 1385–1396.

19 Animal-spirits cycles[1]

Jason Hwang

Are business cycles driven by expectations? Models that posit that they do are hard to test empirically due to difficulties associated with measuring expectations and observing random coordination devices (sunspots). I propose an experiment to capture the salient features of Howitt and McAfee's model of expectationally driven business cycles and investigate whether such cycles arise in an experimental setting. I introduce externalities, uncertainty, and an extrinsic random variable to mimic the crucial features of the model. The results from a pilot session provide preliminary support for the hypothesis that given the right incentives for coordination, expectations-driven cycles do indeed occur.

Introduction

One strand of the vast literature studying the causes of business cycles has emphasized the role of expectations and coordination. Cycles that are expectationally driven can occur if there are significant complementarities in some aspect of firms' decision making, creating an incentive for coordination. A particularly simple model of this kind was proposed by Howitt and McAfee (1992). This model generates unemployment fluctuations that follow shifts in an extrinsic random variable, animal spirits. These animal-spirits cycles arise because the model assumes that hiring decisions are subject to externalities that provide an incentive to coordinate and firms learn to use animal spirits as a coordination device.

Given the unobservability of actual animal spirits or sunspots,[2] the mechanism through which this model produces business cycles is difficult to test with field data. This chapter proposes an experiment that captures the relevant features of Howitt and McAfee's theoretical environment and investigates whether expectationally driven cycles occur in an experimental setting.

Very little previous research has examined the role of animal spirits or a sunspot in experiments. The only published work to date has been a pioneering study by Marimon *et al.* (1993), who show that sunspots can matter if they are expected to.[3] Their results, based on overlapping-generations economies, display expectation-driven price volatility: prices can be volatile even if nothing fundamental about the economy has changed, if participants in the market have been conditioned to associate movements in a sunspot with changes in the fundamentals.

The results I report below corroborate the finding that some type of conditioning can induce agents to base decisions on extrinsic random events. They also support Howitt and McAfee's theoretical result that, with the right incentive for coordination, animal-spirits cycles arise with positive probability. The results are also consistent with Bayesian learning, which Howitt and McAfee show to be able to generate beliefs that converge to an animal-spirits cycle equilibrium.

The model

The following simple setup conveys the main idea behind Howitt and McAfee's model.[4] There is a continuum of identical, infinitely lived firms who decide whether to hire each period. A firm's decision is denoted by h_t, which takes on the value 1 if the firm hires and 0 if it does not. Letting Y_t represent the proportion of firms who decide to hire, a firm's profits are given by

$$\pi_t = \begin{cases} f(Y_t) - c_t & \text{if } h_t = 1 \\ 0 & \text{if } h_t = 0 \end{cases}$$

where $f(Y_t)$ is the firm's revenue. Crucially, the model assumes that $f' > 0$ so that each firm's hiring decision carries externalities for the other firms. It is clear that this setup must generate multiple equilibria, since with appropriate conditions on costs, firms will find it optimal to coordinate their actions by all hiring or not hiring together. Assuming that costs can be either high (c^H) or low (c^L) and are observed after firms have made hiring decisions, the sufficient condition for coordination is:

$$f(0) < c^L < f\left(\frac{1}{2}\right) < c^H < f(1)$$

which says that when no firm is hiring, the revenue from hiring will never justify the cost, while if every other firm is hiring, then the remaining firm will also want to hire, since the benefits from externalities are large enough to swamp even high costs.

Before turning to cycles, it is useful to establish some benchmark results under the assumption of deterministic costs; that is, costs are either always high or always low. Since firms make hiring decisions repeatedly, observing costs after they decide each period, it follows that they will learn to base their decision on their increasingly confident – and correct – forecast of costs for the next period. Two possible equilibira in the case of deterministic costs are the "optimistic" and "pessimistic" paths in which all firms choose either to hire or not hire.

Assuming instead that costs are stochastic yields the main result of the model. To consider the possibility of animal-spirits equilibria, assume that in addition to randomly shifting costs, there is a random variable, extrinsic to the economy, which changes between two states, high and low, and is observed *before* firms make hiring decisions. Under these assumptions, optimistic and pessimistic paths remain as possible equilibria, along with a third possibility: a cycle where all firms hire if animal spirits, the extrinsic random variable, are high and not hire if spirits are low. Howitt and McAfee show that such an animal-spirits cycle can be a rational-expectations equilibrium if agents update their beliefs regarding relevant probabilities according to Bayesian learning. The intuition for this is straightforward. Suppose that firms experience a period of spurious correlation between spirits and costs. During this period, firms will learn to base their decisions on the publicly observed animal spirits, which turn out, temporarily, to be a perfect forecast of costs. Eventually, the correlation disappears and spirits can no longer be used to forecast costs but firms will have learned that they are made better off by coordinating, *regardless of whether costs are high or low*, due to output externalities. If this incentive for coordination induces some firms to use animal spirit as a device for coordination, then the externalities reinforce this behavior, eventually producing a cycling equilibrium.

Experimental design

The model contains four crucial features that an experiment testing its predictions must capture in some way: (a) the presence of externalities, (b) uncertainty regarding costs, (c) an extrinsic random variable, and (d) the timing of events. I present a variant on a standard two-player coordination game which is likely the simplest setup with these features.

Consider a two-player game with the following payoff matrices:

	A	B			A	B
A	10,10	0,0		A	1,1	0,0
B	0,0	6,6		B	0,0	5,5

Random Event X	Random Event Y

Each player chooses A or B without observing a random event that determines the payoffs as shown above. I have chosen to make presentation of the game to the subjects context-free and have therefore used neutral labels. Here choice A may be thought of as hiring, B as not hiring, and random events X and Y as low and high costs. Note that the pure strategy equilibria of the game require coordination, with the exact payoffs depending on which random event has occurred. This introduces the first two required elements of the model into the experiment: externalities and uncertainty. As in the model where a firm would like to follow the actions of the others, here a player would like to make the same choice as the other player. Also following the model, coordination is always better than not coordinating but whether coordinating on A or B is more profitable depends on an unobserved random event.

I introduce animal spirits by showing at the beginning of each round either one of two pictures, one depicting a sun rising over a mountain in full color and the other depicting a snow flake in black and white. Below I refer to the first picture as "bright" and the second as "dark." The previous section noted that Bayesian

Sunspot shown to all subjects
↓
Subjects make choices
↓
Subjects receive feedback on
realized random event, partner's choice and payoffs for the round.

Figure 19.1 Timeline for each round.

learning is consistent with the animal-spirits equilibrium if there is a period of spurious correlation between spirits and costs, during which firms learn that no matter what the costs are, coordination is always profitable. I introduce a "spurious" correlation by correlating the pictures perfectly with random events during the first ten rounds of the game. For the remaining twenty rounds, the realizations of pictures and random events are determined independently by separate coin tosses done prior to the experiment. Also the process of learning described in the model presumes that firms do not have *ex ante* knowledge that coordination with other firms will make them better off – this must be "learned" during the period of spurious correlation. Therefore, I choose not to reveal the payoff matrix to the subjects, in contrast to the standard approach in coordination experiments where payoffs are typically known in advance.

Figure 19.1 shows the timeline for a single round of the experiment. At the beginning, either a bright or a dark picture is shown to the subjects, who are asked to record which picture is shown. The subjects are then asked to write down their choice of A or B. The experimenter then collects the record sheets and fills in the following information as feedback: the partner's choice, the realization of the random event, and the profit the subject made. The feedback gives the subjects a chance to learn, and use to their advantage, the correlation between pictures and random events in the first ten rounds. Further, if learning takes place as the model describes, then the first ten rounds should also teach the subjects that coordination makes them better off and lead, at least in some pairs, to animal-spirits cycles.

Ten economics undergraduate students at the Università degli Studi di Trento were recruited as subjects. See the Appendix in Chapter 7 for the instructions.

Results

Table 19.1 reports the data from the last ten rounds of the experiment. I focus on the last ten rounds since I am mainly interested in behavior observed sufficiently after the initial period of correlation so that the subjects have had a chance to reach any equilibrium. The first two columns show the realizations of pictures and random events. The remaining columns show the choices made by each subject. The subjects' labels indicate the pairings. The second row from the bottom records the number of times changes in a subject's choices coincided with changes in the pictures in a consistent manner. The last row indicates the type of equilibrium reached.

Table 19.1 Data from pilot session

Round	A.S.	Costs	S1-1	S1-2	S2-1	S2-2	S3-1	S3-2	S4-1	S4-2	S5-1	S5-2
21	Bright	X	A	A	A	B	A	A	B	A	A	A
22	Bright	Y	A	A	A	B	A	B	A	B	A	A
23	Dark	X	B	B	B	A	A	A	A	B	B	B
24	Dark	X	B	B	B	B	A	A	A	A	B	B
25	Dark	Y	B	B	B	B	A	A	A	A	B	B
26	Bright	X	A	A	B	A	A	A	B	B	A	A
27	Bright	X	A	A	A	A	A	A	B	B	A	B
28	Dark	X	B	B	B	B	A	A	B	A	B	B
29	Bright	Y	A	A	A	A	A	A	B	B	A	A
30	Dark	X	B	B	B	A	A	A	B	B	A	B
Switched with A.S.			10	10	9	6	NA	NA	NA	NA	9	9
Type of equilibrium			ASC		ASC		Optimistic		NA		ASC	

The first pair (S1-1 and S1-2) clearly appears to have reached an animal-spirits cycle. Both subjects choose A when the picture is bright and B when the picture is dark for the entire duration of the final ten rounds, despite the absence of any correlation between pictures and random events. The last pair (S5-1 and S5-2) exhibits a very similar pattern, following the same strategy in nine of the last ten rounds. The second pair of subjects appears to be converging to the same animal-spirits equilibrium: The first participant (S2-1) switched his or her choices with the pictures nine out of ten times while the second participant did so six times. A closer look at the second subject's behavior reveals that deviations from the animal-spirits strategy occurred mostly in the early part of the last ten rounds. Had the game been played a little longer, it seems likely that the second pair would have converged to an animal-spirits equilibrium.

The remaining two pairs behave very differently from the three already discussed. The third pair appears to have converged to an optimistic path equilibrium, with the first participant choosing A for the entire duration shown in Table 19.1 and the second participant deviating from the same strategy only once. This is consistent with the model, which yields both optimistic and pessimistic paths as valid equilibria under stochastic costs.

More puzzling is the behavior of the fourth pair, whose choices exhibit no discernible pattern. A possibility is that they are converging to a "reverse" animal-spirits equilibrium where the participants choose A when the picture is dark and B when bright. But the evidence for this is weak; the two participants each deviate from this strategy twice in the last seven rounds.

So far inspecting individual behavior indicates that animal-spirits cycles can indeed arise. It is also instructive however to look at the entire pool of subjects. Figure 19.2 shows for each round the number of pairs that succeeded in coordinating. During the first ten rounds, the initial period of correlation, the number of pairs coordinating, gradually increases. This is what one would intuitively expect.

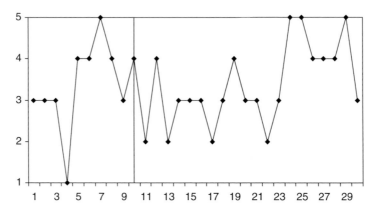

Figure 19.2 Frequency of coordination.

The subjects learn through the feedback of the profits and realized random events that they can use the pictures to forecast random events and at the same time that coordination is profitable. In the eleventh round, pictures are no longer correlated with random events and the frequency of coordination drops. But it increases again, with four of the five pairs coordinating in six of the last seven rounds. This is indicative of the type of learning the model describes. Once the initial period of correlation ends, the subjects use the pictures no longer as a forecast for random events but now as a coordination device since they discover that regardless of the costs, coordination increases profits. This naturally explains the finding that some type of a coordination equilibrium was reached for four of the five pairs by the end of the experiment.

Directions for future research

The results presented here are preliminary but provide initial support for the empirical validity of Howitt and McAfee's model of animal-spirits cycles. Further, they corroborate Marimon *et al.*'s finding that a period of correlation between a sunspot and a fundamental of an economy can condition agents into basing their future decisions on the sunspot even in the absence of any correlation. Future work can build on the simple experimental design used in this chapter in several directions. An immediate extension would be to use larger groups of subjects, rather than pairs, since using pairs probably made it easier to obtain coordination. Also one wonders how important the initial period of correlation was for obtaining cycles. To bring out the importance of initial correlation and stochastic costs more clearly, a more formal 2×2 design may be used, with the nature of costs (fixed or stochastic) and correlation (with and without) as treatment variables. Rematching of subjects and expanding feedback to include the concurrent behavior of other groups may also be considered.

Another exciting avenue for future work relates to a recent literature on coordination failures. Jeitschko and Taylor's (2001) model of "coordination avalanches," for example, share two of the crucial elements of animal-spirits cycles: externalities and uncertainty. In that model, coordination is optimal as in the animal-spirits model but local discouragement of some participants can trigger a global collapse of coordination. An experimental study of their results will require careful consideration with respect to generating correct expectations but would likely feature many of the same characteristics as the experiment in this chapter. Further exploration of animal-spirits cycles and related work studying the role of expectations in different contexts would seem an important direction for future research.

Instructions

See Appendix in Chapter 7.

Notes

1 I would like to thank Dan Friedman for guidance and editorial comments. I also thank Peter Howitt and Steffen Huck for helpful suggestions and Alessandra Cassar for translating the instructions into Italian. I gratefully acknowledge financial support from the 2001 CEEL Summer School on Experimental Economics.
2 I will use the terms animal spirits and sunspots interchangeably.
3 For a recent study investigating sunspot-driven price volatility, see Duffy and Fisher (2002).
4 This is borrowed from Peter Howitt's presentation at the 2001 CEEL Summer School on Experimental Economics.

References

Duffy, J. and Fisher, E. (2002) "Sunspots in a laboratory," mimeo.
Howitt, P. and McAfee, R.P. (1992) "Animal spirits," *American Economic Review*, 82(3): 491–506.
Jeitschko, T. and Taylor, C. (2001) "Local Discouragement and global collapse: a theory of coordination avalanche," *American Economic Review*, 91(1): 208–224.
Marimon, R. Spear, S.E., and Sunder, S. (1993) "Expectationally driven market volatility: an experimental study," *Journal of Economic Theory*, 61(1): 74–103.

20 The restart effect

Jinkwon Lee and Jose Luis Lima

We compare two payoff mechanisms in a finitely repeated linear public good game: accumulated payoff mechanism (APM) and random round payoff mechanism (RRPM). While subjects' behavior must not be theoretically different between both payoff mechanisms, we find clear behavioral difference between them. We also attempt to explain the so-called "restart effect" by a kind of background risk hypothesis that we call "opportunity effect." The results, however, are inconclusive.

Introduction

In a finitely repeated linear public good game, we compare a random cash payoff mechanism for subjects, which depends on the token earning of one randomly chosen round after a whole session is completed (RRPM), to a payoff mechanism based on accumulated token earning through overall rounds (APM). RRPM has been widely used in individual decision-making experiments because it is known to be able to control a wealth effect.[1] However, a generic linear public good game has a unique dominant strategy so wealth effects should not matter. Hence, almost all experiments in the finitely repeated linear public good game literature have used APM.[2]

However, we hypothesize that RRPM may also control subjects' risk attitude, and that might make a difference. Our psychological intuition is that under APM (but not under RRPM), subjects will be less risk averse in early periods and more risk averse (and more attentive) as future opportunities dwindle in the last few periods. Let us call this "opportunity effect."[3] An example from our daily life: many students enjoy life during the first and second years without studying when their final standing is accumulated over 4 years. Suppose that their final standing depends on only one year's grade randomly chosen after 4 years are completed. Then they might pay more attention to classes in early years. This is because they feel different degrees of risk for each year under APM and RRPM. See also Davis and Holt (1993: 85). The opportunity effect is related to the background risk hypothesis suggested by Selten *et al.* (1999). The background risk hypothesis implies that RRPM makes bias. However, if opportunity effect exists, then the difference that RRPM makes relative to APM may be interpreted not as a bias but as the result of controlling risk attitude through rounds.

We use this hypothesis to attempt to explain the "restart effect," which has been a puzzle since Andreoni (1988). He reports that the contribution level to public good at the first round of the restarted run is much higher than the last round of the previous run.[4] This restart effect is found even in the Strangers treatment, intended to isolate learning effects by elimination of any reputation effects possible in Partners treatment.[5] Why subjects start again with a high level of contribution if they learned in the first session that the level of contribution fell down? Should the learning hypothesis be rejected?

The leading explanation is not very satisfying. It points to cognitive dissonance theory, which is based on subjects' psychological discomfort by inconsistent choice with their belief and reaction for reducing it. However, this explanation requires that subjects have enough time to reconsider their previous choice. It may not be able to explain the restart effect when the second run immediately follows the first. See Burlando and Hey (1997).

Our suggested explanation combines the opportunity effect at initial rounds of the second run with the possibility of signaling behavior there and with the possibility of the indirect feedback in the Strangers treatment.[6] When the Stranger treatment is used and the second session is started, subjects may still have an uncertainty about the type of other members though the uncertainty about the game itself may almost disappear. Hence, they may under APM have an incentive for taking the risk to signal others by contributing to the public good to obtain more desirable payoffs through later rounds, Pareto optimal level, at least at initial rounds of the second session if the opportunity effect exists and they think of the indirect feedback.[7] However, the signaling is too risky an attempt under RRPM, because the cash payoff depends on only one randomly chosen round: that is, it controls the opportunity effect. Therefore, the restart effect will not be there and subjects will keep the pace of learning procedure under RRPM while the restart effect may happen under APM.

Experimental design

We follow a generic linear public good game experiment design. Subjects $i = 1, 2, \ldots, N$ are given an endowment e of tokens which they can invest in a private good, x, or contribute to a public good, g, at each round. They must use all endowments at each round. At each round, the token earnings to any subject are determined by $P_i = x_i + \alpha \sum_j^{N=1} g_j$, where N is the number of group members and $e_i = x_i + g_i$. If the marginal rate of return from the public good, α, is chosen such that $1/N < \alpha < 1$, then zero contribution to the public good ($g = 0$) is a unique dominant strategy and full contribution of endowment ($g = e$) for all i is the symmetric Pareto efficient outcome.

In our experiments, there were sixteen subjects divided in four groups of four members each. Subjects were undergraduate students of economics in Trento University, Italy. Each group played two consecutive sessions of six rounds, and subjects were told about this before they started the experiment. Two groups faced the APM in both sessions and their membership was randomly rematched among eight subjects each round: subjects' total cash payoff in each session depended on accumulated token earnings, and the Stranger treatment was used. We call these groups GAPM. The other two groups faced the APM in the first session and the RRPM in the second session: subjects' total cash payoff in the second session depended on six times the token earning of randomly chosen one round after that session is completed, while their total cash payoff in the first session depended on the accumulated token earning. They also were randomly rematched among eight subjects each round (Strangers). We call these groups GRRPM. The conversion rate was 350 Italian lire for each 120 tokens. The participation fee of 5,000 lire was given to all subjects. The token endowment (m) was 100 each round, and the marginal rate of return from the public good (α) was 0.5. Hence, the GAPM and GRRPM were different only in the payoff mechanism in the second session.

Results

The average contribution level to the public good of both GAPM and GRRPM in both sessions is shown in Figure 20.1.[8] Both GAPM and GRRPM in the first session (rounds 1–6), which faces the identical payoff mechanism (APM), appear to have a similar decay pattern though the contribution level of GRCPC is higher than that of GAPM (Table 20.1).[9] Our main interest is in the second session (rounds 7–12). There is a clear difference between GRRPM and APM. However, the direction of the difference is opposite to our prediction. Surprisingly, GRRPM shows a clear restart effect while there is a slight one for GAPM.

Our prediction needs reconsideration, but the evidence suggests related explanations. GRRPM faces a change in the payoff procedure between the first session and the second session, but GAPM does not. It is possible that GRRPM regards the second session as a new game. This requires them to build a new initial belief before the first round of the second session. A higher risk aversion level induced by RRPM may lead subjects to make an initial decision that they imitate their decision in the first round of the first session.[10] The fact that six of eight subjects

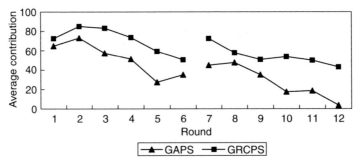

Figure 20.1 Average contribution of GAPS and GRCPS.

Table 20.1 Subjects' token contributions in APM and RRPM

Sessions	Rounds	Treatments	Subjects								Group 1	Group 2	Mean
			1	2	3	4	5	6	7	8			
First session	1	GAPM	100	50	100	50	50	100	20	50	270	250	65
		GRRPM	50	50	100	100	100	50	60	70	320	260	72.5
	2	GAPM	100	50	100	60	100	100	25	50	260	325	73.1
		GRRPM	80	55	100	100	100	80	75	90	320	330	85
	3	GAPM	50	50	60	100	10	100	20	70	190	270	57.5
		GRRPM	90	60	100	100	100	50	80	85	350	315	83.1
	4	GAPM	50	50	100	10	0	100	30	70	190	220	51.3
		GRRPM	70	50	100	100	100	20	70	80	250	340	73.8
	5	GAPM	40	60	50	0	20	0	40	10	120	100	27.5
		GRRPM	60	70	0	50	100	50	65	80	295	180	59.4
	6	GAPM	80	40	90	0	0	0	20	50	140	140	35
		GRRPM	30	50	0	30	100	100	85	10	125	280	50.7
Second session	7	GAPM	50	50	70	70	100	70	20	0	70	290	45
		GRRPM	50	50	100	100	100	50	70	60	310	270	72.5
	8	GAPM	50	10	90	0	100	0	50	30	230	150	47.5
		GRRPM	50	60	0	70	100	50	72	60	282	180	57.8
	9	GAPM	50	20	60	50	0	50	50	30	180	100	35
		GRRPM	50	50	0	100	100	20	67	20	270	137	50.9
	10	GAPM	30	20	0	0	0	0	40	40	50	90	17.5
		GRRPM	50	45	0	80	100	20	74	60	224	205	53.6
	11	GAPM	0	0	70	0	20	0	60	0	70	80	18.8
		GRRPM	10	50	0	90	100	50	50	50	240	160	50
	12	GAPM	10	0	0	0	10	0	10	0	10	20	3.8
		GRRPM	10	60	0	90	100	50	35	0	70	275	43.1

of GRRPM contribute exactly same level as those of the first round of the first session while only two of GAPM do it may support this explanation. Moreover, before starting the second session, the wealth level may affect their building initial belief given that they regard the second session as a different game from the first one.

They may learn again about the new game, they think, based on the new initial belief but faster than in the first session. However, the new learning could not exceed the range for which the initial belief allows: as a result, the decay pattern in the second session may be similar to that of the first session while GAPM seems to keep the learning pace of the first session. The very similar pattern of GRRPM between the first session and the second session may support this view. Hence, these data may show again the importance of the relationship between initial belief and learning procedure.

Related to the effect of RRPM treatment, Figures 20.2 and 20.3 may give additive information. Through all rounds of the second session, the variance of contribution level of GRRPM varies between subjects but the variance in each subject is relatively stable at any level, while the variances both between subjects and in each subject converges to zero as the final round of that session approaches for GAPM. This seems to support that the RRPM keeps subjects' risk aversion as constant through rounds. However, the puzzle is then why their contribution level

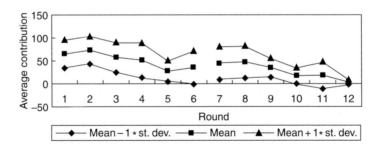

Figure 20.2 Contribution stability in GAPS.

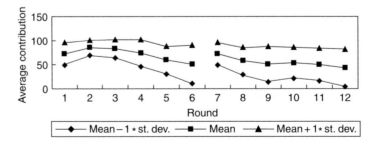

Figure 20.3 Contribution stability in RCPS.

must be stable through rounds if they have learned the dominant strategy and hence their risk attitude does not matter as rounds go. From this may arise the question, that subjects' risk attitude may matter even in an experimental environment where a theory predicts it does not. The answer may be found when we understand the specific relationship between risk attitude affecting subjects' construction of initial belief and learning procedure.

Conclusion and future study

The main result in this chapter is that RRPM and APM made difference in subjects' contribution behavior to the public good though the direction of the difference was different from our prediction: the restart effect was much larger in RRPM than in APM. However, the reason for the difference is not clear. This may be because we attempted to investigate too much in one experiment. The difference between both payoff mechanisms in this experiment may support the background hypothesis in a systematic way, or it may be only an error. Otherwise, it may be systematic in the way being consistent with our original prediction with the opportunity hypothesis. We may need to more carefully investigate this, because this is related to the question of what an appropriate experimental method to reduce biases is. For this purpose, we first need to make it clear whether RRPM and APM have differences in simpler experimental settings to exclude other considerations.[11]

We see that the final round contribution level is highly correlated to that of the first round in this experiment too. This may be an important clue not only for the learning theory in games but also for the practice of experiments in games: the initial belief in an experiment may explain a significant part of subjects' behavior and learning procedure in the experiment. An experiment comparing RRPM to APM from the first session may give a clue for a theory about subjects' initial belief and learning procedure: that is, subjects' risk attitude and attention level may play a role when they build their initial belief.[12] We also could do this in another game experiment such as coordination game in which the risk attitude seems to play an important role in equilibrium selection. Second, we could use the same payoff mechanisms in both sessions to check the restart effect if we obtain the firm result that RRPM and APM make a systematic difference. This may exclude the subjects' uncertainty about the second session game itself that we saw as the reason of the restart effect in RRPM.

Notes

1 The wealth effect is that subjects' risk attitude may change by the change of wealth. It is said that controlling the risk attitude is important in order to obtain unbiased results on the effect of a treatment variable when the risk attitude significantly plays a role in subjects' decision-making. See Davis and Holt (1993) and Friedman and Sunder (1994).
2 There are experiments using a kind of RRPM. See Morgan and Sefton (2000) and Weimann (1994). However, they did it without comparing RRPM to APM, depending on that game theoretical prediction.

3 The opportunity effect may also affect subjects' attention or effort level for a decision-making task, which may affect subjects' behavior in experiments. RRPM may be able to control the attention level too. For the effect of subjects' attention on experimental results, see Ledyard (1995: 170).
4 See also Croson (1996) and Burlando and Hey (1997).
5 Strangers treatment is that the composition of members of a group randomly change at each round while Partners treatment means that it does not change through rounds. In Partner treatment, the restart effect may be possible because of subjects' strategic consideration. Strictly say, the Strangers treatment is a random rematching treatment rather than perfect strangers treatment because the probability that a subject meets the same member more than once is not zero. This may affect the subjects' behavior. See Sonnemans *et al.* (1999).
6 For the indirect feedback, see Davis and Holt (1993: 95). To exclude this, we could use the matching method suggested by them. This method, however, requires a large size of subjects. Since our main purpose in this chapter is to investigate whether RRPM and APM make any difference, we indirectly test our prediction about the restart effect by using our treatments.
7 Signaling is a risky investment while following the dominant strategy is a less risky decision, considering the subjects' concern about the overall payoff through every round.
8 The results, however, may be indecisive because the number of observations are not enough: carefully looking at data show that even the contribution level between two groups in a payoff treatment is significantly different. We may need more observation. Moreover, we must confess that subjects could not understand at the first reading the instruction translated to Italian, and that both GAPM and GRRPM groups were in same room. These also may affect our results.
9 This difference may be explained by investigating the subjects' data given in Table 20.1: there was a subject in GRRPM who always contributes all tokens every round.
10 In real life, imitating their own or others' behavior in previous similar decision tasks seems one of strategies that more risk averse people are likely to choose when there are uncertainties.
11 This work can be done in both individual decision-making problems and games, and is being done by one of the authors. According to Lee's recent experiment for his PhD thesis, for example, RRPM clearly decreases the contribution level to group account, compared to APM in an experiment which uses only one session of ten rounds, four members in a group, partner treatment, and MPCR of 0.5. Moreover, the initial level of contribution between both was clearly different and this difference seems to make the difference at the final round. This may be a clue on the relationship between an initial belief making and risk attitude related to a payoff mechanism, and between the initial belief and learning procedure. An experiment, which measures subjects' risk attitude while investigating its effect on a strategic play, has been constructed and is being run.
12 It may be useful to statistically analyze the relationship of decisions between initial and final rounds by using collected data.

References

Andreoni, J. (1988) "Why free ride? Strategies and learning in public goods experiments," *Journal of Public Economics*, 37: 291–304.
Burlando, R. and Hey, J. (1997) "Do Anglo-Saxons free ride more?," *Journal of Public Economics*, 64: 41–60.
Croson, R. (1996) "Partners and strangers revisited," *Economics Letters*, 63: 25–32.

Davis, D.D. and Holt, C.A. (1993) *Experimental Economics*, New Jersey: Princeton University Press.

Friedman, D. and Sunder, S. (1994) *Experimental Methods: A Primer for Economists*, Cambridge: Cambridge University Press.

Ledyard, J.O. (1995) "Public goods: a survey of experimental research," in J. Kagel and A. Roth, eds, *The Handbook of Experimental Economics*, Mahwah, NJ: Princeton University Press.

Morgan, J. and Sefton, M. (2000) "Funding public goods with lotteries: experimental evidence," *Review of Economic Studies*, 67: 785–810.

Selten, R., Sadrieh, A., and Abbink, K. (1999) "Money does not induce risk neutral behavior, but binary lotteries do even worse," *Theory and Decision*, 46: 211–249.

Sonnemans, J., Schram, A., and Offerman, T. (1999) "Strategic behavior in public good games: when partners drift apart," *Economics Letters*, 62: 35–41.

Weimann, J. (1994) "Individual behaviour in a free riding experiment," *Journal of Public Economics*, 54: 185–200.

21 Zone of agreement bias in integrative negotiation

Fabio Feriozzi, Livia Reina, and Alessandro Scartezzini

Many negotiations offer a potential for integrative agreements (through logrolling) in which the parties can maximize joint gains without competing for resources as in a zero-sum game; nevertheless, negotiators often fail to exploit this potential and settle for suboptimal, distributive agreements. Our aim is to get some insight on the causes that prevent negotiators from reaching integrative, Pareto-optimal agreements. We ran some experiments in which we tested the "fixed-pie bias" of negotiators, and we introduced a new explanation for suboptimality, based on the hypothesis of a satisficing (not optimizing) behavior of negotiators, which leads them to a "zone of agreement bias" (ZAB).

Introduction: integrative negotiation and logrolling

Negotiation has been defined as the process by which two or more parties attempt to resolve perceived incompatible goals (Carnevale and Pruitt, 1992).

Many models derived from game and bargaining theory have treated almost exclusively the conflictual and distributive aspect of negotiation. The focus of negotiation research has recently been shifted from distributive bargaining theory toward the integrative bargaining approach which emphasizes the possibility of expanding or redefining the bargaining space through joint problem solving.

There exist various techniques that are adopted in integrative negotiation: logrolling (or issue-aggregation), issue-disaggregation, bridging, circular barter, cost cutting, and nonspecific compensation (Brett *et al.*, 1990; Hopmann, 1996; Touval, 1999). In order to limit our research, we will focus our attention on logrolling.

The technique of logrolling consists in redefining the issues by aggregating them into interlocking issues. Sub-issues are linked together "to create package agreements out of components that would be nonnegotiable if treated separately" (Hopmann, 1996). This approach is represented in Figure 21.1. On both issues the bargaining spaces of the parties do not overlap, since the preference curves intersect below the line of neutrality or indifference. In a situation of distributive bargaining this would create a stalemate on both issues. However, if we consider that party 1 has stronger interests about issue 1 and is more neutral on issue 2, and party 2 has stronger interest on issue 2 and is more neutral on issue 1, a solution

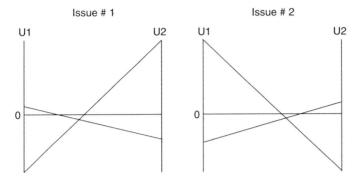

Figure 21.1 Issue aggregation.

can be found by agreeing to let party 1 win on issue 1, and party 2 win on issue 2. If party 1's gains on issue 1 exceed its losses on issue 2, and party 2's gains on issue 2 exceed its losses on issue 1, then both parties will still find the overall agreement beneficial.

In Figure 21.1, bargainers choose a point on the horizontal axis and receive payoffs indicated by the downward sloping line (party 1) or the upward sloping line (party 2). If the bargainers fail to agree on a point, then both receive zero payoff.

Bounded rationality and fixed-pie bias

Research on negotiation has recently begun to focus attention on the study of how negotiators define and perceive the negotiation game. Bazerman *et al.* (1985) suggested that negotiators' mental models are subject to the "fixed-pie bias." They perceive negotiation as a purely distributive or competitive game in which there is a fixed-pie of resources to be divided up among the parties, and better outcomes for one can be obtained only at the expense of another. The authors found that in a negotiation task with integrative potential, individuals concentrate first on competitive issues and it takes them significant experience to overcome the fixed-pie bias and recognize the integrative potential of the situation.

The present research

In the present research, we hypothesize that, besides the fixed-pie bias, there might exist an additional factor that could explain the suboptimality observed in integrative negotiation. This factor is represented by a "zone of agreement bias" (ZAB for simplicity), which might be due to the fact that negotiators behave in a satisficing, and not optimizing, way. In other words, we hypothesize that in a situation like the one described in Figure 21.3, in which the bargaining spaces of the two negotiators overlap in both issues, negotiators explore only a limited part of the negotiation problem's space, and, as soon as they are able to find a suboptimal solution falling within their zone of agreement, they stop searching for the optimal solution falling outside of it, and remain blocked in the suboptimal one. To test our hypothesis, we compare negotiators' behavior under two different treatments (A and B). Treatment A is the one described in Figure 21.2, in which the bargaining spaces of the two negotiators do not overlap in neither issue. Treatment B is the one described in Figure 21.3, in which the bargaining spaces of the two negotiators overlap in both issues (see also next section).

Our hypothesis is that the level of suboptimality will be higher when negotiators have a zone of agreement (treatment B). In this case, indeed, it seems plausible to think that the possibility to find an agreement on the two issues separately could prevent negotiators from exploring the space of more efficient agreements achievable through the aggregation of the two issues. Negotiators might remain blocked in the suboptimal agreements falling within the zone of agreement of each issue, and not consider the Pareto-optimal ones falling outside of it. Negotiators under treatment A, in contrast, not being able to find a suboptimal

Issue # 1

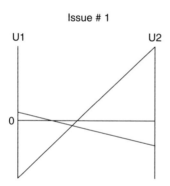

Issue # 2

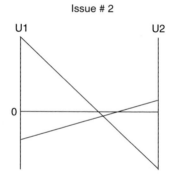

Figure 21.2 Treatment A.

Issue # 1

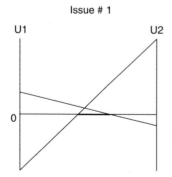

Issue # 2

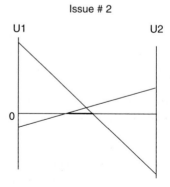

Figure 21.3 Treatment B.

solution, might be forced to consider the two issues jointly and eventually find an optimal agreement.

Experimental design

A total of twenty-eight policy makers (the same experiment has been carried out also with twenty-eight students) were asked to take part in an experiment aimed at analyzing negotiation behavior. Subjects were randomly paired in couples. Seven couples were assigned to treatment A and seven couples to treatment B (see section "The present research"). Each subject was given a sheet with two tables representing her or his incentive in the negotiation about the two issues. The first column of each table contained numbers from 0 to 10, representing the possible agreements on that issue, and the second column contained the points associated to each agreement. Subjects were requested to negotiate with their counterpart on one number from 0 to 10 in the first table and one number in the second table, in such a way to maximize their own total number of points (for instructions see Appendix A). Within each couple a subject assumed the role of player 1 and the other the role of player 2.

Denoting by x and y the value of the first and, respectively, the second number, the payoff tables for player 1 have been obtained as follows:

$$P_{1,A}(x) = P_{1,B}(x) = -50 + 10x, \quad P_{1,A}(y) = -20 + 3y,$$
$$P_{1,B}(y) = -20 + 3y \tag{21.1}$$

where $P_{1,i}(x)$ and $P_{1,i}(y)$ denote the amount of points under treatment i (for $i = $ A, B) associated with x and, respectively, y.

The payoff tables for player 2 are obtained from:

$$P_{2,A}(x) = 10 - 3x, \quad P_{2,B}(x) = 20 - 3x,$$
$$P_{2,A}(y) = P_{2,B}(y) = 50 - 10y \tag{21.2}$$

In Figure 21.4 is represented the space of all possible couples of agreements on issues 1 and 2 under treatment A. Along the line I_1 we can find all the joint agreements inducing a total payoff of zero for player 1 (i.e. the equation of I_1 is $P_{1,A}(x) + P_{1,A}(y) = 0$); furthermore, the arrow indicates the halfspace containing agreements with a total payoff greater than zero. Similarly, I_2 is defined by $P_{2,A}(x) + P_{2,A}(y) = 0$ and the arrow has a similar meaning. The region X contains all the possible agreements in which both players obtain a positive total payoff, and the bold line represents the pareto frontier of such a region. Region X represents the bargaining space that emerges when the two issues are aggregated (through the logrolling mechanism). In Figure 21.5 is represented the space of all possible agreements on issues 1 and 2 under tratement B. Lines and arrows have here the same meaning as in Figure 21.4 but now we can also observe a new region (the box denoted by Z) containing those agreements in which both players obtain a positive payoff on each issue (and then a positive total payoff). It is worth

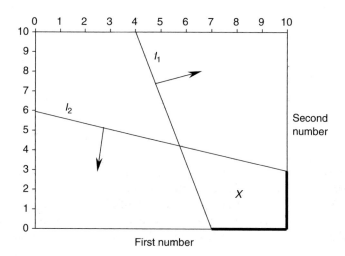

Figure 21.4 Treatment A.

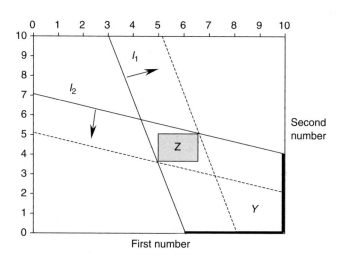

Figure 21.5 Treatment B.

noting that any agreement in the area *Y* Pareto-dominates any other agreement inside *Z*.

Negotiation was carried out face to face and subjects were allowed to speak freely. The only restriction was that they could not show their sheet with the tables to their counterpart. They had about 7 min to reach an agreement on the two numbers. If they did not find an agreement on one of the two numbers they got 0 points for that number. As an incentive subjects were given an amount of gifts (money for the students) directly proportional to the number of points they obtained in the experiment.

Theoretical predictions

If we assume that individuals are not perfectly rational and are subjected exclusively to the fixed-pie bias, we should expect that not all couples of subjects are able to reach a Pareto-optimal agreement, and that the number of couples reaching a suboptimal agreement is the same under treatment B and A.

If, as we hypothesize, individuals behave in a satisficing (not optimizing) way, and are subject to the ZAB, we should expect that not all couples of subjects are able to reach a Pareto-optimal agreement, and that the number of couples reaching a suboptimal agreement under treatment B is higher than under treatment A. In particular, the prediction is that the suboptimal agreements under situation B fall within the cartesian product of the two zones of agreement of each couple. Namely, we expect to observe a high proportion of agreements inside the region Z in Figure 21.5. Furthermore, we expect the ratio of efficient outcomes over the total number of couples to be higher under treatment A. We will often refer to such a ratio with the expression "efficiency rate." In the next section we describe our findings.

Experimental results

Hereafter, within each subject pool we will identify with letters from A to G the seven couples subjected to treatment A, and with letters from H to N the seven couples subjected to treatment B. Tables 21.1 and 21.2 show the experimental results that we obtained in the two subject pools. In order to interpret our results we will use Figures 21.6–21.9 in which the same datasets are reported.

Let us consider first the pool of policy maker. As we can observe in Figure 21.7, under treatment B only two couples out of seven were able to reach the Pareto frontier while the other five ended up with an inefficient outcome. In particular,

Table 21.1 Policy makers

Treatment A				Treatment B			
Couple	1st N°	2nd N°	Time	Couple	1st N°	2nd N°	Time
A	10	0	7	H	6	5	7
B	9	1	7	I	10	0	7
C	10	0	7	J	10	2	7
D	4	5	5	K	NO	4	7
E	10	0	4	L	4	7	7
F	0	0	7	M	6	4	6
G	8	1	7	N	6	NO	7
Mean	7.29	1.00	6.29	Mean	7.00	3.67	6.86
St. dev.	4.02	1.94	1.33	St. dev.	2.68	2.61	0.41
Agreement rate	1.00	1.00		Agreement rate	0.86	0.86	

Table 21.2 Students

Treatment A				Treatment B			
Couple	1st N°	2nd N°	Time	Couple	1st N°	2nd N°	Time
A	10	0	2	H	6	4	5
B	9	1	2	I	6	4	3
C	NO	NO	5	J	5	4	3
D	10	1	7	K	6	4	4
E	10	0	4	L	10	0	5
F	8	0	4	M	10	1	5
G	10	0	2	N	10	0	5
Mean	9.50	0.33	3.71	Mean	7.57	2.43	4.29
St. dev.	0.89	0.55	1.90	St. dev.	2.40	2.04	0.98
Agreement rate	0.86	0.86		Agreement rate	1.00	1.00	

two of them remained blocked in the rectangular region which we previously denoted as region Z, the other two couples surprisingly did not reach any agreement on one issue and in couple L player 1 obtained a loss. The efficiency rate is then 28.57 percent.

Under treatment A, we observe three couples reaching the efficient outcome (10, 0). Other two couples are quite close to the pareto frontier, while in couple D player 1 obtained a loss. Couple F is behaving in a quite odd fashion: player 2 is winning on both issues and player 1 is suffering a very large loss. These facts suggest that we ignore such an extreme case which is probably due to a misunderstanding of the instructions. The overall efficiency rate is then 50 percent (however, we should also take into account that couples G and B are quite close to the Pareto frontier). The discrepancy between the efficiency rates under treatments A and B seems to be significant so that the existence of a zone of agreement bias is actually compatible with our data. The main problem is, of course, the small size of our subject pool which does not allow us to be completely confident with the reliability of our findings. However, we obtained a quite similar result in the other subject pool and that is a good indication about the validity of our hypothesis. As we can see in Figure 21.9, in the subject pool of students under treatment B, four couples remained blocked inside the bias region Z, while the other three were able to reach the pareto frontier, inducing an efficiency rate of 42.86 percent. On the other hand, under treatment A (see Figure 21.8) five couples reached an efficient outcome and couple B is quite close to the Pareto frontier; only couple C was not able to find any agreement on neither issue. The efficiency rate under treatment A is then 71.43 percent.

The discrepancy between the two efficiency rates is not negligible so that the ZAB seems to be at work under treatment B as in the previous subject pool.

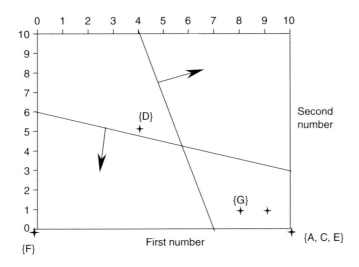

Figure 21.6 Policy makers: treatment A.

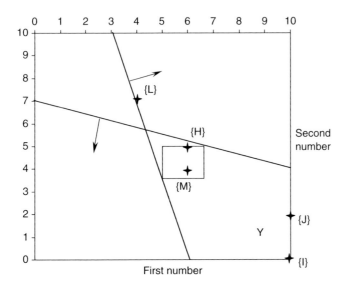

Figure 21.7 Policy makers: treatment B.

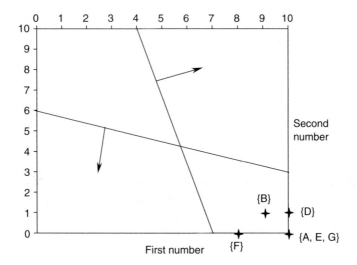

Figure 21.8 Students: treatment A.

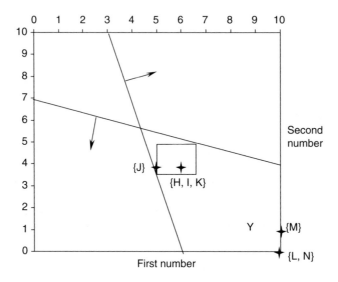

Figure 21.9 Students: treatment B.

Conclusions

The results of the experiments are consistent with our Zone of Agreement hypothesis. The level of suboptimality has been higher under treatment B, that is, when negotiators had a zone of agreement. Under this condition most of the nego-tiators (both policy makers and students) found an agreement on the two issues separately and remained blocked in the suboptimal agreements falling within the zone of agreement of each issue, without considering the Pareto-optimal ones falling outside of it. Negotiators under treatment A, in contrast (with the exception of one couple of policy makers and one couple of students), have all negotiated on the two issues jointly and most of them have been able to find a Pareto-optimal solution.

These findings should be confirmed by a more extensive analysis conducted on larger subject pools, but the indications emerging from our two pilot experiments allow us to be optimistic about the validity of our hypothesis.

Another interesting developement might deal with a situation of multi-issue multilateral negotiation with a potential for logrolling, in which decisions on each issue are made under majority rule. Negotiators indeed might be induced by the ZAB to form a winning coalition (on each issue separately) only with the parties with whom they share a zone of agreement, and not to explore the space of more convenient coalitions outside the zone of agreement.

Appendix

Instructions are in the Appendix of Chapter 7 (section on "Instructions for professional subjects for integrative negotiation").

References

Bazerman, M.H., Magliozzi, T., and Neale, M.A. (1985) "Integrative bargaining in a competitive market," *Organizational Behavior and Human Decision Processes*, 35: 294–313.

Brett, J.M., Goldberg, S.B., and Ury, W.L. (1990) "Designing systems for resolving disputes in organizations," *American Psychologist*, 45(2): 162–170.

Carnevale, P.J. and Pruitt, D.G. (1992) "Negotiation and mediation," *Annual Review of Psychology*, 43: 531–582.

Hopmann, P.T. (1996) *The Negotiation Process and the Resolution of International Conflicts*, Columbia, SC: University of South Carolina Press.

Touval, S. (1999) "Multilateral negotiation: an analytic approach," in J.W. Breslin and J.Z. Rubin, eds, *Negotiation Theory and Practice*, Cambridge, MA: The Program on Negotiation at Harvard Law School.

22 Culture from scratch

Evolution of an experiment

*William Robert Nelson Jr, Elenna R. Dugundji,
Jane Li, and Marco Tecilla*

The purpose of this chapter is to provide the reader insight into the development of a project we call Culture from Scratch. The objective is to determine whether cultures of cooperation and defection can be developed in the laboratory. The broader purpose is to ascertain the conditions under which such cultures will develop, persist, decay, and collapse.

Expectations affect cooperation in Rob and Zemsky's (1997) model of corporate culture. Their agents form expectations based on others' strategies in the previous period. Once expectations are formed, agents prospectively reciprocate to avoid feeling guilty. A worker in Rob and Zemsky's model might cooperate for two reasons: (a) the worker is inherently cooperative (there are unexplained random variations in workers' predispositions toward cooperation); or (b) the worker wants to avoid feeling guilty. Workers feel guilty (guilt reduces utility) if they cooperate less than the mean of workers in their firm. Accordingly, if a worker expects other workers to cooperate then he must cooperate himself in order to avoid feeling guilty.

Gunnthorsdottir *et al.* (2001) provide evidence that predispositions affect cooperation in a repeating public good game. Apparently, people's inherent willingness to cooperate affects the level of cooperation among group members, as assumed by Rob and Zemsky. We hypothesize that if participants' expectations are influenced so will be their contributions. If participants' expectations of others' cooperation are increased, then participants' cooperation should increase as well. This increase in cooperation, above what would exist without our influence over participants' expectations, is the impact of corporate culture. Culture from Scratch seeks to determine whether cooperative and defective cultures can be predictably developed in the laboratory, but most of this discussion will concentrate on cooperative cultures for brevity and clarity.

Pilot session

The idea for the initial experiment was to influence participants' expectations by controlling the order of the games when participants play repeated public good games with the same group. The difficulty of cooperation changed from round to round. Perhaps if people find it easy to cooperate in early rounds they will learn to expect cooperation in later rounds. Cooperation in public good games is most likely when the marginal per capita return (MPCR) is high (Isaac and Walker, 1988). Our early rounds used a high MPCR. People also are more likely to cooperate in games with fewer players, for then there are fewer possible defectors. If two people were participating in a game, the MPCR was 0.7; if three, then 0.6; if four, then 0.5; if five, then 0.4.

The format required participants to play five public good games with the same group during each of two treatments (more details below). Participants were asked to allocate $10 between their private account and the public account. The public account deposits were contributions to the public good. For example, a participant who contributes 3 and keeps 7 when the MPCR is 0.6 and the other members of his group contribute a total of 8, then his payoff is $7 + 0.6 \times (3 + 8) = 13.60$.

We ran two treatments during June 2001. Subjects were the graduate students and professors at the CEEL Summer School. All three groups of five participants played both treatments. In treatment A, intended to create cooperation, one round of each public good game (with each of the above MPCR's associated number of players) was played in order from the easiest to the hardest – two-person games to five-person games. In treatment B, intended to create defection, games were played in the reverse order – from five-person games to two-person games. The order of the treatments was also reversed in the different groups to control for order effects.

Figure 22.1 shows two histograms of the data collected during the five rounds where all five participants are playing in the three groups. One histogram shows the "cooperate" run and one shows the "defect" run. The mean contribution for the "cooperate" run is 2.6 and the mean contribution for the "defect" run is 2.3. The distributions show sharp peaks representing approximately half of the counts at zero contribution. This suggests a twofold approach in our subsequent quantitative analysis: that is, regression not only on the actual contribution, but also regression on the binary choice of simply whether to contribute or not.

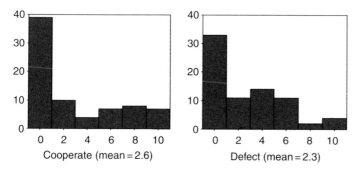

Figure 22.1 Individuals' contributed amounts aggregated across groups, for the "cooperate" run and the "defect" run ($N = 75$ per histogram).

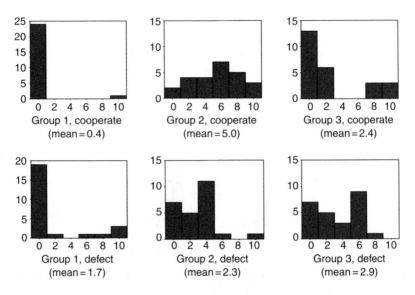

Figure 22.2 Individuals' contributed amounts by group and by treatment ($N = 25$ per histogram). Groups 1 and 3 played the "defect" run first. Group 2 played the "cooperate" run first.

In Figure 22.2, we see the same histograms for the cooperate run versus the defect run, but now broken down by each of the three groups. Here, we see a dramatic qualitative distinction between, for example, the behavior in Group 1, which is heavily skewed towards zero contribution in both the "cooperate" run and the "defect" run, and the behavior in Group 2, which is more bell-shaped for both runs. Furthermore, we have the perhaps initially counter-intuitive result that for both Groups 1 and 3 the mean contribution actually seems higher for the "defect" run versus the "cooperate" run. It is extremely important to recognize, however, that for Group 2 we ran the "cooperate" run first, and for Groups 1 and 3 we ran the "defect" run first. Although we have not run the experiment on enough different groups to be able to make any firm conclusions, this does suggest the hypothesis that there is a "memory" effect between the two runs, that in fact the two runs of "cooperate" and "defect" are *not* independent treatments when performed subsequently on the same group, and that the order does matter. More concretely, we might hypothesize that once a culture of defection is established, it may be difficult to revive cooperation. Further experimentation is necessary to test this hypothesis.

In Figure 22.3, we see histograms showing the effect of the rounds aggregated over the groups and across the runs. There is a clear qualitative shift in the shape of the distributions from earlier to later rounds. Recalling Figure 22.2, we seem to have only one clean, independent treatment of the "cooperate" effect and five runs that may be said to be influenced to varying degrees by the here stronger

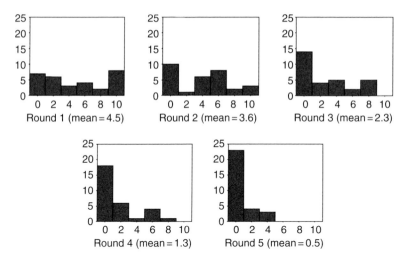

Figure 22.3 Individuals' contributed amounts by round, aggregated across groups, and treatments ($N = 30$ per histogram).

"defect" effect. It is thus reasonable to suppose that the overall aggregate effect may be having more defection in later rounds.

Results for ordinary least squares (OLS) and ordered probit (OP) regression with contributed amount as the dependent variable are given in Table 22.1. OP analysis may be slightly more appropriate than OLS, given that there are fixed upper and lower bounds on the amount that participants can contribute, namely zero and ten units, respectively. Furthermore, the allowed contributed amount is discretely quantized. Nonetheless, both OLS and OP show similar results. The model specifications with only a dummy variable for whether the run is theoretically a "cooperate" treatment or not, plus a constant (and for OP, the according thresholds), are poor fits and the coefficient for the cooperate dummy is not statistically significant. Adding dummy variables in the regression to account for group-specific and round-specific effects greatly improve the fit of the model. The coefficients for the effect of Groups 2 and 3 relative to Group 1 and the effect of Rounds 3–5 relative to Round 1 are all highly significant. Adding variables to the regressions with the group average contribution in the previous round and a participant's own contribution in the previous round,[1] improves the fit of the model still further, although as might be expected, some significance of the group and round dummies is taken away.

Results of binary logit and binary probit regression analysis on the choice of whether to contribute or not are shown in Table 22.2. As is to be expected theoretically unless observations are highly skewed, values for the coefficients for the binary logit model specification are approximately 60 percent higher than those for the binary probit model. We repeated the same model specifications for the binary choice of whether to contribute or not as we did earlier for

Table 22.1 Estimation results for some models of the individuals' contributed amounts, using ordinary least squares and ordered probit regression

Dependent variable	Own contributed amount					
	OLS estimation			*Ordered probit*		
Constant	2.293	2.927	2.085	0.040	−0.066	−0.529
	6.324	*4.812*	*3.301*	*0.314*	*−0.238*	*−1.711*
Cooperate dummy	0.307	0.307	0.198	0.008	0.026	−0.183
	0.598	*0.713*	*0.479*	*0.046*	*0.135*	*−0.876*
Group 2 dummy		2.560	1.307		1.630	1.116
		4.860	*2.097*		*6.180*	*3.670*
Group 3 dummy		1.600	0.761		1.182	0.864
		3.038	*1.358*		*4.436*	*2.977*
Round 2 dummy		−0.900	−1.740		−0.329	−0.885
		−1.324	*−2.504*		*−1.179*	*−2.831*
Round 3 dummy		−2.133	−2.483		−0.831	−1.221
		−3.137	*−3.773*		*−2.904*	*−3.960*
Round 4 dummy		−3.133	−2.811		−1.318	−1.336
		−4.608	*−4.279*		*−4.380*	*−4.331*
Round 5 dummy		−3.933	−3.066		−1.914	−1.638
		−5.784	*−4.393*		*−5.761*	*−4.655*
Previous own contribution			0.179			0.063
			1.929			*1.472*
Previous average contribution			0.366			0.262
			1.979			*2.931*
Threshold 1				0.181	0.282	0.297
				4.769	*4.894*	*4.866*
Threshold 2				0.350	0.533	0.564
				8.676	*9.165*	*8.968*
Threshold 3				0.566	0.833	0.897
				14.954	*16.651*	*15.781*
Threshold 4				0.683	0.985	1.071
				16.418	*18.585*	*17.669*
Threshold 5				1.004	1.381	1.519
				21.584	*24.842*	*24.465*
Threshold 6				1.115	1.513	1.666
				24.283	*27.981*	*28.007*
Threshold 7				1.315	1.747	1.917
				22.478	*25.360*	*26.595*
Threshold 8				1.484	1.947	2.121
				26.829	*31.318*	*32.971*
Threshold 9				1.588	2.060	2.239
				22.029	*26.349*	*27.453*
N	150	150	150	150	150	150
R-squared	0.002	0.327	0.394			
Adj. R-squared	−0.004	0.294	0.355			
Init. log likelihood				−274.32	−274.32	−274.32
Log likelihood				−273.76	−235.56	−226.08
Rho-squared				0.002	0.141	0.176
Adj. rho-squared					0.079	0.107

Note
t-Statistics in italics below the estimated coefficient values.

Table 22.2 Estimation results for some models of the choice whether to contribute or not, using binary logit and binary probit regression

Dependent variable	Decision whether to contribute or not					
	Binary logit			Binary probit		
Constant	0.241	−0.162	−1.017	0.151	−0.126	−0.579
	1.037	*−0.257*	*−1.324*	*1.039*	*−0.340*	*−1.327*
Cooperate dummy	−0.322	−0.637	−0.797	−0.201	−0.382	−0.472
	−0.981	*−1.362*	*−1.596*	*−0.981*	*−1.420*	*−1.667*
Group 2 dummy		4.670	3.831		2.728	2.288
		5.975	*4.557*		*6.501*	*4.928*
Group 3 dummy		3.120	2.757		1.827	1.630
		4.621	*3.865*		*5.001*	*4.165*
Round 2 dummy		−0.944	−1.431		−0.517	−0.834
		−1.164	*−1.672*		*−1.140*	*−1.732*
Round 3 dummy		−2.070	−2.200		−1.162	−1.255
		−2.447	*−2.617*		*−2.536*	*−2.709*
Round 4 dummy		−3.014	−2.643		−1.736	−1.547
		−3.469	*−3.030*		*−3.633*	*−3.225*
Round 5 dummy		−4.164	−3.411		−2.398	−2.007
		−4.534	*−3.622*		*−4.783*	*−3.816*
Previous own contribution			−0.045			−0.031
			−0.438			*−0.529*
Previous average contribution			0.412			0.236
			1.853			*1.902*
N	150	150	150	150	150	150
Init. log likelihood	−103.97	−103.97	−103.97	−103.97	−103.97	−103.97
Log likelihood	−103.37	−58.71	−56.71	−103.37	−58.24	−56.22
Rho-squared	0.006	0.435	0.455	0.006	0.440	0.459
Adj. rho-squared	−0.013	0.358	0.358	−0.013	0.363	0.363

Note
t-Statistics in italics below the estimated coefficient values.

contributed amount. The previously observed pattern of results is confirmed. In contrast to the earlier regressions, however, a participant's own contribution in the previous round is not significant in the full specification. Also notably, the group-specific effects in the binary choice models are the most significant variables at the 99.95 percent level of confidence. In the earlier regression with contributed amount as the dependent variable, the group-specific effects are less pronounced; the dummies representing the rounds and the variables with the amounts contributed in previous rounds play a more significant role.

Paid test session

The experimental design was "improved" between the pilot session with unpaid subjects and the test session with paid subjects. The paid session was run about

5 days after the unpaid pilot. In order to increase the probability of cooperation in the easy rounds, we increased the MPCR from 0.7 to 1.5 in the two-active-participant games. The MPCRs in games with more active players were also changed. If two people were participating in a game, the MPCR was 1.5; if three, then 1.0; if four, then 0.75; if five, then 0.6. The Nash strategy is to contribute all ten when MPCR > 1. Examples and a quiz were added to the instructions to increase the probability that participants understood the game.

The ordering of the rounds was also changed. In the paid test session we repeated and combined the number of players into two new treatments. The first, called the "peak treatment," is meant to create cooperation and has the following sequence of group sizes: 2-2-3-3-4-4-5-5-5-5-4-4-3-3-2-2. The alternative "pit treatment" runs 5-5-4-4-3-3-2-2-2-2-3-3-4-4-5-5, and is meant to create defection. Each group played both treatments and participants were aware of the order that games were being played in each treatment.

We hypothesize that the peak treatment will create cooperation during early rounds when cooperation is the privately most profitable strategy and cooperation is easy. We will see if cooperation persists from the rounds where cooperation is easy to when cooperation becomes difficult and then becomes easy again. The predictions are the same, but in the opposite directions for the pit treatment.

In theory, the causation should lead from experience to expectations, from expectations to actions, and from actions back to expectations. In the pilot design only actions were measured. In the paid test session, participants' expectations were also measured. In each round, participants were asked to estimate the mean contribution of other members of their group. We paid them for the accuracy of their estimates using a quadratic scoring rule. This mechanism provides participants the incentive to make accurate estimates. Having expectations data allows us to test the hypothesized causality regardless of the pattern of contributions. Participants were paid for one of the rounds from each treatment rather that for all rounds played. Too much time would have been required to calculate all of the payoffs from all of the rounds, for this session was run using paper and pencil.

Cultures of cooperation did not develop consistently. Surprisingly, during early rounds of the peak treatment participants deposited less than the total amount in the public account, even though total contribution was the Nash strategy. (In the initial rounds with two active participants and an MPCR > 1.) Without this seed of cooperation, participants will not expect cooperation and a cooperative culture will not form. Incomplete cooperation during early rounds occurred despite thorough instructions that included examples and a quiz. Participants' quiz answers were checked and corrected prior to playing the games (see Andreoni, 1995; Houser and Kurzban, 2002, for studies of confusion in public good games). Because of the apparent confusion, some problems like running the experiment with paper and pencils and no apparent treatment affects, no more space is spent discussing this session.

Computerized test session

Despite ambiguous evidence supporting our ability to create cultures of cooperation and defection in the laboratory, we decided to design a computerized version of the experiment. Participants' expectations of the mean of other participants' deposits were also collected in each round. Participants were paid according to their estimates' accuracy by employing a probabilistic quadratic payoff mechanism.

An unpaid computerized pilot was run during November 2001. The rounds followed the following format: 2-2-2-3-3-3-4-4-4-5-5-5-5-5-5-4-4-4-3-3-3-2-2-2-2-2-3-3-3-4-4-4-5-5-5; that is, cooperation was easy in the beginning and then became hard. Then cooperation became easy again and finally returned to being hard. Participants in this treatment played the thirty-six live rounds in just over 23 mins. Again there was less than total cooperation in the initial rounds with two active participants and an MPCR of 1.5. Because participants did not cooperate in the early two-player rounds, they did not expect cooperation in the later rounds when cooperation became more difficult. Low cooperation persisted until the MPCR became greater than one. During the last twelve rounds, where the difficulty of cooperating increased for the second time, essentially all participants contributed all of their money to the public account. We interpret the data optimistically. By the second build up from easy to difficult, participants learned how the public good game works and contributed all their money to the public account during the two-person game. This cooperation persisted throughout the remaining three rounds.

Recent improvements

Changes have been made to simplify the experiment, thus reducing confusion. The number of participants in each group will always equal four and only the MPCR will vary. Investigating the effects of changing the number of players will be saved for the future. Instructions will be clarified by directly telling participants the private marginal cost or benefit of contributing to the pubic account. Another computerized version of the experiment is under construction. Participants will be paid according to their deposits and the accuracy of their estimates' by employing a probabilistic quadratic payoff mechanism.

We anticipate running 1.5 h sessions, with two 36 round treatments, the order of which will alternate in different sessions. Rounds in one treatment move cooperation from easy to difficult to easy to difficult. The Peak treatment's MPCR looks like: 1.25, 1.25, 1.25, 1, 1, 1, 0.75, 0.75, 0.75, 0.5, 0.5, 0.5, 0.5, 0.5, 0.5, 0.75, 0.75, 0.75, 1, 1, 1, 1.25, 1.25, 1.25, 1.25, 1.25, 1.25, 1, 1, 1, 0.75, 0.75, 0.75, 0.5, 0.5, 0.5. The new pit treatment is the reverse order of the peak treatment. Participants will know that groups will be reassigned between treatments and that participants will play the second treatment with all new group members. Participants will be paid according to the sum of: their own private account, their public account, and their own estimate based payoffs from all of the rounds in one of the treatments. The pay treatment will be randomly selected.

In our sessions to date, only occasionally did cultures of cooperation develop as we anticipated. But we think cultures will develop in future sessions, when participants' confusion is reduced. The theory of culture that we are testing requires two causal relationships: (a) people's expectations or others' cooperation must depend on and correlate with their experiences; (b) people's actions must depend on and correlate with their expectations regarding cooperation. Both correlations required for expectation-based cultures to develop are present. When all of the appropriate data from the paid test session and the computerized pilot are combined, the correlation between observation and expectations is 0.77, and the correlation between expectations and actions is 0.67. Both correlations are significant beyond a reasonable doubt. If we can limit confusion, and participants cooperate in the early rounds, when the MPCR > 1, cultures of cooperation are likely to develop. Cultures of defection are also likely to develop when the initial rounds played make cooperation difficult.

Broader research agenda

The purpose of this experiment is to determine whether a culture of cooperation can be developed in the lab. The broader purpose of this project is to learn about the creation and destruction of cooperative and defective cultures. The rudimentary cultures of cooperation we expect to develop are our "cultures" in a conventional scientific sense. Our cultures of culture will be used similarly to how biologists use cell cultures in Petri dishes. The critical similarity is the experimental control available once cultures of cooperation and defection can be predictably created in the laboratory. Cultures of culture will facilitate testing questions such as: What causes the cooperation within an organization to be fragile rather than robust? How does the size of a team affect the fragility of its culture of cooperation? If a member of a defective group is transferred into a cooperative group, does he remain defective, does the group become defective, or does the transplanted member become cooperative? These inquiries are academically interesting, pragmatically valuable, and abundant.

Notes

1 In our analysis we have chosen to impute values for Round 1 for the own previous contributions and the average previous contributions by using mean values, rather than dropping the records listwise. This is primarily out of consideration for the fact that we have already so few data points, but it also allows us to conveniently compare R-squared and rho-squared across our model specifications, by retaining the same number of observations.

References

Andreoni, J. (1995) "Cooperation in public goods experiments: kindness or confusion?" *American Economic Review*, 85: 891–904.
Gunnthorsdottir, A., Houser, D., McCabe, K., and Ameden, H. (2001) "Disposition, history and contributions in a public goods experiment," Working Paper, George Mason University.
Houser, D. and Kurzban, R. (2002) "Revisiting kindness and confusion in public goods experiments," *American Economic Review*, 92: 1062–1069.
Isaac, M. and Walker, J.M. (1988) "Group size hypotheses of public goods provision: an experimental examination," *Quarterly Journal of Economics*, 103: 179–199.
Rob, R. and Zemsky, P. (2002) "Social capital, corporate culture, and incentive intensity," *Rand Journal of Economics*, 33: 243–257.

Index